My Quest for El Dorado

With Best Wishes

Ross Salmon

ROSS SALMON

My Quest for El Dorado

"The Indians have bows of gold and arrows too. Their adornments as well as cups and utensils are also of gold.

It is a land of fierce and hostile Indians who guard what they call the Territory of the Inchi Paititi."

Extract from the chronicles of the Spanish Conquistador Gamoa.

HODDER AND STOUGHTON

LONDON SYDNEY AUCKLAND TORONTO

British Library Cataloguing in Publication Data
Salmon, Ross
My Quest for El Dorado

Salmon, Ross
My quest for El Dorado.
1. Bolivia—Description and travel—1951—
2. El Dorado
I. Title
918.4'04'5 F3314

ISBN 0-340-24205-1

ISBN 0 340 242051

 Printed in Great Britain for Hodder and Stoughton Limited, Mill Road, Dunton Green, Sevenoaks, Kent by Lowe & Brydone Printers Limited, Thetford, Norfolk.
Hodder and Stoughton Editorial Office: 47 Bedford Square, London WC1B 3DP

To my dearest wife Rosalie I dedicate this book. Without her love and encouragement I should have given up the search long ago.

Contents

1 Beginnings 13

2 Quest 19

3 Incallacta 36

4 Beni 68

5 Following the Paititi 85

6 Iscanwaya 117

7 Towards Chapare 145

8 Chuamayu 154

9 The Indians of Sacapampa 165

10 The Patchamama ceremony 180

11 The Callawayas 195

12 Calling the condor 208

13 The Moxos 226

INDEX 247

Illustrations

Between pages 136 and 137

The ruins of Incallacta

A sacrificial altar

The fortress city of Iscanwaya

Callawaya women

Mosetene Indians

A meeting of the *amautas*

The sacrificial victim

The condor comes down

The golden 'language plate'

Fortress wall near the Moxos

All photographs from the author's collection

Sierra Nevada
de Santa Marta
Barranquilla
Cartagena
Lake Maracaibo
Sierra de Perije
R Orinoco
Santa
Martica
VENEZUELA
GUYANA
R Magdalena
Bogota
COLOMBIA
ECUADOR
PERU
Lima
Cuzco
R Beni
R Mamore
PLAINS
Trinidad
OF BENI
La Paz
Cochabamba
Santa Cruz
PACIFIC
OCEAN
CHILE
BOLIVIA
PARAGU

AREA OF THE KNOWN INCA EMPIRE
- from Bogota South through the Andes to Chile
Land 500 - 1800 metres
1800 - over 6000 metres
0
400 Miles
0
400 Km
NAM
FRENCH GUIANA
B R A Z I L
TO
ROSSO
ATLANTIC
OCEAN
Rio de Janeiro

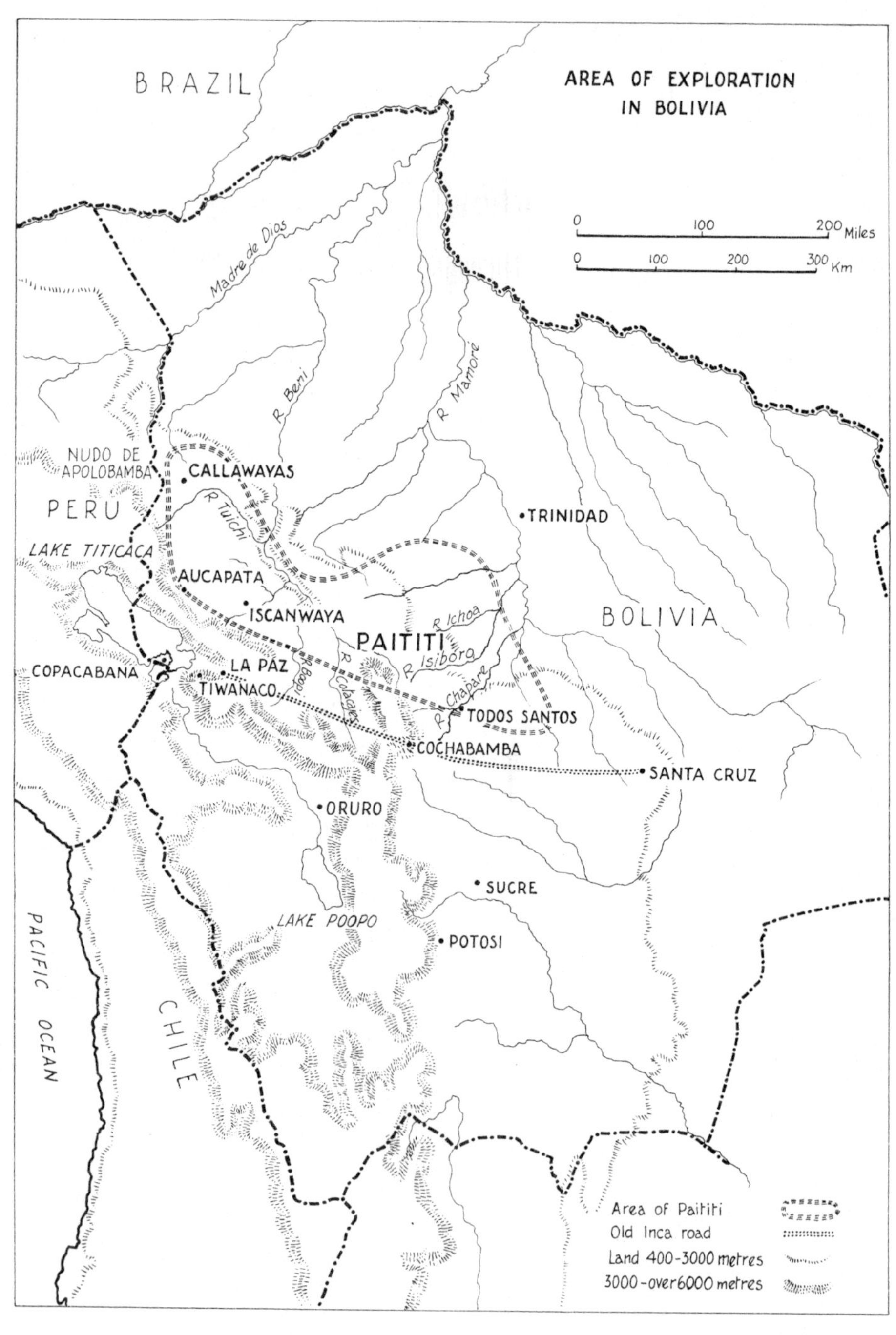
AREA OF EXPLORATION
IN BOLIVIA
BRAZIL
0 100 200 Miles
0 100 200 300 Km
Madre de Dios
R. Beni
R. Mamoré
NUDO DE
APOLOBAMBA
CALLAWAYAS
PERU
R. Tuichi
TRINIDAD
LAKE TITICACA
AUCAPATA
ISCANWAYA
R. Ichoa
BOLIVIA
PAITITI
R. Isiboro
COPACABANA
LA PAZ
R. Bopi
R. Cotacajes
TIWANACO
R. Chapare
TODOS SANTOS
COCHABAMBA
SANTA CRUZ
ORURO
SUCRE
LAKE POOPO
POTOSI
PACIFIC OCEAN
CHILE
Area of Paititi
Old Inca road
Land 400-3000 metres
3000-over 6000 metres

CHAPTER ONE

Beginnings

MY SEARCH FOR THE Lost Empire of the Incas began twenty-five years ago. Going straight from school into the excitement of war gave me a love for adventure, and when I was demobilised the thought of a steady career in England never occurred to me.

I decided instead to work for a giant beef enterprise, with factories in Brazil, cattle ranches in central South America, a chain of butchers' shops all over Britain, and its own shipping company. I imagined myself being trained as a high-powered company executive, flying my own plane, buying up millions of pounds' worth of beef on the hoof. But I had to start at the bottom as a ranch assistant on the plains of the Orinoco. Life turned out to be pure cowboys and Indians, and pretty primitive, too. The only whites on a ranch about the size of Devon were the manager and myself. The fifty or so cowboys were local Indians, and this was my first meeting with the descendants of the indigenous peoples of South America, and my first chance to learn their language, their customs and way of life.

Venezuela was just emerging as one of the richest countries of the New World. The immense wealth pouring out of the oil-fields of Maracaibo was transforming the country almost month by month. You could see the steady improvement in amenities of all kinds and in the standard of living of the Venezuelan people. No longer were they satisfied with a steady diet of piranha fish, crocodile steaks, turtles and wild birds. They wanted the roast beef and two vegetables of the western world. This spelt good fortune for our cattle company, because prices rose as demand outstripped supply.

Eventually I was given a ranch of my own to manage in the

next-door republic of Colombia, and I remembered the expensive meat of Venezuela. Colombia had no oil and very little industry. Outside the cities of Bogota, Medellin and Barranquilla, life had changed little since the early days of the Spanish conquest. There was not much money, and little demand for beef. A reasonably fat steer fetched only £5 in Colombia, and there were too many of them on offer even at that give-away price. Why not ship some of the two thousand five hundred cattle on my ranch into Venezuela, I thought: the enormous profit would more than pay the freight charges.

The only snag was that by the time I had rounded the cattle up from distant paddocks, collected them on the river bank, shipped them by paddle-steamer down the River Magdalena to Barranquilla, freighted them right out into the Caribbean to miss the sand bars, brought them round to La Guara and up the mountain road to Caracas—a journey of two weeks at least—they would probably be dead. But there was a much shorter route from the Magdalena Valley into Venezuela, though, at first sight, it looked just as difficult. If we blazed a once-and-for-all trail through the tropical forest into the jungle-covered hills to the east of the Magdalena, it would mean a cattle drive of no more than a few days. With a bit of vegetation to pick at along the way, the beasts might not arrive in such bad condition.

I put the idea to the Indians and the *mestizos* who worked as cowboys on my ranch, but they put up a strong objection. Those hills—the Sierra de Perije—were, they said, inhibited by groups of cannibal Indians who would never let people pass through. My first reaction was incredulity, but clearly they believed they were telling the truth. They even mentioned tribal names: the Yuko, the Dobokubi and the Kunaguasaya. My Indians were not prepared even to discuss a trail though the hills. They dismissed the idea with damning finality.

I decided to wait a few months until my next visit to Bogota, when I went to see Professor Dolmatoff, the world-famous Colombian anthropologist, and I explained my problem to him.

He suggested that I spend the next year reading about the mountain Indians. "And when you have read those manuscripts that deal with your area and the eastern Cordillera, you can read the archive material written by the Spanish *conquistadores*," he said.

So I returned to my ranch to research the Indian story. Night after night, I read, studied, wrote and read. I was immediately convinced by the arguments of many professional anthropologists that the first men to migrate into the Americas about twenty thousand years ago came from the Far East into Mongolia; across the Bering Straits when they were solid ice; into Alaska; and gradually down into the whole American continent.

I needed little persuasion to accept the Asiatic origin of the first American Indians. Indeed, the Indians who worked on and lived around my ranch all had the general stature of the Oriental, as well as his high cheek-bones, wide-set slanting eyes and fine hair. There were linguistic links, too, especially the extreme tonal values of their vocabulary.

The pre-conquest history of the South American peoples can only be inspired guesswork or, at best, intelligent deduction, because they left no written language. It is true that much has been learned from first contacts with the little-known tribes of the northern Andes, but even evidence gathered by intelligent scientific observers must be questioned on the basis of one significant doubt.

Almost all the Indians would have had a fleeting contact with one of the hundreds of missionaries who poured into South America; so how shall we ever know how much the missionaries' teachings changed or even coloured the Indians' own stories of their legends, customs and way of life?

To me the accounts of the *conquistadores* and the early explorers made horrific reading. Harmless, friendly Indians suffered rape, robbery, torture, murder and enslavement at the hands of the early settlers. First it was the Spaniards looking for gold, silver and precious stones. Then it was a growing army of fortune-seeking immigrants from Europe and America, who took over the Indians' territory and ripped their way of life into shreds. But in all my reading I found out very little about the Indians of the Sierra de Perije. The Spaniards did not mention them, nor did recent accounts of explorations by American oil prospectors, because no one had achieved friendly contact. The occasional missionary had either disappeared without trace or had been driven out by these Indians, who clearly hated the Blue Eyes, as they called non-Indians.

I remember one incident where an American missionary with money to spend had wanted to take a short cut. He flew over the

Sierra de Perije in a helicopter and dropped packets of food to the hungry Indians. On to each packet he pasted a photograph of himself, so that the Indians would come to associate his face with these presents of much-needed food. A few days later he confidently lowered a rope ladder from his helicopter and climbed down into the Indian village. He was greeted by a fusillade of arrows and killed instantly.

The few eye-witness accounts that were published referred to the ferocious Caribs or the Motilon Indians, but these names meant nothing. Almost any Indian was called a Carib by the early settlers. The word means 'cannibal' and, by law, the only Indians the Spanish were officially allowed to enslave and mistreat had to be cannibals. Many Indians were therefore classified as Caribs. Motilon means 'with short hair', but a number of primitive tribes used to shorten their hair, and still do so today, by their traditional method of singeing it with a red-hot piece of wood. To say that the mountains were inhabited by Carib and Motilon Indians was, therefore, quite meaningless in terms of identification or classification.

There was only one thing to do. I had a solid foundation of deep study and years of experience of survival in the primitive environment of the South American jungle, and so I simply had to carry out my own exploration.

So, with the assistance of Jimenez, my captain of cowboys, I laid plans. Jimenez became quite enthusiastic when he realised the personal benefit that might come his way if the ranch prospered as the result of successful exploration. His vast knowledge of the area amazed me until he told me that he had been born and brought up about one hundred miles to the east of the ranch, in the foothills of the Sierra de Parije.

"The Indians up there in the hills are scared stiff," he explained. "They used to rule this valley before you Blue Eyes came here. They were all-powerful, and they fled to the mountains rather than submit to your gods of war. They kill any invaders today because they know that, if Blue Eyes conquer their hills, there is nowhere left to go. They are cannibals; they eat their own and enemy dead, because there is so little food up there in the mountains. Here in the lowland jungle they could hunt and kill monkeys, deer, and pigs, and they could catch fish in the rivers. Up there in the hills, it is too cold for animals and fish, and the Indians are very hungry."

Our first expeditions into the hills were painfully slow. Jimenez was from a primitive Indian family and he knew that the only way to achieve peaceful contact was to proceed with extreme caution. The two of us slogged our way into the hills, always unarmed and always taking one Indian from the last village to guide us to the next. These Indian guides knew which path was the accepted line of communication between neighbouring villages, and they knew at which point to stop and shout at the top of their voices to announce our approach. In this way our arrival could never be misunderstood as a possible attack. Even so, when we arrived, the village was always deserted. Clearly, the frightened Indian inhabitants were hidden in the surrounding trees and bushes, watching us carefully to ascertain whether we presented any threat to them; so we always spread our meagre equipment on the ground to show that we were unarmed; then we sat and waited.

When the Indians slowly filtered back into the clearing, both Jimenez and the guide from the last village spoke to them in Quechua, and they always succeeded in making friendly contact. We lived with the first tribe of Yuko Indians for about six weeks, and I spent the first month writing thousands of Indian words, phonetically, then trying to converse. This was an awesome task, because the Indians were too unsophisticated to help. For example, I heard them refer to a stone as a '*timpari*'; so I held up a cooking pot, and said questioningly, '*Timpari*?' expecting them to say, "No, not a *timpari*. It is a . . . " Instead of volunteering the right word they just screamed with laughter. So it took me three or four months living with several Yuko tribes before I could converse even crudely, and even then I needed help from Jimenez. But once I did start to talk to them I gained a tremendous amount of invaluable information.

One particular family group of Yuko Indians, living under their primitive lean-to shelters made out of leaves and twigs, were at starvation level. My suggestions that they come back to the Magdalena valley and live in a reservation there were coldly brushed aside. I tried to point out to this group that they were doomed. A diet of maize, potatoes, and bugs out of rotted tree trunks, together with the effects of disease and congenital conditions due to years of inbreeding, meant that their precarious survival was coming to an inevitable conclusion.

The Chief's answer was extremely interesting. "The Injka will soon return, slaughter your Blue Eyes' nation in enormous battles and restore us to our homeland in the valley where we were happy." I wrote down the word 'Injka' phonetically, and, of course, it was so similar to the word 'Inca' that it immediately filled me with excited anticipation, and I encouraged the Chief to tell me more.

"The Injka ruled over all the kingdoms of all the tribes in the world," he told me. I realised that his idea of the world did not extend beyond central South America, but that was still a pretty large empire to control.

"You Blue Eyes think you have defeated the Injka, but you haven't," the Chief continued triumphantly. "They are there, hidden in large cities in the jungle and in the mountains. They are only waiting for their god of war to appear to lead them into battle and destroy you Blue Eyes. We know where they are, and we know their god will come to rescue us."

How much of this story of the hidden cities of the Injka was I to believe? On the one hand, I was hearing the story from a primitive tribal chief who had never before had contact with anyone outside his own little Indian community. So it was his own genuine story, not tarnished or coloured by any contact with other travellers such as myself. On the other hand, it is a story which has been told and retold throughout history. When a formerly proud and powerful nation finds itself threatened or defeated by an even more powerful enemy, it is a common enough tactic to rally the oppressed nation round a god of some sort who will seek revenge and retribution. Were there still descendants of the Incas living hidden somewhere? Were there great secret cities in the hills? I longed to find out. The idea fascinated me. But no sooner had I won the Chief's friendship than I was in an aeroplane crash in the jungle. I was the only survivor, but I had fractured almost every major bone in my body from skull to ankle, which put an abrupt end to my days as a ranch manager. Two years in hospitals in England killed my hopes of ever taking up such a marvellously challenging life again but it did not kill the burning ambition to continue my search for the lost Inca empire.

CHAPTER TWO

Quest

AS I GRADUALLY RECOVERED from the disastrous effects of the air crash, I made slow progress towards fulfilling my ambitions. But my all-consuming hobby had to be contained within the limitations imposed by having to earn a living. It was obvious that I would never be supremely fit again, but once I had recovered a reasonable degree of mobility I was able to return to South America to continue my exploration of the Sierra de Perije.

As well as the Yuko (the little men of the mountains), I met family groups of the Dobokubi (the big men of the jungle) and the Kunaguasaya (the men who live near the water). None of these groups had ever had any contact with white men before, yet all told me the same legend. With only minor differences in emphasis they all said that there were Indians hiding in the jungle, who would one day emerge to do battle with the Blue Eyes to win back the fertile valleys from which all those Indians had been driven.

The Yuko, the Dobokubi and the Kunaguasaya all believed this oft-repeated story. Their insistence persuaded me to believe in the possibility at least that there was indeed a large community of Injka (or Inca) Indians living somewhere in the vast wilderness of the South American jungle. After all, we know from the chronicles that no Inca group ever surrendered to the Spanish. So what happened to those who were not killed?

I had earlier started working on a part-time basis for B.B.C. television, and this had taught me the rudiments of making films. Eventually I was lucky enough to win an international award which brought offers to make films around the world.

This meant that I could, in most cases, select the country of my choice, be paid to make a film for a commercial organisation there, and then have time to make my own documentaries of the indigenous peoples of that country. On the strength of my explorations and documentary films I was invited to lecture at universities in America, and my visual evidence of the migration of man gradually attracted the attention of a few members of the academic world. Uppermost in my mind all the time was the question of what had happened to the Inca nation.

Three fruitless expeditions, spanning some fifteen years, got me nowhere. But at last a major break came when Professor Hugh Jones of Cambridge University introduced me to Dr. David Davies of London University. For many years Dr. Davies had been studying the history of the Incas. He, too, believed that there was a lost Inca empire yet to be discovered in the unexplored area of the Andes, though it was nowhere near the northern and eastern Cordillera where I had been searching. We talked for hours, checked over maps, exchanged information on our own original researches, and reached the conclusion that Bolivia was the only area of South America that fitted almost all the right conditions. If indeed there was a lost Inca empire it must be here, we decided, and David had further, more recent explorations to back up his hypothesis.

There were only two alternatives: to explore and find the empire or to admit defeat.

Inca legend stipulated that it had been founded on the shores of Lake Titicaca (at least half of which is in Bolivia), and had then spread northwards into what is now Peru, where the seat of government had been established at Cuzco. Bolivia was therefore the Inca birthplace, and from its green fertile valleys had come the food for the empire. But surely, I thought, once the Spanish invaders had looted and destroyed the cities of Peru, they would have advanced further and wiped out the Incas in Bolivia.

David, who had studied the Spanish chronicles, was sure that they had never overrun so far south. They might have sent out exploratory foray parties, but their lines of communication were insufficiently sophisticated for them to have been able to remain in safety. Moreover, there was little to loot in Bolivia; the small scattered farming communities were concerned with growing food; there were few cities to ransack.

Pushed slowly back from the northern areas, the retreating

Incas might well have had time to rally further south and to have built new cities on the fertile lower slopes of the Bolivian Andes, well away from the Spaniards. It has been suggested that there were once thirteen million people living under Incan rule, and my surmise was that they could not all have suddenly disappeared. Thousands of these Incan subjects died in smallpox and influenza epidemics. Thousands committed suicide to escape the terrible burden of labour, tax and tribute imposed by the Spaniards. Many more died in the silver mines of Potosi, and millions were killed in battle because, as the *conquistadores* themselves admitted, no Incan army ever surrendered. Some married Spanish soldiers, but it is irrefutable that thousands escaped—some to the jungle, some to the inaccessible mountain and hill areas. It is the descendants of these people who, I thought, might have inhabited the Lost City of the Incas and whose descendants might still today be living in remote areas.

I quite realise that in the most rigid interpretation of the classification 'Inca', these people cannot be called direct descendants. Strictly speaking, all those who were living under Incan rule when the Spaniards came were not technically members of the original Incan ruling group, but were subject peoples of differing names and cultures on whom the Incas had imposed their rule, their language and their authority. But in this book I shall go along with the majority of South American anthropologists who call the millions of peoples who lived under Incan rule 'Incas'. This is not incorrect for, in the broadest sense, they were after all members of the Incan empire, and whatever name they may have had before they were conquered has been lost in the mists of time.

What had particularly excited David was an invitation from the University of Cochabamba to examine an Inca ruin called Incallacta, which nestled in the lower slopes of the Andes, south east of La Paz.

The Director of the Inca Museum at the university was Mrs. Geraldine Byrne de Caballero O.B.E., the English widow of a rich Bolivian who had owned the fertile valley where the ruin had been discovered. Since Geraldine was also the British consul, she was able to smooth away many difficulties, and so we decided to make Cochabamba the starting point for our journey of exploration, and Incallacta the target of our first expedition.

Ramon and Carlos, two young men on the staff of

Cochabamba University, offered to guide us and to help with the carrying of my heavy filming equipment. One look at my greying temples and spreading midriff obviously told them I should need assistance.

Soon after we abandoned our jeep and set off on the long march across the hills, I was forcibly reminded that twenty odd years had passed since my original explorations. The sight of yet another valley to cross, and yet another steep, rocky hillside to climb became a much more daunting prospect than it used to be. The loaded haversack, with my tent and sleeping-bag strapped to it, did not rest easily on my shoulders any more. It seemed to drag heavily around my waist and down on my hips much of the time.

The fact that the hills rose from two to four thousand metres above sea level had one great advantage. They were above the insect line, so that there were no mosquitoes or flies, and very few small menacing insects of the creepy-crawly kind. Nor were there any snakes, lizards or reptiles. The air was crisp, with temperatures similar to those of a pleasant English summer day. The one disadvantage at four thousand metres was the lack of oxygen. Climbing, particularly, became a tantalisingly slow-motion operation.

After we had laboriously crossed two ranges of stark, barren hills and waded two rushing rivers, my heart sank as I saw yet another expanse of empty countryside ahead of us.

The quizzical scepticism of Ramon and Carlos did not help, either. They had never approached Incallacta from this direction before, and clearly they were puzzled that the ruins were still not in sight. For the tenth time that day I pretended to film the countryside. The time taken to unload and set up the camera and tripod and go through the motion of filming provided me with a much-needed rest without actually forcing me to admit that I was on the point of exhaustion.

Suddenly we came across a high stone wall half-hidden by bushes and small trees growing alongside it. A whoop of triumph from Ramon and Carlos announced that this was part of Incallacta's defensive wall. All we had to do was follow this wall for a few more miles, and we'd reach the ruins. I just thanked God that those last wearisome miles were downhill towards the tumbling, rocky river in the valley, for I knew that was just about as far as I could walk without collapsing in an ignominious heap.

At first a line of dwarf trees growing on the cascading, uneven slope of the hillside hid the imminent panorama of the ruins from my frantically-searching gaze. Then, in one moment, the depression and despair were swept away on a tide of exultation. Not far below me, the steep hillside levelled out into a huge, rocky courtyard which jutted out, overlooking the sweep of the valley beneath. That flat stadium was half-covered in scrub and stumpy trees, no more than a metre high, which could not hide the stark outline of a very large stone-built city.

I picked out the stone walls of many houses and buildings, and in the centre of the city a much more substantial stone wall, five to seven metres high, surrounded by a grassy area about the size of two or three tennis courts. There were also magnificent stone arches, high gables and doorways. The sheer size of many of the constructions gave an air of dignity and majesty to the ruins, which refused to give way to an atmosphere of decay and disuse.

So this was Incallacta, the Inca city which had been built as a fortress four hundred years ago, in 1556, to guard a vital pass through the rugged Andes mountain range. I stood there for some minutes in a state of breathless excitement. What might easily have turned out to be the pitiful crumbling remains of a few stone walls was, in fact, the impressive façade of a large, ruined city. Maybe it had been abandoned for four hundred years or so, but such was the superb quality of masonry and construction that not even the ravages of tropical storms or the spreading undergrowth could destroy or hide completely the outline of houses, a temple, a parade ground and city walls. At once I began composing essential film shots to illustrate the lonely grandeur of Incallacta and its supreme setting as a fortress guarding that pass through the Andes. It was easy to see that the only way in which a significant body of men could have travelled on foot through this mountainous country would have been along the banks of the river which sliced through the deep valley below.

On the banks of the river there was a strip of land about four hundred metres wide which was flat; if it were not exactly a clear highway, at least it was easier to walk along than the cruel rocky slopes that cascaded down from the clouds on either side. To travel along this valley you would have to pass within a hundred metres of the forbidding walls of Incallacta. The fortress city was built on a large granite mound which stretched almost across the valley at its narrowest point. It was as if nature had cut a wedge-shaped piece of granite cake, and placed it gently but firmly across the valley floor; the thick end melted into rocky wall on one side and the sharp end almost joined on to the sheer slopes on the other side. Only the width of the rushing river stopped the granite from forming a bridge across the valley floor.

If a master tactician had set out to devise a completely impassable barrier, he could not have chosen a better site. And it was on this wedge-shaped rampart that the Incas built their fort, to provide the most effective sentry-box it is possible to imagine in this almost impenetrable mountainous area. To make the citadel even more secure and safe from attack, they built a wall two metres high out of stone blocks right round the perimeter of the fort, and in this wall they placed strategic peep-holes through which they could shoot arrows or hurl rocks at any intruders desperate enough to try to scale the sheer rock-face leading up from the valley below. An impregnable citadel indeed, within whose walls lay the well-preserved remains of many buildings made of stone blocks, cut and fitted together precisely, a monument to Inca skill in construction.

As I clambered slowly down the narrow, often treacherous pathway towards the citadel, I had the premonition, justified as it turned out, that this was to be the gateway to our adventurous journey of discovery.

When one thinks of lost Inca cities, one imagines them to have gold ornaments, idols and artefacts strewn around, unclaimed, like old tin cans and broken bottles at a popular picnic site. But there was no heap of gold to be seen when we set foot in the city. Nor did we expect it on this occasion. Incallacta may be truthfully described as a lost Inca city, inasmuch as it had never been filmed, photographed or written about. But it was known to perhaps half a dozen scientists from the university and, of course, to the Indians who still live in the small isolated communities further along the river bank. Any gold that was abandoned in exposed areas of the city has no doubt been swept up by local Indians over the years, and traded for clothing, machetes and agricultural tools.

As we pitched our tents in the valley beneath the fortress city, I could almost see David's mind searching and digging, even before he unpacked the tools of the professional archaeologist's trade. I left him planning his own campaign of excavation and discovery, while my thoughts floated into the cloudy past, to a similar exploration trip in Colombia twenty-five years ago. Was this, my next tentative step on the long, frustratingly difficult path, at last reaching its rainbow's end?

Ramon and Carlos led the way down into the valley. On the river bank was an old Indian hut which they had been using as a base camp for the past year while they studied the remarkable Inca ruins on the hillside two or three hundred feet above.

The river, fed by the holy Inca waterfall at Incallacta, came rushing down from the slopes that rose sheer above us. Perhaps it was more of a mountain stream than a river; it was only about twenty feet wide, and ankle-deep, but there was sufficient volume of water, even in the dry season, to set up a steady roar of protest as the water rushed over and around the rocky outcrop and small boulders where the steep land began to level out.

With so little depth of soil on this stark Andean countryside, there was no dense growth of vegetation. The trees on the river bank and the lower slopes of the hills were no more than four metres high, stunted and not very thick on the ground. Clearly the inhospitable terrain offered little support for vegetation, and it was easy enough to walk around, gathering firewood. There were two vital jobs to complete before darkness fell: to get the camp-fire blazing and to prepare a bed for the night.

The fire was easy. But the old Indian hut was very dirty, so we decided to pitch our tents between the hut and the river bank, and, in order to take the sharp edge off the stony floor beneath the tents, we packed leaves and bush cuttings under our sleeping-bags.

By the time we had eaten a modest supper and washed in one of the rocky pools cut into the river bank, we were thoroughly exhausted. There was the physical fatigue caused by the seemingly endless trek all that day across the hills in the rare atmosphere, but mental exhaustion was even more acute. It was not just the ecstatic excitement of that first sight of a little-known Inca site. It was more the deep, sustained thrill of anticipation, as we considered the prime importance of this magnificent fortress. This was indeed a foundation stone on which to build our theories. It was surely the gateway to our lost Inca civilisation, because such a magnificent fort must have been built to defend an area of prime importance.

There was much work to be done in Incallacta itself: archaeological digging and excavation to be done, photographs and film to be taken, theories to discuss; above all, we had to find out if there were Inca roads leading out of the city into the dark, forbidding sierra all around us.

In spite of the uncomfortable bed and the chilly damp rising from the thundering river a few yards away, we were soon asleep. But not for long.

The years I had spent in the South American jungle gave me the confidence to be totally unafraid of the wild life, for no animal would seek out a human and attack him without provocation; but that same experience and knowledge stimulated one disquieting thought. Would our presence be resented by the local Indians living in isolated communities in the surrounding hills? Did they regard Incallacta as a sacred city? Would they try to drive us away? This was my only lingering doubt as a shallow oblivion crept over me.

I was ready to wake at any sound cutting through the steady roar of the rushing water. And soon there was a growl like that of a dog who is having a mock battle with a bone. Was it human or animal? I was ready to run from any Indian threat, but animals were something I hadn't expected. There'd been no sign of animal habitation in the hills all that day. A jaguar? Certainly not. No jaguar would live so far from its jungle home. A puma? That was possible. In the United States they don't call it a puma. It's the mountain lion, and it lives in the Rockies, I seemed to remember, so why not here in the low Andes?

I didn't known how long I held my breath whilst I listened, but it was long enough to follow the sound of this creature moving alongside my tent and away towards the river.

In a way the special tent I was using gave me a feeling of security, for it zipped up like an envelope all round me. The smallest insect could not get in. Nothing could get in without slashing its own entrance through the canvas roof. So I became easier. As time passed without further disturbance, I felt relieved enough to deride my fear. To think that a puma might materialise from the mountainside, make straight for my tent and slash it open was a ludicrous idea only to be found in a schoolboy thriller.

There had been some creature, though. Slowly and gently I unzipped the flap of the tent and looked out: nothing but the inky blackness of the trees silhouetted by the dark purple backcloth of the tropical sky; no sound but the steady seething roar of the river against the calm stillness of the surrounding hills.

I looked at my watch. It was five o'clock in the morning. There was so little of the night left that it hardly seemed worth going back to sleep. So I got up and walked quickly over to the hut. Our two guides were sleeping peacefully on the floor, fenced in by what remained of the single walls.

They'd all be wanting coffee when they woke up and, since the embers of the fire were still glowing on the stone platform we had built at the entrance to the hut, I rekindled the fire with a handful of twigs. I stood inside the hut just to be on the safe side and watched the fire burst into life. We kept each other company, the blazing fire and I, until dawn sent a shimmering sheen of pale light across the night sky.

By the time the others had woken up and dipped into their coffee cups, the mysterious noises of the night seemed a long way away: unreal almost, not worth mentioning, even. I would never have risked possible ridicule in telling the story, but for Ramon's observation over breakfast. Quite casually and quietly he mentioned that two pumas had been wandering around during the night. Had we been disturbed? Not the one puma which I thought I might have heard, but two pumas, he assured us.

"No," said David increduously, "didn't see or hear a thing."

After a scant breakfast (we were too weighted down with camping and filming equipment to carry much food), Carlos led the way up the narrow stony path that snaked up the hillside to the city walls of Incallacta.

It was not exactly a feat of mountaineering to ascend the steep pathway, even with filming equipment, but it was still a pretty hard slog in that rarefied atmosphere. It was yet another indication of the supreme tactical genius of the Incas who founded the fortress city. This was the one pathway leading from the valley to the city boundaries. Every other approach from the valley was shielded by a sheer granite rock-face which would have been impossible to scale without modern mountaineering equipment. Quite clearly a relatively small band of soldiers armed with bolas slings, truncheons and spears could have held Incallacta secure against an army of invaders who could have approached only by the clearly-defined pathway, and not more than two abreast. They would have been sitting ducks.

Carlos and Ramon escorted us around the ruins, summarising

the theories they had evolved during their months of close study. The lay-out followed that of other Inca cities in Peru, described by the first Spaniards.

The plateau on which the city had been built was almost pure rock, unable to support the growth of anything more than meagre scrub. It was not difficult to pick out the outline of several groups of houses, an enormous temple in the centre of the parade-ground area and, of course, the defensive wall surrounding the city.

The stone houses which, as in all important Inca cities, were built for the chief, the religious leaders, the soldiers and the selected virgins, were carefully constructed of large stones, cut and shaped to fit together without any form of cement. In most cases the walls still stood at least two metres high, and only the thatched roofs were missing.

There was also quite a large area where the plateau of rock joined the steep hillside, which was much more overgrown with vegetation. Here we discovered the ruins of many adobe huts which must have collapsed during tropical rainstorms and so provided a bed of earth where bushes and trees could grow much more vigorously. Obviously this was where the mass of the city's inhabitants lived. The small groups of stone houses for the élite were on the other side of the temple, overlooking the huge waterfall which cascaded down from the hillside into the valley below.

Almost every important city of the Incas was built near a waterfall, which played an important part in their religious life, for they believed in purification of the soul by immersion of the body in clean running water. If Incallacta followed the pattern of other Inca cities, the substantial square houses of two rooms nearest to the waterfall would have belonged to the priests and religious leaders.

Next to these houses was a group of eight smaller dwellings of one room each, where the selected virgins would have lived. It was the custom among the Incas for the priests to choose the most attractive young girls of the tribe, and to shut them away in their small colony within the city walls to undergo a few months of practical teaching, religious instruction and purification. Then, when a young man was picked out for the very prestigious job of priest or soldier, he was given one of these girls. Some of the virgins suffered a less welcome fate. They were sacrificed to the Sun God in ceremonial rituals twice a year. There is no knowing exactly what attributes the Incas considered necessary to qualify a girl as an attractive virgin. We do know that the Spaniards considered Inca women to be very pretty, and certainly pictures and descriptions portray them as sexually desirable, gentle creatures. It could be that the Inca men had quite different ideas. If they were anything like the Yuko or the Kunaguasaya, for example, physical strength would be far more important in a prospective wife than a beautiful figure, and the ability to chop firewood more of a necessity than aptitude in love. In fact, physical love-making was certainly of less importance to the Inca men than to most of us in the western world. The extremely inhibiting effect of the altitude made Inca men sexually undemanding, a fact that made sense to me when I remembered my state of collapse after a short walk in the thin air of that altitude. It reminded me, too, of an ancient Inca custom reported by the *conquistadores*.

When the young soldiers and priests had been given their pick of the virgins, the girls who were left over provided a little entertainment, after a purification ceremony beneath the cascading waterfall. The naked girls would gallop across the river and start the long slow climb up the hillside across the valley. When they reached the far bank of the river, all the unattached males of the Inca city set off in pursuit. The idea was that any girl who was caught by one of the pursuing horde of young men was thrown to the ground and claimed as his personal prize. According to their chronicles, the Spaniards watched this custom, and were greatly amused to note that, after a lively chase in the rarefied atmosphere, the Inca men were usually too whacked to claim their booty. The effect of the altitude and the general lack of sexual prowess among almost all the Inca men worked to the advantage of the *conquistadores*, who said that the women enjoyed their advances and that, whenever they captured an Inca town, they always found a significant group of the female inhabitants who welcomed them almost literally with open arms.

The temple, built at the very heart of the city, was the focal point of life for the whole Inca community. Like many cultures before them, the Inca worshipped the sun, and the religious leaders held tremendous power, subordinate only to the Inca chief himself and his representative in each town who, of course, had the support of the army in his area. For though the Inca and his powerful military force laid down the strict social organisation within the Inca empire, the religious leaders commanded and controlled day-to-day life in almost every other direction.

The temple at Incallacta was built in the heart of the city, and its stone walls still stand three and a half metres high; it is the largest Inca building ever discovered in Bolivia and, according to the archaeologists of the University of Cochabamba, the largest temple so far discovered anywhere in the Inca empire. A massively overpowering edifice it must have been, measuring eighty-four metres long by twenty-seven metres wide, with the ridge-shaped roof supported by pointed stone walls which must have been five metres high at each end.

As I stood there alone in the centre of the temple floor, with my hands resting on the solid stone altar, it was not difficult to imagine the sumptuous splendour of this setting at the time of an Inca ceremony.

In one wall running the length of the temple there were twelve narrow doorways through which the Indians would have entered in single file from the parade-ground area outside. With a huge thatched roof supported by massive timbers, it would have been fairly dark inside, but built into all the inside walls of the temple were little alcoves with a stone shelf in each. These forty-eight shelves would have been filled with gold ornaments lit by blazing torches, which would have provided an awe-inspiring setting of regal splendour.

After a breakfast of biscuits and cheese, Ramon and Carlos led us two *gringos* along the footpath that snaked unevenly alongside the narrow rushing river on the valley floor. It was easy enough two pick our way in and out of the scattered shrubs and bushes, and easier still when we came to an area of rock the size of a football pitch with no soil at all and, consequently, bare of vegetation.

David's sharp eyes never stopped darting like a rapier in battle. When he stopped in his tracks it took a moment or two for my own eyes to focus on what he had seen. On the far side of this naked stone parade-ground were half a dozen mounds of small stones. Each mound was about as high as a dining-room table and about four times as big in area.

"Could be burial mounds," said David. "Worth investigating." And he was gone with Ramon by his side. Carlos and I strolled a little further along the valley, where we made an exciting find. We had come to a point where the river changed direction a few degrees, and where the tumbling waters were funnelled through a narrow cleft in the rocks. Here there were stepping-stones across the river bed, so conveniently placed as to suggest that a human hand, rather than nature, had placed them there. The stepping-stones led to a paved area on the far bank, and from this neat stone platform led a distant pathway. This was no animal trail. It was a precisely-landscaped pathway of smooth stone bricklets. Obviously it led up the hill, and eagerly I followed it, hoping to find a vantage point from where I could look back to Incallacta.

It is common knowledge that Inca tracks and roads were supreme feats of engineering and construction, made out of rocks and stones that were individually shaped and fitted to form a smooth, hard surface, all without the aid of any form of cement.

This stone track was almost two metres wide: just about right for two men or one man and his llama to walk along together side by side. My spirit of adventure and achievement was heightened by the thought that I was certainly walking in the footsteps of the legendary Inca travellers of four hundred years ago.

I needed some stimulus to keep going, I must admit. From a distance I must have looked like someone in a slow-motion film as I began to drag one foot laboriously after the other. The expected handicaps of middle age and overweight were compounded by the steepness of the path, as well as by the thin air of that altitude. Carlos was blessed with youth and the enormous lungs of those born in the mountains, and he was striding along. Eventually I accepted his offer to carry my camera case, even though I had written my own rule that I should never be parted from the priceless equipment which was essential to the success of the exploration. As I gasped for breath and stopped every quarter of an hour, Carlos quietly advised me to keep going at all costs, even very, very slowly. He understood the problems of lowland people exerting themselves at altitude, but experience told him that to stop even briefly is the immediate prelude to total surrender.

So I kept myself going with a masochistic drive that sometimes bordered on despair. After two hours of this self-torture, we at last reached a small plateau about the size of a tennis court. This was where I set up the camera to film the magnificent view, looking down on Incallacta one hundred metres below us across the valley. I filmed long shots showing the whole ancient Inca settlement: the ruins of many stone houses, the walls of the huge Temple of the Sun, and across the narrow ravine to the smaller Temple of the Moon. From this position on the hillside above the city I could show on film the superb strategic position of the Inca fort: how it guarded the narrow, vital pass through the Andes leading to the little known, unexplored sierra looking out over the immense dark canopy of the Amazon jungle.

I would accept that some other European or American traveller may have actually seen the city, although no pictorial record exists to prove it, but even if a foreigner had been there and told no one, I am almost certain that no one had ever stood on this particular plateau, looking down on Incallacta.

We stood in silence, Carlos and I, both overawed by the greatness of the engineering skills of Inca Indians all those years ago. Carlos broke the silence. With stunning casualness he said, "Look at the Temple of the Sun and the priests' houses above it." He drew the outline with his hand as he spoke. "Can you see the shape of the puma?"

It was probably a full minute before my racing thoughts were finally drilled into some sort of order, before each fleeting shred of memory fell into the pattern of a clear picture. Of course. The animal shapes of a genuine Inca city were quite clear at Incallacta. Carlos obviously knew this from his previous studies of the city. I had to draw on my memories of the Incas in Colombia and the legends of the Dobokubi to realise the significance of the animal shapes. No Spanish chronicle talks about Inca cities having been built in the shape of animals, but the Injkas of Colombia told me to look for the outline shapes of the puma, the condor, the llama and the jaguar in the capital cities of the Incas. Each shape can be seen. The shape of a puma's head was outlined by the grouping of the priests' houses. The Temple of the Sun outlined the shape of the puma's body in one direction, and the neck and head of the jaguar in the opposite direction. The sharp pointed ears of the llama were also the claws of the condor. All the animals were there, silhouetted by the dazzling sunlight against the dark earth of the plateau on which the city had been built. At once I took longer shots of the whole city, over which I would be able to superimpose the animal shapes on the screen when I returned home. This was indeed a vital piece of evidence which helped me to convince myself that this was without any doubt an Inca city.

It must have taken many hundreds of Inca men several years to build this large city. The engineering skills and the sheer hard labour of carrying those huge stones, shaping them, and hoisting them ten or twenty feet to the top of the walls, was a task of formidable proportions. Why did they build it?

Certainly it was brilliantly sited to protect and guard the entrance to the Andes along the pleasant valley. But what treasure was there of such importance to the Incas that they went to such lengths to guard it? And how far away was it? Where was it exactly, and how did one get there? Only the last of these questions could be answered at once. There was only one route by which to travel away from Incallacta on foot, and that was the Inca road on which I stood.

As I walked back down the track towards our camp on the river, I knew that exploration along that Inca road would have to be the next step of the journey.

Halfway down the hill I caught sight of David in the valley immediately below the boundary wall. He was still investigating those heaps of stones, and I saw that he and Ramon had thrown aside the top layers of stones from some of the mounds.

I stood and watched until a movement on the hills on the far side of the valley caught my attention. It was a llama, and as my eyes focused I could see that it was not alone. On the rocks around the llama sat four Indian women, dressed in their long cloaks and flat-brimmed hats. They appeared to be sitting motionless, looking down on the spot where David was working. I asked Carlos if this represented any kind of threat, but he admitted that he was baffled. He'd noticed that these women and others had been watching all of us all day.

"Where from?" I asked incredulously.

"Up there," Carlos said, pointing to the broken rocks of the ridge above. "One of them is still there."

I couldn't see anything, but it seemed a little sinister. "Where do they come from?" I asked.

"Here," he replied with pursed lips, indicating the line of the hills. It was a disquieting realisation that there were Indians living around here. We hadn't seen any signs of human habitation on the last part of our journey in, nor indeed in the hills on either side, but Carlos, who knew the area, seemed quite unconcerned. We continued our descent and joined David and Ramon, who were obviously pleased with the interesting discoveries they had each made.

"Look at this! Inca brain surgery, trepanning," said David, as he lifted a piece of bone from the top of a skull, as if he were neatly removing one piece of a jigsaw puzzle. "This one shows a pre-frontal leucotomy. See this hole near the temple. This is the one spot where the surgeon can safely put his knife through the skull—probably the most delicate brain surgery performed today. The Incas obviously knew how to carry out this most skilful operation."

"Doesn't look as if the victims lived, though," I observed.

"Oh, yes. They might have died of old age," insisted David. "We'll take the skulls back to the university. The medical people can soon tell us whether the patient lived or not, just by examining the skull."

"Funny shape, some of the skulls," I pointed out. One adult skull tapered off almost to a blunt point at the top, rather like and inverted ice-cream cone. One much smaller skull, obviously that of a child, was beginning to assume this extraordinary cone shape, as well.

David was perplexed, but Ramon had the explanation. He told us that they had a number of similar skulls in the Inca Museum at the university, and, although the early Spanish explorers often wrote about the Inca ritual of head-shaping, they did not agree about the reason for it. Pencil drawings by the Spaniards show that the Incas tied strong cloth bandages around the heads of babies and continued with this very tight bandaging until puberty and beyond. One Spanish drawing shows a baby lying on its back with a heavy plank of wood tied firmly across its forehead, pinning it to the ground.

Obviously both these methods were used, and both worked effectively, but the Spanish chroniclers did not agree about the reason. Garcia said that it was purely a device to give what the Incas considered an attractive personal appearance, and that this particular beauty treatment was reserved for the Inca nobles. Certainly the chiefs, the ruling class and the state governors also had wooden wedges driven into the lobes of their ears so that they grew up with the physical distinction of huge lobes that almost touched their shoulders. So there could be some basis for the theory that a misshapen skull was also considered to be the distinguishing mark of an Inca nobleman.

Juan Cajmarca, the son of an Inca princess and a Spanish officer, had another theory altogether. This was that the Incas were great disciplinarians, and would not tolerate disobedience or tantrums of any sort, even from those of very tender years. He tells us, for example, that Inca mothers never held their babies while they suckled, in case the infant started to cry as soon as it was put down. Instead, the baby lay on its back while the mother knelt above it, and dangled a breast for it to feed from. Cajmarca says that any child that was at all fretful or emotional had its head tightly bandaged soon after it was born, so that it grew up to be tractable and well behaved. The Incas believed that the human emotions were located in the frontal lobes of the brain, and the effect of squashing the front of the skull was to iron out the problem areas. A brain surgeon, to whom I told this story, agreed that such a drastic treatment might have the desired effect, but it might also turn the child into a cabbage.

There can be little doubt, however, on the evidence of these skulls and many more that have been excavated, that the Inca culture produced brain surgeons of considerable skill and expertise.

David was so excited about his discoveries that I felt a shade guilty about bringing him back to earth with the news that groups of local Indians had been spying on us all day, but he seemed unconcerned.

Since our camp-site was outside the city walls, I slept uneasily that might, nagged by fear of possible retribution from local Indians, and daunted by the prospect of arousing their anger even further by continuing our exploration of Incallacta next day.

CHAPTER THREE

Incallacta

I WAS AWAKE BEFORE daybreak, at that calm and peaceful moment when the sun, just below the horizon, is beginning to ruffle the dark velvet smoothness of the night sky.

The embers of the previous night's fire needed only a little encouragement to glow once again, and soon the coffee pot began to bubble with life, to be followed by a pot of dehydrated stew for our breakfast.

During the day David continued his excavations, while Ramon and Carlos seemed to enjoy helping me with my filming. They were both invaluable guides, since they had already carried out many hours of study during several trips to Incallacta on behalf of the Cochabamba University, and they knew about recent research, carried out by other academics, relating to the Inca occupation of Bolivia.

Ramon told me that Incallacta had been built by the Inca Huayna Capac only a short time before the Spanish invasion.

An original document, written by the first Spaniards to establish a permanent frontier post at Cochabamba in 1556, had just been discovered, and assessed by a team of anthropologists under Don Alfonso de Morales, the Director of Historic Archives at the university. The lengthy document is called 'The Redistribution of Land of the Inca Huayna Capac in the Central Valley of Cochabamba'. It was written by the early *conquistadores* from the accounts of Inca officials, who were speaking of the immediate past, within living memory, so that the document is likely to be quite accurate, according to Don Alfonso and his team. It is the only written account of life in that area when the first Spaniards arrived, and the only description of the Inca government in

Bolivia immediately before the Spanish invasion. It tells of the first visits to the Cochabamba valley by Huayna Capac's father, Topa Inca Yupanki, about the year 1500, during the meteoric expansion of the Inca empire. Yupanki's army quickly conquered the Aymara-speaking tribes living in the valley—the Charcas, the Caracaras and the Chichas—and designated the area a granary of the Incas.

The conquered tribes were neither enslaved nor subjected to Inca rule. They were embraced by a benign socialist rule which, in return for labour, offered them food, clothing, housing, protection and a new religion. The indigenous tribes had to grow maize, fruit, potatoes and the coca leaf but, in accordance with normal Inca practice, they could retain one third for themselves. One third had to be paid as a *mitimae* (tax) to the Incas living on the High Plateau, and one third was used to feed the Inca governor and his staff, who ruled the area, the Inca soldiers, who were sent to protect them, and the priests who introduced and taught the Inca religion.

Yupanki must have regarded the Cochabamba valley as a vital acquisition, because at Cotapachi he built four thousand silos, in which to store maize and potatoes, and he extended the Inca road from Cuzco to Tiwanaku for another 400 miles to Cochabamba, so that this valuable food supply could be moved easily to the centres of population in the high mountains.

Maize and potatoes formed the basic diet, and coca was vital to the well-being of the people living at high altitudes. The fact that coca was used as currency, and was much more valuable than gold, for example, supports the theory of scientists in Bolivia's Department of Anthropology that not nearly enough emphasis is placed upon the importance of the coca crop in Inca times.

Many people in La Paz and smaller cities at that altitude still chew a lot of coca today. I did, and I found it of great benefit, for it helped to overcome the problems caused by breathlessness, and enabled me to undertake physical challenges that would have otherwise been quite beyond my capabilities. Raw coca is not a drug, but it is, of course, the basic ingredient of cocaine. Nothing has been written about cocaine being used by the Incas but, since the drug is made illegally by Indians in many remote areas of Bolivia today, it seems likely that it was manufactured in Inca times.

According to the researchers at the university, Huayna Capac built Incallacta and a line of smaller forts in the hills around Cochabamba to protect his invaluable food supply against the Guaranee Indians from the jungle of eastern Bolivia, and against the Charcas, the mercenaries of South America. The Charcas were a large and fiercely hostile tribe living in the Andes of southern Bolivia in the area where the Spaniards eventually established the mining towns of Potosi and Sucre. They were well-organised, highly-trained warriors who rented their army to whichever tribe was willing to pay them as allies in a dispute over territorial rights with a neighbouring tribe.

When the Incas first came the Cochabamba valley, almost all the indigenous tribes of the area put up some resistance, and many of them employed the Charcas in a vain attempt to repel the Inca invasion. Ramon showed me the evidence of much rebuilding and repairs to the walls of Incallacta, which supported his theory that the city had been sacked on more than one occasion.

As I filmed the magnificent temple walls I was once again filled with awe and admiration for the strength and engineering skills of the builders. What was even more breathtaking was that all the hundreds of rocks had been quarried at a site on the top of the hill two kilometres to the east, and then transported down the very steep slope to the plateau on which the city had been built.

So far everything about Incallacta indicated that it was Incan. Ramon offered further evidence when he suggested that the lay-out of the city was astronomically aligned. The twelve narrow entrances in the side wall of the temple were precisely placed so that, as the sun moved round the horizon, its rays lit up an alcove opposite each entrance in turn. In each alcove there might have been a gold figure, representing each month in the year, which would have been lit up at dawn for approximately thirty days until the sun moved round the horizon to light up the next figure.

On the hillside just above the city was an agricultural calendar. This took the form of a curved stone wall built in four sections, each one two metres long and joined to the next section by a buttress wall thirty-three centimetres wide. The wall was built in such a way that the sun lit up each buttress in turn at different times of the year, thus indicating to the Indian farmers when to sow, reap, fallow and prepare their land according to the four seasons. We know that any important Inca city incorporated one of these agricultural calendars, because the Spaniards wrote about them, but this one at Incallacta is the only one known to exist today.

According to Ramon, the Indians who built Incallacta incorporated these calendars for telling the month and the quarter of the year, though I was not there long enough to test the hypothesis myself. They also had a clock to tell the time of day, and this I could verify from my own observations. At one edge of the city, alongside the forty-eight stone silos for storing food, the builders had placed a large stone about two and a half metres high, looking something like a gigantic inverted ice-cream cone. The top of the stone, or the sharp end of the cone, had been chiselled and shaped like a child's brick in a construction set. There were four sharp edges and four flat faces at different levels. As the sun moved moved across the sky each day, it lit up each of the four faces of the rock for a period of three hours. By looking at the rock one could, with a little practice, tell the time of day within half an hour or so.

Ramon, who had climbed on to the rock, told me that it was almost certain that each face of the rock had been covered by a sheet of gold, which would have reflected the sun's rays for miles around. There were holes in the rock-face which could have been cut to take the pegs clamping the sheets of gold.

We continued our exploration of the ruins as far as the boundary wall next to the priests' houses; this was built right on the edge of the city plateau where it broke away steeply to the canyon floor twenty metres below. It must have been a superb defensive system, for it would be almost impossible for an invader to scale the sheer rock-face of the canyon wall while subjected to a barrage of arrows, stones and bolas fired by the soldiers from behind the stone wall.

On the top of the canyon precipice was the foundation of what had once been a suspension bridge which, according to university sketch maps, had crossed the narrow gorge through which the waterfall thundered. This would have connected the plateau, on which the main city was built, with a much smaller piece of flat land which also protruded from the hillside. The suspension bridge had long since fallen down, and the only way to cross today is to take the narrow precipitous footpath which leads from the city down to the waterfall, cross by the rock platform which the Incas had built for their frequent purification ceremonies, and then climb the narrow footpath on the other side.

Even though the two young Bolivians carried all my filming equipment, I became very panicky during the walk along that footpath which was no more than thirty centimetres wide, with a sheer drop on one side. It was just like walking along a window-sill on the fourth storey of a block of flats.

It is purely psychological, this business of vertigo, as I found out when I turned to face the cliff with my back to the steep drop, and proceeded down the path sideways like a crab. As long as I stared directly into the hillside and clutched at whatever small plants were growing out of the cracks in the surface, there was no panic. I turned round just once to look down at the footpath ahead and the whole canyon almost leapt to meet me.

The two Bolivians who had watched me struggling to climb the hills in that thin atmosphere and had poured scorn on my nervous reaction to the Indians spying on us, were beginning to show their frustration. Clearly they had no fear of heights, and my slow progress did not exactly label me as an ace explorer.

The footpath up to the smaller plateau across the ravine was not so difficult, and soon I was standing on the stony courtyard, about half the size of a half a dozen tennis courts. In the centre was the ruin of the Temple of the Moon.

The circular stone wall stood about one and a half metres high and enclosed a piece of absolutely level land the size of one tennis court. In the centre of this enclosure was a huge, solid rock nearly two metres high, with a smooth top surface the size of a large dining-table. This was the sacrificial stone, Carlos explained, and the four shallow channels—one at each corner—were cut so that the four legs of whatever animal was being sacrificed could be held in position with one leg strapped into each channel. Or the arms and legs of a person? I suggested. People were sacrificed as well on special occasions, the Bolivians agreed. The victim was usually a virgin.

At one end of the smooth surface of the top of the sacrificial stone, a great bowl the size of a dinner-plate had been hollowed out. This, I was told, was to catch some of the blood of the victim whose heart had been cut out. After the ceremony the bowl of blood was left as an offering to Inti, the Sun God.

On the hillside overlooking the remains of the Temple of the Moon I could see what appeared to be straight lines carved into the surface, but almost hidden by the low undergrowth. I walked up the hillside and cut my way through the covering of shrubs and low bushes to find that many lines of steps had been hacked out of the surface, one line above the other, like the terraces of a soccer stadium. Obviously that is exactly what they were: seats for thousands of spectators, all of whom would have had a magnificent view of any ceremony being staged in the Temple of the Moon below.

While I was filming this scene, I met David again at the mouth of an enormous cave in the hillside. The entrance was about the size of an average three-bedroomed semi-detached house and, although it was partly hidden beneath a dark canopy of vegetation, there was enough light to see the first ten metres into the tunnel. Then it curved to the left and disappeared into total darkness. Being alone, David had not ventured into the inky blackness of the cave, and I certainly did not relish the prospect of joining him on such a journey by the light of the one small hand-torch we carried.

There was plenty of evidence to show that the cave had been inhabited at one time. There were elementary and somewhat crude carvings on the wall: a small stone kiln; shelves and small alcoves chiselled out of the rock-face; two pieces of human skull; stone maces and stone axes, together with innumerable small pieces of bone that might have been human or animal. Clearly this very large cave was worth a thorough investigation, but there was no knowing what danger one might have to face in the dark interior, and so we decided to postpone the investigation for another time, when we could come prepared with powerful lights and with guns for self-protection.

Round the camp-fire that night I told David about my conversations with Carlos and Ramon, and in particular about a discussion I had had with one of the local Indians, who had told us that, across the hills, were other stone ruins of the cities of 'the people of yet before'. He had pointed in the direction of the Inca road leading across the valley and up into the distant rocky hills. Was Incallacta perhaps one of a line of Inca forts guarding the four or five wide valley passes through the rugged Andean hills of this area, and not just 'another lost city of the Inca'?

David agreed that we should break camp next morning, and walk the Inca road to investigate these other ruins. Ramon and Carlos offered to accompany us for another two or three days, to show us the ruins of the four fortresses they knew but, with regret, they would not be allowed to travel outside the limits of the State of Cochabamba, because they did not have permission from the military who controlled Bolivia.

During the next two days we walked along the old Inca road from Incallacta, heading westwards back towards Cochabamba. None of the three forts or the five look-out points we visited was as large as Incallacta, but all were built of stone in similar style to that of all the other Inca ruins. The three forts, called Puca Puca, Pamparacay and Incaracay, appeared to have been constructed purely as forts to accommodate soldiers and their families, who may have been quite self-sufficient. There were no temples, parade-grounds, areas where priests and agricultural workers lived apart, or silos to store food for a significant population. David found a cave in the hillside which had been used as a cemetery. It was full of human skeletons, and this suggested that Incaracay had been a permanent garrison with a settled community of soldiers and their families who had lived and died there. David's excavations also disclosed a number of interesting objects which he laid out so that I could film them. There were dozens of stones, from the size of a cricket ball to the size of a child's football. Some had holes in the middle, so that they could have been used as bolas to sling at an enemy, or they could have been used as hammers by ramming a shaft of wood into the hole in each stone. He had also found a number of small stones in the shape of human heads fifty centimetres in height, and there were smaller figures, in the shape of men and women, made in gold, all of them complete with sex organs.

Another piece of gold had an unusual shape which puzzled us at first. There was a shaft thirty centimetres long, rather like the shaft of a large carving knife. On the end of it was a crescent-shaped blade, so that the instrument had the outline of, say, a knife handle welded on to the silhouette of a new moon. Ramon had the answer. "It is an Inca surgeon's knife," he said. "We have found them in other ruins in Bolivia."

The crescent-shaped blade was hardly sharp enough to cut a Sunday joint, but Ramon assured us that it could be sharpened to match the edge of a razor blade. Indeed he recalled an account (though he could not remember names or details) of an American surgeon consultant who had demonstrated to his students by actually performing a brain operation with an Inca knife. What had impressed the medical world, so it was said, was that the ancient surgical instrument could cut through skin or bone or delicate brain tissue with equal efficiency, whereas our present-day surgeons use different instruments for each stage in a major brain operation. Since I wrote this I have talked to Professor John Gillingham, Head of the Department of Neuro-Surgery at Edinburgh University. He confirms both the story and the skills of Inca neuro-surgeons. I can quote him.

While my own thoughts and efforts were concentrated on the problems of filming both the spectacular setting and the skilful construction of the fort which was built to guard a pass through the foothills of the Andes, David spent his time excavating and studying. That evening he put forward a theory that was to change all our plans. Unfolding our map of the area, he marked every fortress and every look-out point we had visited, and they ran in a half-moon shape from Cochabamba to Incallacta. All were near to the old Inca road joining Cochabamba with Santa Cruz, and together they guarded every pass through the lower Andes in the south-east corner of Bolivia; quite clearly each one was constructed to guard against possible attack from the south and the east.

The glib explanation that had always been accepted was that the forts were built to guard Cochabamba and the south-east quarter of the Inca empire from attack by the Guaranees but, as David pointed out, Indians attacking on a large scale from the direction of the Brazilian jungle could have driven straight to the heart of the Inca empire in Bolivia by making a long detour around to the unguarded south-western flank. A more logical explanation for this particular line of forts, set quite close together, might be that they were built to guard the much more local area to the north-east of Cochabamba, called the Yungas de Corani. We immediately asked Ramon and Carlos to tell us all they knew about the Yungas area, and in particular whether there could have been anything that warranted such elaborate protection in Inca times.

Both the young Bolivians were perplexed at the suggestion, and could think of no reason why this area could be of any value in Inca times any more than it is today. They admitted that very little was known about the vast tract of sub-tropical jungle to the north of the Cochabamba–Santa Cruz road, because it was still quite undeveloped. The only inhabitants were small groups of

Indians, often no more than five or six families, living a primitive existence in total isolation. There were no towns, villages or organised communities at all, and the rare exploration expeditions undertaken by the university had not uncovered any prehistoric remains of any consequence.

Carlos then remembered that a Bolivian timber company had bulldozed a mud track from the Inca road into the Yungas for a distance of about twenty kilometres to a forest of hardwood trees. We might be able to borrow the university jeep with its driver, travel to the woodmen's camp, and then walk a short distance to Tablas Mayu, the last Indian community before one reached the vast unexplored area of the Yungas de Corani, the Yungas de la Victoria, and eventually the unknown unexplored Cordillera de los Mosetenes.

Back in Cochabamba, Mrs. Byrne de Cabellero, the British consul, introduced us to the Rector of the university, who was enthusiastic enough about our project to offer us the jeep, a driver called Rafael, and maps of the area.

Next day we made the hair-raising journey to Tablas Mayu. The first half of the drive along the old Inca road towards Santa Cruz was extremely uncomfortable, as the jeep leapt in and out of pot-holes across shallow crevasses cut out by the small streams which rushed down the hillside and crossed the road in a steady torrent. The second half of the journey was really very frightening. We stopped in the tiny hamlet of Corani to buy more food before we took to the mud track which was pitted and scarred by the tyre marks of the timber lorries.

We were travelling slightly downhill most of the time and, when we reached a line of steep hills, the road became much more solid, since it had been hacked out of almost pure rock. The trees and scrub thinned out considerably and no longer towered above us, since the topsoil here was obviously not deep enough to support a dense forest.

The lack of vegetation growing alongside this rocky shelf of a road did, however expose another threat: the sheer precipitous drop of about one hundred metres to the valley below.

Rafael proved to be a competent driver. He drove quite carefully along what was often no more than a narrow ledge cut out of pure rock, but there were occasional hazards like a short stretch of wet mud or a mini-waterfall cascading from a lagoon on the hillside, and several times David had the front door of the jeep open, ready to jump.

I was in the back seat at the time, surrounded by our equipment. Feeling fatalistic about the whole adventure, I tried to comfort David by pointing out that, although our wheels were often no more than a metre from the terrifying drop, it must be much worse for the tractors and lorries of the timber company. I tried to get some support from Rafael, and he had the good sense to agree at first. Then he pointed out that the huge tyres of the lorries had a much better grip on the surface than those of our jeep and, having a much higher clearance, these lorries could travel in each other's wheel-marks like a train on rails. Finally, with no sense of timing at all, Rafael pointed out a stone cross at the roadside with a name engraved on it.

"They sometimes go over the edge," he volunteered. "Like that one. There's another one just round the bend."

By now we had passed the last camp where they were felling trees, and Rafael told us that it was a matter of luck whether or not we could proceed along what was basically a wide footpath through the jungle to reach Tablas.

After many stops and much hacking down of thick scrub we eventually arrived at an area of forest which had been cleared. There was a long, low stone wall stretching into the distance on either side, with a wide home-made gate in front of us.

"Tablas," said Rafael. "We made it."

David jumped down to open the gate, but Rafael called him back.

"We don't go in until we are invited," he said. "We don't even open the gate."

"It'll be dark soon," David pointed out, but Rafael insisted that the Indians knew we were there waiting, and they'd come out soon, and invite us in, if they liked the look of us.

"If they don't?" I queried.

Rafael just shrugged his shoulders philosophically.

In Bolivia dawn breaks and night falls very quickly. There's no gradual awakening or period of dusk. It takes no more than half an hour for broad daylight to become total darkness, which is exactly what happened while we clicked our fingers, waiting. Eventually Rafael split the calm peace of the jungle by blazing away on the jeep's horn. If they hadn't known we were there, waiting, they certainly did now. They probably knew back in Cochabamba, judging by the deafening noise we were making.

But it worked. Within moments an elderly Indian, dressed in well-worn trousers and a native tunic, came and opened the gate, and stood there blinking in the headlights of the jeep.

Rafael dipped his lights, got out and went over to talk to the man. They had a very earnest discussion for quite a long time. Obviously it was not a case of "Hello, do come in." Negotiations were going on at length.

Eventually Rafael came back and, as the Indian stood to one side to hold the gate open, we drove in.

Inside the compound was a small clearing where we parked the jeep, unloaded our kit and followed the Indian along a narrow footpath through the trees, up a rocky slope to another boundary fence and another gateway, and eventually into the village itself, cowering quietly in the darkness. I could only make out the vague shapes of several houses and the dark shadows of one or two people moving stealthily around, apparently oblivious of the presence of strangers.

The Indian led us to a large wooden hut with a thatched roof, and then walked away briskly.

"This is their maize store," Rafael told us. "It's nearly empty now, and we can put our sleeping-bags in here for the night." He said nothing about food, water, or lavatories; so I improvised on all three counts.

David and I shared the biscuits and fruit juice we'd bought in Corani and, while Rafael disappeared in the direction of the village houses, we laid out our sleeping-bags by the light of our torch, and stretched out.

It was barely seven o'clock in the evening, much too early to sleep, in spite of our early start and our hard day's work. Time for useful discussion, we thought, and that is what might have happened if we hadn't been overrun by jungle rats as soon as we switched the torch off. Perhaps it was a hyperbole to say that we were overrun. It just seemed like it. By the time I had grabbed the torch and shone it on the floor, there were only three rats there, and they scurried away into the heap of dried maize.

Early next morning I followed some Indians to the village clearing—their parade-ground—which was alive with people preparing for the day's work. They did not look at all as I had expected; most of the men wore trousers. Most wore sleeveless cloaks made out of tree bark or animal skins, but one or two had ancient and ill-fitting sports jackets. All had relatively short hair, even if it was untidily cut. The women were clothed in voluminous ankle-length dresses made out of the mass-produced cotton material, with a flower pattern, which you can buy in any multiple store. Most had their long black hair tied back with pieces of coloured braid, and those with infant children carried them in large slings on their backs, knotted round their shoulders. Their appearance was simple in the extreme, but certainly not so primitive as I had expected. Rafael explained that this particular Indian community was the nearest to the recently-constructed main road from Cochabamba, and had probably traded with civilisation for several years. Certainly there had been a great deal of trading and intermixing since the timber merchants had entered the forest and set up their camp only ten kilometres away.

The houses in Tablas were quite simply constructed. The walls, about two metres high, were made of skinned saplings tied together with vines, and supported by a much larger tree trunk sunk into the ground at each corner. Most were thatched with palm leaves, but two had corrugated iron roofs which looked incongruous in that wild jungle setting.

Inside many of the houses there was a collection of cooking-pots and pans, knives, forks, plates and scissors, as well as candles, oil lamps and boxes of matches. Lengths of flowered cotton material, occasional pairs of shoes and socks, wide-brimmed hats and axes and shovels were other items that must have been purchased in Cochabamba's shops.

I wondered what the Indians could have used for money. "Coca and gold," Rafael told me. "Coca leaves were always a very important part of the diet of the Incas of the high plateau, and most of our people living high up in the Andes still need coca even today. There is an ancient road which the Indians travel from the Yungas here, leading to La Paz and to Cuzco and Lima in Peru. The Indians take the coca to the big cities once a year, and traders come here to buy gold."

"What gold?" I asked.

"Small decorative pieces which they dig out of the tombs," Rafael replied. "And there is gold in most of the rivers here," he added. "They pan for gold. They don't find it in any great quantity, but they don't want much. They are almost self-sufficient."

I followed a small group of men and women and children along a footpath through the forest until we came to a large level piece of land which had been cleared of trees, apparently by the slash-and-burn method. The crops were thriving here. There was maize almost ready to harvest, as well as coca, potatoes, yucca and bananas. There was a handsome selection of fruit and vegetables to eat with the meat of the wild animals of the jungle. During the days David and I spent at Tablas we saw the Indians bring in a wild pig, monkeys, chigwirees, birds and toads, which all went into the stewing-pots.

Making friends with the Indians was not easy at first, in spite of their previous contact with civilisation. Their early reaction was apprehension, and suspicion wherever we tried to break down the barriers. It was as if they were always looking for an ulterior motive in our every gesture of friendship, as if we were planning to take advantage of them or do them some harm at every turn. This was not an unreasonable attitude on the part of a people who, over the years, have been slaughtered, enslaved, robbed, raped and tortured by white men ever since the Spanish conquest; a people who, even in recent years, have been sold into slavery, or who have been given presents of poisoned food and clothing infected with killer diseases.

I read reports in *Time* magazine in 1974 of a missionary in Brazil who was brought to court for selling Indian children and, in the same magazine, I read the story of the Venezuelan ranchers who invited a tribe of hungry Indians to share a specially prepared feast and then machine-gunned them all to death.

These events did not take place in Bolivia, but such stories travel fast, and there is not much doubt that unscrupulous prospectors and colonists heap similar atrocities on the Indians all over South America from time to time. There is enough exploitation to breed apprehension, if not stark fear, among many Indians, as well as dislike, if not actual hate.

It was a situation I had faced often enough in Colombia and Venezuela in my ranching days, but I reckoned I knew how to break the barrier of suspicion. The answer I found was to give and give in an attitude of sincere and genuine friendship and absolute generosity, starting with the children. Generally the stories of appalling treatment and atrocities have not filtered down to them. They are more open-minded than their parents and, like children the world over, they love sweets. So I started by giving them a toffee each, making sure I showed them how to unwrap the paper! Then I'd make a toffee disappear by sleight of hand,

and we'd all play 'hunt the toffee!' We played blind man's buff, and I made a complete fool of myself by falling over, or having a mock battle with a tree. Idiotic things had the kids in stitches, even the ten-to-twelve-year-olds. Their mothers and fathers watched with benign indulgence and, when it was time to hand out some more toffees, I'd suddenly find the adults in the queue as well. I followed this initial contact by sharing whatever goodies I had with all the members of the tribe, and it was just as well that David and I had brought a quantity with us. This was certainly the way to open the doors to friendship.

The Indians had the strangest ideas of what was the most prestigious present we could give them. Top of the list was an ancient canvas hat of mine, which I gave Ilyapa, the headman of the village. A pair of David's worn-out socks, the old torch batteries, a biro and a piece of paper, spare boot-laces and a packet of soup powder were all received with awe and amazement.

I hit on the idea of recording the Indians' speech, and I played it back to them, to their intense wonder and amusement. Then David played his trump card. He carried an Instamatic camera and, without saying anything, he rattled off half a dozen photos, and peeled them out of the camera after they'd been developed. He handed each one to the assembled group, who at first were struck dumb with amazement, as if they were seeing the first pictures of the moon. Not a word was said. There was no reaction except incredulity at first; then, when the penny dropped, they all started laughing and jostling for position to pose in front of David for yet another photograph.

This response was perfect. I had half-expected the reaction I have had many times before when trying to film primitive Indians. I have known many who disapproved whole-heartedly, because, in some way, they had the idea that I was taking away a piece of their soul. Perhaps it was because David gave each one his own photograph and did not take it away that they were reassured. Anyway, they loved it.

At once I sensed a breakthrough, and I got out my 16-m.m. movie camera, which I had not expected to use for some considerable time. First of all, it can be mistaken for a gun, and secondly, if I explain that it is a camera to take their likeness, there is always this misgiving about stealing their souls. This time I wasted just one reel of film as I let them watch me loading it in the camera; this obviously impressed them as pure black magic.

Then I unwound the wasted reel of film, and gave them each a small piece, which they examined minutely and carried off as tenderly as a white woman might carry off a mink coat. For the children it was a hilarious pastime as they draped the film around themselves and each other. There were hoots of delight when I allowed a tight coil of film to unleash and spring at them like a snake. And then they had a cream-cracker each.

David and I were fast becoming extremely popular, as I knew we would. We were both generous benefactors, and yet quite undemanding ourselves. I also sincerely believe that the fact that I played the fool and smiled and laughed a lot was a critical factor in our favour. I judged that the people from civilisation with whom the Indians would have had contact (and very unpleasant memories, too) would have been stern, officious and probably threatening. We took care to be none of these things, and our hopes of a more amiable reception were certainly being fulfilled.

For Tablas was a stepping-stone. This was no lost Inca city, nor even part of a forgotten race. These people were only one stride from being civilised, but I hoped that they would know something about the people from the jungle to the north, even if there had been only a fleeting contact in the distant past. Obviously they would not be readily forthcoming. To give them sweets and presents was one thing, but to invade deep into their territory would certainly be discouraged, if not prohibited.

I carried out a plan of campaign which now in retrospect gives me cause for shame. At the time it seemed the only way to break down what appeared to be the last barrier leading to our goal: knowledge about the hinterland behind Tablas.

Every time one of the Indians performed some task for me or, in conversation, explained some important aspect of their way of life, I gave him a biscuit or a sweet—a bribe which set a precedent now followed by all other whites who have any dealings with this group. In retrospect it seems a despicable way to behave. I concentrated on one of the sons of Ilyapà, the Chief. He was called Huaqui, and I think he was the eldest son, because he was often detailed off to look after me. Or this may have been because he was one of the few who undersood some words of Spanish, and the only one who could speak it a little. His name meant 'brother'.

We sat talking most evenings, and I handed out a regular supply of toffees and biscuits and sultanas, whenever Huaqui told me what he knew (or made up) about the life of this particular *ayllu* (kinship group).

During a conversation one evening I discovered that he was obsessed with the idea of owning one of my shirts. I could well understand this tremendous desire because, as far as I could see, none of the others owned a shirt; so I popped the jackpot question. "Will you take me to the people in the hills?" I asked, pointing northwards. "If you will, you can have this shirt."

Desperation flooded across his face. His eyes darted to the hills and then back again to my face, as if seeking confirmation. "This very shirt," I assured him, to my eternal shame. It was a rotten trick. He wanted to take me, of course, but for some reason he just couldn't resolve the obvious problem which such a move would create.

"It's a long journey," he blurted out, almost in tears. "My father will not let me go now at harvest time. There is so much maize to collect before we sow the potatoes. Will you let me have the shirt if I tell you how to get there?"

I relented at once, and agreed to let him have it, even though the knowledge of how to get there might be worthless to us without someone to guide us. In the past I have found it essential to have one person from a familiar community to introduce me to the next, who can otherwise be extremely hostile. However, that was a bridge to cross later. First I had to know where I was heading.

Hauqui just sat there scuffling the mud and leaf-mould with his finger-tips. He was now deep in thought. He appeared to be battling with his conscience, as he wiggled his feet and flicked his head from side to side. Finally he looked longingly at my shirt, got up and started to walk to the edge of the clearing. He did not invite me to go with him. He looked round only once, briefly, to see whether I was following. For half an hour we walked at quite a brisk pace, crossing two rushing streams that cut sharp slices into the rocky hillside, and passing near fields of cultivation.

The narrow overgrown trail started to climb quite steeply, and I was struggling to keep Huaqui in sight; so I called out to him to slow down. He stopped, but did not look round or speak. He was acting as if he were ashamed of what he was doing, and wanted to get it over as quickly as possible.

As soon as I caught up he marched on, until he came to a piece of relatively flat land from which the trees had been felled, but their stumps and roots were still there in the ground, like an untidy collection of miniature dining-tables in a dwarf's restaurant. Obviously, when the remains of these trees had rotted or been burnt, this was going to be an allotment for growing food, and since nearly all the vegetation had been cleared from this hilltop site I had a much better view of the surrounding countryside than ever before.

Huaqui pointed to the jungle-covered hills and valleys to the north, and rattled off a fusilade of words at such speed that I understood nothing.

"Slowly," I said. "Slowly, slowly, to let me understand. Then the shirt is yours," and I touched a sleeve just to emphasise exactly what I meant. I suppose it was a battle of wits between the rich white man with the colourful shirt and the poor reluctant Indian boy, who was having to sell his soul. It was a confrontation which gave me no great pleasure at the time, and which fills me with shame in retrospect. But I was quite desperate to get the vital information I wanted, and I distinctly remember trying to salve my conscience by reminding myself of the tremendous journey I had made, of the twenty-five years I had spent searching, and of the possible importance of the discovery if I could win our one-sided battle.

Desperate now, I took off my shirt, sprayed my naked arms and shoulders with insect repellant to keep away the mosquitoes, and stood there with the magic shirt in my hand. I knew it was the key to open the door to that pot of gold at the end of the rainbow that was so tantalisingly close. To the scantily-dressed Indian boy, that shirt must have seemed like a king's ransom, also tantalisingly close.

Suddenly he surrendered. Slowly and distinctly he told me to follow that great river (below us in the valley) until I reached the foot of those hills. "Cross the river Mayka where there is a stone house, and on the other side there is a path through the trees leading to the top of the hills, to the 'land of no trees'. Go straight down the hill, cross a river and walk on where two rivers meet to make one river. Follow down the river Pakari ('the start or the origin'), past the rivers that flow into the Pakari until you come to the river Yanakaka, which comes in from this side" [indicating the left].

I stopped Huaqui at this point because, even with a clear view of twenty kilometres in front of us, I was by now completely lost. I made him start all over again, and I wrote brief notes on my cigarette packet. I asked him how I was to know which was the river Yanakaka, and he explained that there was a waterfall where it joined the Pakari.

The journey already sounded daunting but there was a long way to go yet. From the waterfall we had to follow the river Yanakaka up to its source in the hills of Thapka (the pig), and look for the 'land of small trees' (a clearing?), where 'the people of yet before' used to live. "From this Kapachachal (ancient site) a path leads across the hills [pointing northwards] until it arrives at the cities of Intisuyu."

Until Huaqui made the last statement I had very nearly given up all hope of making what looked like an impossible journey. But the word Intisuyu set the adrenalin pumping once again. The word Inti in Quechua means 'sun' or 'God', and the fact that he referred to cities in the plural was exciting news as well. I probed him on the question of numbers. both of cities and inhabitants, but he was quite genuinely vague.

"*Kapa, kapa, kapa,*" he said, stabbing the horizon with his finger tip. 'Village, village, village', in various parts of the distant jungle, which did not really give me much guide. "More people than here," he continued, but that did not mean very much either. More people than in Tablas could mean hundreds or thousands. Either Huaqui did not know the answer, or else he had no way of communicating the picture he had in his mind. But he had told me enough to keep his end of the bargain and, for a moment, his eyes sparkled with emotion, as I gave him the shirt. He did not put it on. He just passed it from one hand to the other, pulling it into all sorts of shapes and patterns as he did so. Then he placed the shirt on my back, but kept a tight hold of one sleeve. The message was obvious. It was *his* shirt, but I could have the benefit of its protection as we walked back to his village.

Huaqui's directions were so precise and in such detail that I supposed he had made the journey to Intisuyu himself on more than one occasion; so he must know the people living there.

I questioned him closely about the Indians 'over the hills', and especially about the sort of reception I might get. His answer was both surprising and disappointing.

"They know about you Blue Eyes," he said. "Their *Sinchi Kooto* (leader or chief) is a Blue Eyes; but be sure to let them know you are coming. Start calling to them from Kapachachal."

The idea of announcing your arrival when you are still a long way off is a perfectly normal procedure among the indigenous peoples of the South American jungle. It was a rule I had always obeyed during my explorations in Colombia and Venezuela. It is common sense, really. If the Indians in a remote village are given ample warning of your approach it gives them time to look you over and a pair of middle-aged Englishmen would hardly be classified as a potential threat to the security of a native community. Two figures suddenly emerging from the jungle shadows without warning, and walking into a village parade-ground unannounced, would be a different proposition altogether. No matter how harmless the visitors might be, almost any group of persecuted Indians would attack first, and make sure they eliminated any potential threat.

Huaqui's statement about their leader being a Blue Eyes was a most disturbing thought that filled me with apprehension. It was possible that Huaqui was talking about an albino Indian (and there are quite a lot of them in the South American jungle), or it could well be that we had been beaten to it. Perhaps a party of Europeans had already discovered out lost city, and were living there even now. Judging by our own experiences, it would not be unreasonable to suppose that, once a friendly contact had been established, a white man might conceivably be made a group leader among primitive Indians.

There was much to discuss with David, particularly the journey which I knew we would have to attempt in order to contact the Indians of Intisuyu.

"Of course we must go," said David with what was, for him, an emotional ring to his voice. "See if you can get Rafael to come back for us. We don't want him with us." Neither of us wanted Rafael to carry the news back to town if perchance we were about to make an important discovery, and so I put the proposition to him. I offered to pay him well if he would return for us in exactly two weeks, with a leeway of two more days in case we did not keep exactly to our schedule. Rafael agreed to this plan and so, to make sure he did come back, I told him that we were not carrying much money with us—it was all in Cochabamba—and so I would pay for both journeys when we returned. Rafael agreed reluctantly.

David and I then set about planning our route, but the information given me by Huaqui did not tally with what we could see on the map. The various maps we possessed all differed and seemed inaccurate. The large-scale government map was incomplete; many rivers had no names, and large areas ahead of us were blank. The one given to us by the university seemed the best, but even that did not match the contours we ourselves could see around us. We would need a guide. We would also need food.

In return for biscuits, a cigarette lighter and the promise of some clothing, we were soon supplied with maize bread, coca leaves, dried potatoes and dried wild-pig meat.

While Illyapa was in a happy frame of mind, I produced one of my vests, and offered it to him if we would let his son Huaqui come with us as a guide. Quite obviously he did not want to let his son go, and yet he wanted that vest very much indeed: I could see that, and so I invited him to try it on. Slowly he acquiesced and, after I'd shown him which were the head-hole and the armholes, he pulled it on over the top of his tunic. Fortunately I am so large that my voluminous vest was big enough even to fit over the top of everything! It was also fortunate, from my point of view, that all the Indians passing by at that moment stopped in their tracks to admire the new cloak, as they called it. Clearly my methods were working. It was now an offer that could not be refused.

"Go now, but come back quickly," Ilyapa said to his son Huaqui, and, having given his instruction as succintly as that, he turned on his heel and was gone. Apparently there was no need for any discussion. As in most Indian families, discipline in this *ayllu* was absolute. We were going on our journey, and that was that.

I have no doubt that Hauqui would have been quite prepared to start out immediately. He could have got up and walked away without any change of clothing; without weapons or food; without a moment's thought, because this was his environment, his life. For David and myself it was a strange and unknown world, and we needed a little time to prepare, and to work out plans for every crisis we might meet on the way.

We packed our food and a flask of purified water into the blanket which Hauqui spread out. When it was full, he slung it over his shoulder in the same way as the women carried their babies, so that his hands would be free, he explained, to wield the machete and cut our path through the scrub and jungle. I was left with a haversack containing one tent, medical supplies and other small essential items, while David carried the camera, film and another machete.

The trek over the next three days into the rolling, jungle-covered hills was a gripping adventure from beginning to end, but I think it was only the intense excitement at the prospect of discovery and success that took the edge off the sheer fatigue during what was a gruelling and difficult journey.

Huaqui was a superb guide and leader, who seemed equal to every problem we posed, and every difficulty the terrain presented.

The first stage of the journey was down the very steep, rocky slope to the river Matamonte, and just before we reached the river we came to a very large courtyard of flat land almost as big as a soccer pitch, and what attracted our attention at once was the fact that it was hardly overgrown at all. There were no large trees, only saplings and young trees that could not have been more than ten years old, and the bushes growing in small clumps had not spread out to cover the whole area as they had on the terraces above.

It did not seem unreasonable to suppose that this had been an area of cultivation until recent years. Excitedly I put this suggestion to David and, unwilling though he always was to accept any of my ideas without conclusive proof, he had to admit that this was the most likely explanation. As an immediate check, I asked Huaqui if his people had ever used this clearing for cultivation.

"No," he said. "There are too many insects. It is too far from the village and we have good land nearby. This was land cultivated by the Intisuyu, or so my father says."

On hearing this, David sprang into life, his weariness forgotten, as he dumped all his kit, and announced his intention of carrying out a survey of the area. I agreed at once, because it gave me the chance to sit and rest awhile; so, as David and Huaqui strode away across the clearing, I parked myself on a stone nearby and got out my camera to see if it had been damaged yet. All seemed to be well, and so I relaxed and lit up a cigarette. Surveying the scene around me, I realised that I was sitting in the centre of a semi-circle of stone seats. As they were somewhat overgrown with grass and small plants, their arrangement was not at first obvious. When I got up, walked around, and cut away some of the vegetation, it was quite clear that the semi-circle of seats had been placed there deliberately by human hand. They were spaced evenly about one metre apart; some were square-shaped, others triangular. Looking back at the larger stone on which I had been sitting, I could see that it had been carved in the shape of a throne with a high back and two arm-rests. It must have been carved, and it certainly looked as if the whole setting had been arranged as some kind of court, with the leader on the larger throne and his council sitting in a semi-circle around him.

I put my camera on its tripod and prepared to film the scene; I became so engrossed in the work that I did not notice any movements in the bush around the clearing, nor hear any sound at all except the whining of the camera. I lifted the tripod and camera a few metres to the right towards the edge of the clearing, to change the angle of the next shot and, as I crouched down to adjust the level of the tripod, I saw a slender black shape streak across the open space in front of me. I was so shocked that I stood up as if someone had stuck a sharp nail in my behind. My shoulder caught the hand-hold of the camera and the whole apparatus threatened to tip over. Instinctively I caught hold of the toppling camera and pulled it back upright. That could have taken no more than two seconds, but when I looked again the animal had gone.

I told myself that there was no reason to be scared of this fox or wild cat with the sleek black coat. It was obviously terrified of me, judging by the speed of its retreat and, as I kept repeating to myself, there are no wild animals in the South American jungle which actually hunt humans with the intention of killing them. The only danger from jaguars, pumas or wild pigs comes when you threaten their young, or inadvertently trap them with no means of escape. They will get out of your way if they possibly can. This had always been my experience during the years I lived deep in the Colombian jungle. Just to be on the safe side, however, I packed away my camera, and tucked the tripod under my arm so that the three steel tips were pointing in front of me. It could be a weapon with which to defend myself.

I also called out to David and Huaqui to return at once. I don't think there was any panic in my voice, but I remember feeling easier when I heard them both crashing through the bush nearby. They dashed into the clearing, saw that I was unharmed, and demanded to know what was wrong.

"A black animal just dashed across the clearing," I told David. "I didn't see much of it, but I think it was a black puma, or it could have been a fox. I just don't know for sure. It had a sleek, shining coat—that's all I can say for certain."

David was obviously nonplussed; so I described the bare facts to Huaqui.

"*Uyasti rekasti*," he declared authoratively. There was no argument, no room for discussion. He had given his decision. Later I asked him again to tell me which animal I had seen, and I wrote down his answer phonetically. Since then I have asked many Bolivians who speak Quecha and Aymara to translate this for me. No one has been able to do so, but some did tell me that it sounded like a black panther, which has been seen only rarely in the South American jungle, but, unless anyone can translate Huaqui's words *uyasti rekasti* for me, I shall never know for sure what animal it was.

"Might there be others nearby? A family of them?" I asked Huaqui.

He shook his head. "No more," he said. "That one has gone away."

He was not at all concerned. Pretending that I was not really worried either, I launched into a spate of words about my exciting discovery of what appeared to be a throne carved out of stone at the centre of a semi-circle of smaller stone seats.

"And look," I continued triumphantly, "the smaller seats run alternately: a square one and then a triangular one."

"*Yayee wack'as*," said Huaqui. "The people over the hills."

A *wack'a* in Quechua means 'a sacred place', and *yayee,* so I'm told, could mean 'Advice' or 'Decision'; so probably Huaqui's words could be taken to mean 'a sacred place for decisions' or a form of council chamber.

The trouble was that Huaqui did not speak either pure Quechua or pure Aymara, but a sort of mixture, an obvious dialect or bastardisation of both languages. I found it impossible to understand a complete sentence of his, and I had a great deal of difficulty in picking out a few key words, even when I knew what he was talking about. On this occasion, however, it was David who was doing the talking in short staccato phrases—the headlines one uses to impart important information at great speed.

"An enormous city," David said jubilantly. "Another clearing beyond the trees near the river. Stone walls. Stone barricades. Could be six or seven boundary walls, one inside the other like a jam roll. This could be the remains of a very large city. Come and look."

In a few minutes we arrived at an area of relatively level land which fell away gradually in small steps towards the river below. It was not so open as the other clearing had been. There were trees and bushes growing, but they were well spaced, and it was easy enough to walk between them, and to pick out many lines of stone walls about one to one and a half metres high.

"These are the boundary walls, the barricades or the defences," David explained earnestly, as he traced the curving lines of stones. Obviously he had already assessed the significance of the stone remains during his previous walk. Abruptly he turned to the left and stepped over one low wall, and then another and another.

We stepped over six walls before we came to what appeared to be the stone ruins of small rectangular houses in the middle of the encircling fortifications. For two hours we scrambled about, following the lines of tumbledown stone walls before we began to appreciate what we had discovered. We found the remains of at least fifty small rectangular stone buildings that we assumed must have been dwellings. There was no larger building which might have been a temple, nor any open space which might have been a parade ground; so at first sight it appeared to be the ruins of a small city. Surrounding the tightly-packed houses were fortifications of a kind we had not seen before: eight concentric stone walls running right round the city, and spaced no more than one and a half metres apart. We followed the outer circular wall, and estimated that its length was three to four kilometres, but there did not appear to be an obvious gateway in and out. Certainly there was nothing elaborate, with stone arches and massive pillars, like the gateways to other Inca cities.

We made a more detailed study of what little remained of the walls. The construction was crude compared with that of Incallacta, and far below the standard of some of the fortresses we had seen on the Cochabamba to Santa Cruz road. The stones used for the construction of the walls at Incallacta had been squared off so that they rested quite neatly one on top of the other, but here the Indians seemed to have been satisfied to collect a heap of stones of all shapes and sizes, and just put one on top of the other, using generous dollops of wet mud in which to bed the stones and hold them in position. They were not shaped or cut or fitted together with the supreme engineering skill demonstrated in many Inca buildings. Was this an Inca city at all?

The concentric circular stone walls surrounding the city were something we had never seen before in any other ruin. Nor had we even read reports of this kind of defensive system. Was it a formidable defensive barrier, or did the walls form a corral for holding animals? On the evidence of our first visit it was impossible to say. David and I agreed that, if the world showed any excitement at the announcement of our discovery, we could always come back and continue the work. For the moment it was time to eat, to prepare for the imminent arrival of darkness, and to sleep off the fatigue of a hard day.

Next morning we started the trek along the banks of the Matamonte and, as we descended into the dense jungle, the mosquitoes began to attack, even through a layer of clothing. "Very angry the mosquitoes around here," Huaqui volunteered; so, as well as putting on more insect repellant, I took a dose of Vitamin B. This was the method we used in Colombia to combat the mosquitoes. The Vitamin B tablets make you smell horrible, like a dirty animal in a farmyard—so horrible, apparently, that even mosquitoes cannot face up to landing on your skin.

Despite the presence of so many ferocious insects, the valleys of the Yungas of Corani proved a most hospitable and attractive setting. We were resting on a convenient stone bench on a piece of level land, and I surveyed the scene in depth. The gentle slopes of jungle-covered hills funnelled down to clear rivers; the whole panorama was of fertile, hospitable land rolling into the distance. It must have seemed attractive to primitive man thousands of years ago. There would have been wild fruit, lush vegetation, fish in the rivers, maize and coca growing in the valleys, and areas of level land on which to build villages and grow crops.

We strolled along in comparative comfort for two kilometres before Huaqui held up his hand and called a halt.

"*Ttiwacachana*," he said, pointing to a few metres ahead. I had no idea what this word meant, but it soon became obvious that it was 'quicksands'.

The narrow streams that rushed down the hillside continued their cascading path across the dry river bed, cutting a narrow valley through the sand until they reached the river. At this spot, however, the hillside levelled out, and the two streams slowed abruptly and spread into a wide delta like the mouth of a river before it reaches the sea. Here the wide belt of water oozed out towards the river like spreading treacle and, since it never stopped flowing gently across the river bed, it formed a semi-permanent surface of soggy wet mud and sand.

"If you walk on that, you fall to join your ancestors in the middle of the earth," said Huaqui, and, to emphasise the point, he heaved in a heavy piece of rock which slowly sank out of sight.

I would have guessed that the river was no more than waist-deep at this point, and I expected that we would have to cross over or walk in it for twenty metres, to bypass the quicksands.

"No," said Huaqui. "We have to climb the bank and walk along the hillside."

I looked at the river bank and could see that, because the water dribbling down the hillside had kept the earth moist and fertile, the jungle and undergrowth were particularly luxuriant. There was no obvious open trail; so it was going to be another slow, laborious fight every metre of the way.

"Why not walk in the river?" I insisted.

"No, you cannot walk in the river," Huaqui replied obstinately. "We go this way," indicating the jungle.

It was strange at first that neither Huaqui nor any of the primitive Indians ever offered any explanation. They just did not understand that a total stranger could be mystified or ignorant about the environment. On reflection, one realised that they had little or no contact with anyone brought up outside their area. They only knew their own people, brought up in the same circumstances as themselves, having acquired much the same knowledge from personal experience. They had never been strangers in an unknown land themselves, so they had no point of comparison when it came to understanding a stranger's point of view.

It is also true that, among many Indian tribes in South America, life is a rich panoply of personal experience, rather than the acquisition of knowledge through teaching. In Tablas, as with the primitive Indians of Colombia with whom I lived, I cannot recall a mother or a father saying to a child, "Don't touch the hot stone, because it will hurt," or "Don't touch that animal, because it will bite you." They would simply say, "Those stones are hot," or "That animal bites." The child then had to learn by personal experience that hot stones burn, and that animal bites are painful. In Huaqui's mind the simple admonition that you cannot walk in the river was a perfectly adequate piece of advice by his standards. If I wanted to find out why, I could learn by personal experience. Reluctantly I decided to trust his judgment and accept the strenuous long haul up the hillside.

In the branches of one particularly healthy bush I spied a bird's nest with four greeny-blue eggs in it. I could not be sure, but I thought they were the wild-turkey eggs which, I remembered, had made delicious eating on my jungle treks in Colombia. I was just thinking that maybe I would collect the eggs and cook them for our supper that night, when Huaqui turned round and shouted, "The birds will attack all of us."

He was hopping up and down, displaying more emotion that I had ever seen, desperation and fear predominating.

"What do you mean?" I asked.

"You are going to take the eggs," he said, as if he were accusing me of the most dastardly crime. "All the birds of that family would attack all of us . . . in the eyes, the nose and the mouth. We cannot see any more tomorrows."

"I did not take any eggs," I assured Huaqui, trying to calm him down.

"You take eggs," he remonstrated, "before sun goes out. Inti tells me."

I had no answer, because he was absolutely right. I was going to take the eggs, but how could be possibly know? Was he some sort of mind-reader, or did he have extra-sensory perception? That was a question I was going to ask myself again and again before my adventures were over.

I explained to David what had happened, and he told me that he had heard of several cases in other South American countries of a concerted attack by dozens of birds, which pecked out your eyes and cut your face into ribbons, but he could not remember the name of the bird. David was not in a talkative mood. The dysentery from which he had been suffering for nearly two days was beginning to weaken him.

At last we came to a piece of level land, where we turned and started our descent back to the river.

In many respects it was an easy journey, but it was slow,

monotonous and boring. Above all, it was terribly disheartening to realise, when we reached the river bank again, that we had spent most of the day in making no more than one hundred metres of real progress along the river.

From then on it became much easier, and we fairly strode along the dry bed of the river, the only inhibiting factor being the loads we carried, and the dysentery, which was making David feel ill.

After two more days slogging along the river bed, fighting our way along a narrow overgrown footpath through the hills, and then walking more easily along another river bed which had almost dried out, we reached the point where, as we could see from our map, the Rio de Oro (River of Gold) came tumbling down the hillside to our left.

"We follow this river nearly to the top of the hill," said Huaqui, "and there we find the ruins of Capachachal."

"Does anyone live there?" I asked.

"Not now," Huaqui replied. "There are some houses of the Mosetene tribe in those hills to the left, but we shall not try to meet them, because they are not friendly people."

"Will they not see us?" I asked anxiously.

"It is a very long way for them to see us," said Huaqui, "and they will not hurt us if we do not enter their land."

Two hours later Huaqui announced triumphantly that we had reached the ruins of Capachachal.

I had half expected that we would come to a large clearing in which we would be able to pick out the stone ruins easily enough, even if they were screened by a covering of creepers; but this expectation was wide of the mark. In fact, if we had not had Huaqui to guide us we would have never found the ruined city in a hundred years.

Huaqui stopped suddenly in front of a barrier of green jungle.

"There," he said, pointing into the trees. David and I looked blank.

"That is the boundary wall," Huaqui insisted, pointing no more than twenty metres ahead. We could see nothing but the matted undergrowth, but still, as if by mutual consent, we edged a few metres nearer. We could still see nothing; so I turned to look at Huaqui questioningly.

"I do not enter," he said shaking his head. "I wait while you go in."

"Go in where?" I asked in puzzled amazement. Huaqui merely nodded at the thick green barrier ahead; so I took the machete from him and chopped away at the undergrowth clinging around my waist. In this way I edged another five metres into the luxuriant vegetation with David right behind me.

Suddenly my machete blade richocheted off a chunk of stone with a metallic ring of protect. In an instant, David pushed his way through to be at my side, and he dropped on to his knees to examine the stone obstacle.

"Give me the machete," he demanded. as he got to his feet, and at once, in spite of all his troubles with dysentery, he was hacking away at the bushes, to reveal the remains of a stone wall no more than one and a quarter metres high, which ran at right angles to our path.

"It is a boundary wall," David exclaimed triumphantly, as he bent forward and peered through the trees to his right. "Look, you can just see the line through the undergrowth. Let's go into the ruins, and see if it is any clearer," he added as he climbed carefully over the stones where he had cut down the worst of the jungle barrier.

"If this is a lost city," I said, "we've got an answer to all those disbelievers who say that there cannot be a city that is still undiscovered in the South American jungle, since everything has been seen from the air. I could film our arrival, and show that you really can't see overgrown ruins from two metres, much less two kilometres up in the sky."

David grunted his approval, because, once inside the city wall, his attention was riveted on the tumbledown stone walls, which were covered in a thin film of moss and lichen. The trees and bushes were not so tightly packed as they had been along the approaches, but they formed a canopy which effectively denied us any panoramic views, or any chance of appreciating the plan of the city.

Huaqui's refusal to enter was not unexpected; most South American Indians believe that ancient cities are inhabited by the spirits of their ancestors, and they are invariably frightened by these spirits, whom they consider to be mischievous or downright wicked. Huaqui's refusal to enter the ruins meant that David and I had to hack our way through the thick undergrowth, and then cut down the scrub and bushes whenever we wanted to examine or film typical stone walls and buildings.

I was concerned to see the weakening effect the dysentery was having on David, and it was disturbing that the anti-diarrhoea tablets I had given him were having so little effect. I persuaded him to reinforce the tablets with very strong antibiotics, and by the next day there was a slight improvement.

By the end of the second morning we had cleared enough of the undergrowth in one small area to be able to see some of the buildings; we had also made a narrow pathway through the middle of the ruins, which showed us enough for David to suppose that we had uncovered a significant city built of stone.

He was prepared to identify one large building as a temple, similar in construction to the one at Incallacta but, with a measurement of thirty metres by twelve metres, less than half the size. Alongside this, the largest of all the buildings, were the ruins of six small dwellings just like the priests' houses at Incallacta, all with well-preserved stone floors. Next to them were the remains of approximately twenty small stone buildings. We could not be sure exactly how many, without clearing the considerable amount of bush and scrub and secondary jungle that grew over all. We cut a narrow footpath only until we reached another boundary wall forty metres beyond the temple, and found that, as at Incallacta, there was a narrow canyon, a rushing stream and a waterfall beyond it.

David pointed out that it would need a gang of workers to clear and to excavate the whole city, but we should make up our minds whether a much more ambitious expedition would be worth while at a later date.

What we found during the next twenty-four hours left us in no doubt that we had made a significant discovery of another lost city and, if we were to believe Huaqui, this might have been the capital city of quite a large community who lived in these valleys in years gone by. Since there were no trees more than one hundred years old growing in the ruins, it is reasonable to suppose that this particular city, and probably the associated ruins throughout the area, had been inhabited long after the Spanish conquest.

The lay-out of the buildings was similar to that of Incallacta and some other Inca cities. The method of construction by carefully shaped and fitted stones was in the Inca style, and the boundary wall, the fortifications, the temple and the waterfall all fell into the traditional pattern. Many of the artefacts we found were also identical with those in other Inca cities, and the fact that we found a number of pieces made of gold lying in stone alcoves and on shelves suggested that this might be a post-conquest settlement never discovered before.

The pottery was beautifully made and painted predominantly in red and yellow. We also found such typical articles of the Inca period as a surgeon's knife, a gold-alloy axe head, a gold necklace, and some small statuettes. I am not prepared to go into great detail about the amount of gold in the city ruins, because, as I shall report later in the book, I have made a firm promise to the Bolivian authorities.

Suffice it to say that, by now, David and I were thoroughly convinced that we had made a really important discovery, and that we would lead a large-scale expedition back to the ruins to carry out a full scientific study. We each gave a solemn understanding not to reveal the location of our discovery until we had both agreed to do so, and we shook hands on that.

Meantime, it was quite clear that David's condition was slowly deteriorating. We were a long way from help, and so the next priority was to get him back to civilisation and under medical supervision. The return journey was even more arduous than the original one, possibly because the adrenalin never flows so fast in retreat, but six days later we drove into Cochabamba and David went straight into hospital. Unhappily for him, they diagnosed a severe case of amoebic dysentery, and, since we did not have the necessary money to pay for treatment in the hospitals out there, they advised his immediate return to London.

I arranged our flight back to England, knowing that we could still proceed with our plans to announce our discovery, and we hoped to attract enough interest to finance our return trip and realise our ambitious plans for a future expedition.

My expectations were shattered by two unexpected developments. First of all David's illness was even more serious than we feared, and even after a long spell in the Hospital of Tropical Medicine in London, his chances of returning to South America on another expedition in the near future seemed bleak. The second setback, just as frustrating, was the blank wall of disbelief that greeted our claims to have discovered part of the Lost Empire of the Incas.

Angry and bitterly disillusioned, I was determined to go it alone if I had to, and to finish the story that had started twenty-five years before.

CHAPTER FOUR

Beni

FROM THE RUINS OF the city called Capachachal, we brought back a pocketful of the smallest gold figures we had found, as well as a gold axe and some of the stone maces and bolas. These genuine artefacts, together with my film and photographs, would be sufficient evidence, we thought, to back up our claim to have made a major discovery, and the fact that there were articles of gold still lying around suggested that this particular ruined city had not been discovered by the Spanish *conquistadores* or by subsequent exploration parties because, in either case, the gold would surely have been swept up. The Indians of Tablas Mayu were too scared to enter the ruins, as Huaqui had demonstrated. They had an overwhelming fear of the spirits of their ancestors.

David and I were hopeful that we would now be able to persuade even the most sceptical of academics that this was indeed the Lost City of the Incas. We did not know at that time, as I was to find out later, that it was merely 'another lost city of Incas': one of several in Bolivia. So when we arrived back in England, we did not hesitate to tell press and television reporters about our discovery and we produced the gold artefacts as supporting evidence. There was no question of trying to sell the gold articles. Melted down, their value would not have been much more than one thousand pounds, and their value to us as evidence was worth much more. In our minds this was only one aspect of the whole story but, unfortunately for our plans, it was the only the part to attract immediate interest. The discovery of the gold became the focus of attention all over the world, and our hopes and aspirations were blasted away by the explosive press reports that followed. Such phrases as 'a fortune in gold in the city of the

Incas' and 'the city of gold for which explorers have been searching for centuries' were all too common.

Gold was what some reporters considered to be the most important and noteworthy aspect of our claims, but we had never laid undue emphasis on this. It was no more than one important piece of the evidence. Unfortunately, the enormous publicity echoed around the world and backfired on us completely. To start with, it triggered off an international incident.

David and I had made a vow that neither of us would reveal the exact location or the country of our discoveries without the agreement of the other, so that our own studies could be completed in secrecy. It was a great shock, therefore, when David came out of hospital a few weeks later, to be told by the Foreign Office that the Bolivian government, through the National Institute of Archaeology, had made an official complaint about the so-called theft of gold from their country. The only solution, of course, was to return all the articles to Bolivia, and David offered to help. He said that, although he would not be fit enough to accompany me on another expedition into the interior, he hoped to recover sufficiently to be able to attend the International Archaeological Conference in Ecuador in two months' time. He offered to go there by way of Bolivia, to deliver the artefacts in person and to find out why the Bolivians refused to support our claims.

When I saw David again after the International Conference, I was dismayed to learn that, on arrival in Bolivia, he had been thrown into prison, and branded as a common thief. Only the intervention of the British Ambassador plus the return of the artefacts had secured his release. He was too shaken and disillusioned to ask for a conference with the Bolivian scientists about our work over there.

Disheartened by this unexpected setback, I settled down for the winter to my normal everyday work as a reporter for the B.B.C., but all the time I kept remembering how tantalisingly close I had been, possibly, to reaching a successful conclusion to a search which had intrigued me for most of my life.

There was no point in considering another expedition until the next dry season started in May. When the time approached, I made up my mind to take the film of our first expedition back to Bolivia, in one last attempt to vindicate myself.

Having financed the previous trip, and having expended another thousand pounds on film stock, processing and printing, I had very little money left. So I secured a bank overdraft and flew out to Bolivia in May.

I called first of all on the British Ambassador, and he advised me to go at once to see Dr. Carlos Ponce Sangines, the founder and director of the Bolivian National Institute of Archaeology. The Ambassador told me that Bolivia is the only country in South America with such a national institute, and that Dr. Carlos is one of the most respected archaeologists in the Americas. The fact that, through pure ignorance, I had failed to make contact with him on the previous trip guaranteed a pretty hostile reception. The atmosphere at that first meeting was decidedly chilly to start with but, after half an hour (my fluent Spanish certainly helped tremendously), Dr. Carlos began to soften. Somewhat grudgingly to begin with, he listened to the story of my sincere belief that our expedition had made some notable discoveries. He accepted my apology for having ignored his institute solely because I had been unaware of its existence, and eventually my obvious enthusiasm broke down the remaining barriers. By the end of that long meeting we had formed a friendship, the basis for an excellent working relationship, that was to last for the rest of my time in Bolivia. But first I had to get to the roots of his disenchantment with the work we had been doing and with the modest claims we were making.

The prime reason for his anger and resentment was the emphasis which newspaper reports had placed on the discovery of a fortune in gold. He pointed out that one of his principal duties was to control the parties of bona fide students and scientists who wanted to work in his country, and to fight off the waves of robbers, vagabonds and fortune seekers, who were an absolute menace to the genuine scientific work of his department.

"If you tell them you've found a fortune in gold, we'll be invaded by *huaceros* ('grave robbers'). In the past they've blown some of our most valuable ruins to smithereens with sticks of dynamite. They torture and kill local Indians in their private battles, and behave in an even more barbaric way than the *conquistadores*—and that's saying something. You can have no idea of the extent of the exacerbation caused by these rogues, whom we treat as criminals, for they are robbing us of our national heritage, and robbing the world of a unique opportunity to write its history."

The Doctor's forthright accusations were absolutely justified from Bolivia's point of view and left me conscience-stricken to think of the part I had played in the betrayal of the country which I regarded as the land of discovery. In order to salvage a vestige of pride, I pointed out to the Doctor that we had never stressed the gold angle, but had always explained that we had only brought these artefacts back for scientific purposes. What was even more to the point was that we had not pinpointed the location of our discoveries. Indeed, we had never even mentioned Bolivia.

Dr. Carlos was adamant.

"You have been responsible for a small influx of thieves already, as well as stimulating an embarrassing amount of interest from reputable scientific bodies around the world. Don't think for a moment that they haven't been working furiously to follow your tracks. Information has reached me that a considerable amount of money has been spent on private detectives for this purpose, and already, I can tell you, the *huaceros* know you were at Incallacta, and they have been scouring those ruins in case that was the source of your gold."

I apologised profusely for all the trouble we had unwittingly caused, and made it clear that I deplored this universal preoccupation with the mythical fortunes in gold, which, if they were ever found in Bolivia, obviously belonged to the government. I told Dr. Carlos the full story of our expedition behind the line of ruined forts into the provinces of Chapare and Cochabamba, and our contact with the primitive indigenous people in this isolated and apparently unexplored area of Bolivia.

Then, encouraged by the Doctor's new attitude of cautious acceptance, I asked if the National Institute would help me in filming and writing about the story that was so desperately important to me. I promised that I would stick to the scientific facts presented to me: I would co-operate with the National Institute, and publish with their approval; eschew all references to caches of gold unless they had a vital bearing on some scientific aspect of the story, and never identify the location of a site without permission.

Dr. Carlos extended his hand in friendship, and the first point we discussed was the value of our original claim to have found the lost city of the Incas and possibly a lost empire of Incas in the province of Cochabamba. The Doctor was not nearly so sceptical as I thought he would be. In fact, he did not for one moment imply that these remarkable claims could not be true. He merely cast doubts in the form of questions which our sketchy evidence did not answer.

"Very little large-scale exploration has ever taken place in that area," he admitted, "and I agree that there could be significantly large communities living in some isolated areas which have never been seen either by travellers or from the air, since no planes travel that route. It is extremely unlikely, however, that we are quite unaware of the existence of all these isolated communities, even if we have not made permanent contact with them. Odd members of these little-known tribes regularly opt out of their way of life, or are thrown out of the tribe for some serious misdemeanour, and come to join civilised communities. They give us much information about the people they have come from, and missionaries are working constantly all over South America. There are three groups working in the unexplored areas of Chapare now, and as soon as they make friendly contact with one tribe, they get detailed information about other tribes of the area. It takes a long, long time, I admit, but gradually we are building up a picture, and I should think that we know about your community of five villages without having made permanent contact yet. There are many such communities between Cochabamba and the Brazilian border.

"You talk about finding the Lost City of the Incas there in the jungle. I believe that you have found a city of stone ruins which we don't know about, but I want a lot more proof before I will accept it as an Inca city. Even if you can convince me that it is indeed a city built by the Incas, and that you were the first to discover it, then which lost city of the Incas is it? There are at least ten such lost cities that we have discovered in Bolivia in the the last decade, and there are probably many more yet to be discovered."

Dr. Carlos must have seen the bitter disappointment on my face, and he tried to soften the blow.

"Mind you, there is an important story to be told about the extent of the Inca empire in Bolivia and, indeed, there is much evidence to show that quite possibly the first settled cultures in South America were founded in our country. There is a momentous documentary to be filmed and written about the significance of our recent work in this field, but there is no one great Inca city of gold, of that I am certain."

"But what about all the stories written by the *conquistadores*?" I protested. "Many of them spoke about El Dorado or Paititi, about Indians who used gold knives and spoons and goblets, and even constructed buildings of gold. Maybe the city was never discovered by the Spaniards, but so many accounts were written about it that there surely cannot be any doubt about its existence."

"We believe it was all a gigantic confidence trick perpetrated by the Inca leaders," Dr Carlos replied. "Remember that when the first Spanish arrived, the seemingly inexhaustible supply of Inca gold suddenly assumed a value far in excess of what it had been worth to the indigenous peoples of that era. The Incas in Peru saw the invaders inflict the most unbelievably barbaric tortures on their people to find out where the gold was stored away.

"The Spanish conquereors were utterly merciless in their quest for gold, and the only relief granted to an Inca villiage was when the ruthless gold-seekers actually marched off to loot another remote Indian settlement.

"So what did the Inca leaders do? They decided that the best way to get rid of the Spaniards was to dream up a fabulous treasure-trove of gold in some far-distant place. They invented El Dorado, and located it in the jungles of the Great River. Presumably they meant the Amazon, which to them would be virtually the other side of the world, and about as far away as they could hope to entice the Spaniards. That is how the myth of the Lost City or the City of Gold originated. In my opinion there is no such city and there never has been in the history of South America."

"But what about the legendary Colonel Fawcett?" I protested. "He was a man of unquestionable integrity, and in fact he was employed by your own government to draw up an exact border with Brazil. He said he found the Lost City, and the people who knew of his unimpeachable reputation believed him."

"He probably did find a lost city," the Doctor agreed. "It might have been Inca, but it is doubtful, because the Incas did not settle in the tropical forests, as far as we know."

"What about his story of the gold treasures he found there?" I continued.

"Yes, there might have been a great quantity of gold," the

Doctor agreed. "There is plenty of gold in the rivers that run into the province of Beni on the eastern borders of Bolivia, and that is where Colonel Fawcett was working. Whichever indigenous culture inhabited the area in prehistoric times could have extracted the gold from rivers, and used it in exactly the same way as the Aymara, the Inca and the Mollo cultures did in more recent times.

"Since he found a quantity of gold articles in the ruins, Colonel Fawcett may have thought he had stumbled on the mythical lost city. It is even more likely that his modest claims were embellished and exaggerated by others, and a ruined city with a few thousand dollars' worth of gold trinkets which the Spaniards never found suddenly becomes a treasure-trove worth millions.

"Much the same thing happened to you over your own story. It is these wildly improbable accounts of fortunes in gold which attract the scoundrels and vagabonds of the world, who disrupt and seriously threaten all the worthwhile scientific archaeological work we are trying to do."

Dr. Carlos Ponce Sangines was happy to allow me to make a documentary film but not to help me search for the Lost City of the Incas, for he felt that to be a waste of time, because to him it was pure myth. Moreover, the Bolivian Archaeological Institute considered it to be of no scientific value and not worthy of the deployment of their resources.

I was crestfallen for, although I did not hanker after hidden mounds of gold, I did still want to follow up my ideas. However, I could see that I would get nowhere without Dr. Carlos's co-operation, and if I had first to make a rather dull film about the early Inca occupation of Bolivia in order to win his approval, then I was happy to do so.

To prove my change of heart I was asked to film recent excavations of early Inca sites which were being carried out at Samaipata and Comparapa under the aegis of Dr. Victor Bustos. Then it was suggested that I might like to visit the prehistoric ruins on the plains of Beni. Although this did not at first appear to be furthering my quest, I would at least be delving into Inca culture and, as Dr. Victor pointed out, a deeper knowledge of the Incas, where they came from, how their empire had been formed and why it flourished, would help me to understand them better.

Samaipata and Comparapa were similar to Incallacta, but the

plains of Beni were the site of a pre-Incan culture.

The plains of Beni lie in the flat lowland area to the east of the Andes; they flood to a depth of one metre every wet season, when torrential rains cascade down from the hills, making the many rivers which race to join the Amazon overflow. The earth of these plains is not porous; so the flood water lies there for at least four months of the year. Today the vegetation is poor, and few people live there, but the theory is that, once, this area was densely inhabited by one of the earliest civilisations in South America, perhaps the ancestors of the Incas and of all the other cultures of the Andes.

I first flew over the area in a small Cessna with Kenneth Lee, an American geologist. We looked down upon a vast brown billiard table dotted with green billiard balls at irregular intervals, as if the gods had been interrupted in the middle of a game. These large green balls were mounds of earth, more or less circular, with lush green forests of trees growing on the upper half. They appeared to have been constructed in groups of three or four, and each group was joined to the next by a canal.

It was patently obvious that the canals had been dug by hand, because they travelled in a dead straight line from mound to mound, unlike the natural tributaries of the river Mamore, which followed the natural contours and wriggled and curved every few metres like angry serpents writhing on the floor.

We flew low over the mounds and saw ample evidence of how, in ancient times, the apparently well-organised intelligent people had controlled the flood-waters in a manner which is not copied today. We saw hundreds of thousands of hectares of land which today produce nothing, but which in ancient times must have provided food for unknown thousands of indigenous people who lived there.

Kenneth Lee had already measured one of the mounds and estimated that the circular hill of earth was four hundred metres in diameter, with a height of ten metres above the flat surface of the plains. If one thousand Indians at the most had packed themselves into this area, it would mean that approximately two hundred of them would have been able to dig the earth to build the mound. Other men would have been occupied in hunting and growing food for the rest, since it is doubtful if the women and children would have been able to do much of this heavy work.

On that assumption, Kenneth Lee estimated that it would have taken at least ten years to build a mound of that size above the flood-waters, allowing for the fact that work could only be carried out during the six months of the dry season.

If one accepts these approximate figures, the conclusions are staggering. Satellite pictures taken by the Americans at Bolivia's request showed that there are more than forty thousand of these mounds in the lowlands of Bolivia and Ecuador, and probably twice that number in Colombia, Venezuela and Brazil. Until excavations are carried out all over South America in the decades to come, we shall not know for sure that all these mounds were constructed by the hand of primitive man, as they certainly were in Bolivia; but all the present evidence suggests that there could have been a prehistoric civilisation, numbered in millions, in South America's lowlands east of the Andes.

What may be even more significant in years to come (as a world food shortage begins to bite) is that South America has millions of square kilometres of land with a potential to grow food for a hungry world, once we catch up with the technological brilliance of the indigenous Stone Age Indians who lived there long ago.

The satellite pictures also produced evidence to support the theory that this was one huge, organised culture, perhaps the biggest unified culture the world has ever known.

The photographs show that in each group the mounds were joined by footpaths of mud raised above the level of the floods, as well as by a network of straight canals. Most staggering of all, it can be seen quite clearly, and without any room for argument, that it was possible in those prehistoric times to travel by canoe along the canals joining the rivers, from the coast of Brazil to the Carribbean.

Dr. Victor told me that during his excavations he would be looking for further evidence to substantiate the theory that these people must have been part of an enormous culture, possibly with a unique social and religious organisation as well. After several long flights over the plains, he picked out the three mounds we would excavate during that dry season. The first two would be Loma Mendoza and Loma Ortiz, because both these mounds had been cut in half by the bulldozers which were carving out the first road between Trinidad and Santa Cruz. It was partly a case of salvaging what artefacts which these machines had crushed and shattered on their journeys through the mounds, and partly the urgent need to evaluate the archaeological significance of what they had uncovered. A bulldozer is no friend of the archaeologist, of course, but the fact that two of the mounds had been sliced through the middle like Christmas puddings would probably uncover enough vital information to enable Dr. Victor to assess the value of excavating other mounds in a scientific manner.

The local government at Trinidad lent Dr. Victor a jeep, and we spent the next fortnight studying the two mounds in detail. During the evenings I discussed the findings with Dr. Victor, and made a note of his evaluation and his conclusions.

We measured Loma Ortiz and estimated that it covered approximately fourteen hectares. The mass of earth had been constructed in a circular shape and we measured the diameter fairly accurately at 450 metres. The mound is inhabited today by one family of indigenous *mestizos,* who live in a small wattle and adobe building, which they had built near the top of the mound. They kept one seedy-looking cow of the Spanish Longhorn type, a runt bull, and three younger cattle which they were apparently rearing for beef. There was also a small plot of maize and wheat, some potatoes, yucca and sugar cane. The small-holding seemed to be run in a haphazard fashion, with cattle and chickens running free. During the time we were there the four children of the family took it in turns to shepherd the cattle and keep them away from the growing crops. There were no fences or enclosures, and no kind of housing for the livestock, nor was there any obvious building for the storage of the various harvests. Judging by the small heaps of maize cobs in the two rooms of the family house, it seemed likely that the inhabitants kept their small supplies under their own roof.

The bulldozers revealed that the mound had obviously been built and inhabited at three distinct levels. The first was five metres above the level of the flat plains, the second ten metres, and the third fifteen metres, which is the height of the mound at the present time.

I suggested to Dr. Victor that this indicated a gradual rise in the level of the flood-waters over a long period of time, but, in the manner of a cautious scientist, he would only admit that this would be only one piece of evidence to support such a theory. There might be more evidence, he thought, as a result of excavations.

As the bulldozer had sliced through the mound, it had smashed thousands of pieces of pottery; scattered fragments littered the raw surface. Dr. Victor was dismayed and disconsolate as he surveyed the damage, but such vast quantities of broken shard suggested that the number of people inhabiting these mounds in prehistoric times had been huge.

Rough-and-ready first analysis indicated that one and a half million cubic metres of earth had been moved in the construction of Loma Ortiz alone. The earth had been dug by hand with the help of primitive wood or bone tools, and so the amount of earth dug and carted by one man in one day could not have exceeded one cubic metre. This would suggest that a group of one thousand men could not have constructed the mound in less than four years. Of course, the mounds were inhabited during the process of being built, and this might indicate that fewer than a thousand men were engaged in the work over a much longer period of time.

But the method of construction of the mounds suggests a highly organised culture with a central government capable of distributing food, clothing and tools to the workers and their families whilst they were digging away.

Another point which hinted at an excellent overall organisation was the presence throughout the mound of significant numbers of living creatures and their bones. We found bones of deer, ant-eater, wild boar, capybara and giant rats, and a tremendous number of wild-bird skeletons. This wildlife would have been marooned with the Indians on the mounds during the wet season. Hundreds of stone axes and hardwood arrowheads would seem to indicate that the people were expert hunters, but they must have been careful to limit the numbers they killed so that no species died out. Perhaps they 'farmed' wild animals, or perhaps the numbers they could kill were strictly controlled by a ruling class. However it was managed, it was clearly successful and by primitive standards the Indians must have lived well. For in addition to meat they had an abundance of fruit and vegetables which they had grown both on the mounds themselves and on the flat surrounding lands. We found no remains of their foodstuffs, but at the time the Spaniards arrived in Beni, in about A.D. 1600, the Indians were growing maize, potatoes, yucca, manioc, pumpkin, cotton and tobacco. Presumably they cultivated the plains during the dry season and stored the surplus in their huts in the mounds.

Maize, for example, takes about ninety days to ripen in that tropical climate, and so they could have taken two harvests before the plains were again covered with water. By retreating a short distance up the slope of the mound to the terraces they had constructed, they could have planted and harvested yet another crop before the flood-waters reached the height, and a further smaller crop could have been harvested near the top of the mound on land which the flood-waters never reached.

Careful inspection of the site revealed that these prehistoric peoples had possessed advanced engineering skills which had also enabled them to cultivate crops on the level lowland right into the dry season. They had sophisticated and effective methods of both irrigating and fertilising the land.

In the middle of one large area of about two hundred square kilometres an enormous mound of earth had been built, rising perhaps five metres above the level of the plains. In the centre of this mound was a basin, with a diameter of one kilometre and, when we flew over the top of it, the basin was filled with water. It was, in fact, a huge man-made lagoon. On closer examination we found a channel cut down one side of the mound. When the retaining wall of the lagoon was lowered a metre or so at a time, it would allow some of the water from the lagoon to drain away into a channel which was obviously man-made, since it ran in a straight line across the surrounding level land. Whenever this main channel ran near to one of the camps of cultivation of one of the other mounds, a small ditch joined it. When we examined the point where the smaller irrigation ditch joined the main channel, the junction was blocked by bricks and tree trunks. Once the debris was removed, the water from the main channel would overflow along the ditch at the side and run down to water the crops growing in the cultivated plot at the foot of the mound. Thus the people of the Mound culture had provided themselves with a bountiful supply of cultivated food and the likelihood of three harvests a year.

I observed that the quality and the quantity of the maize and yucca could not been very high, since the earth in which it was grown was so poor and lacked nitrogen and phosphates. Dr. Victor then took me on a two-kilometre walk to a point where one of the many tributaries of the river Mamore curved right round for nearly three-quarters of a circle. The area of land enclosed by this bend in the river was at least two hectares. Even though we were well into the dry season, the surface of this area was still soggy, for it was covered in a stinking layer of dead and dying aquatic plants and other rotting vegetation.

Dr. Victor pointed out that the Indians had taken advantage of the natural curve in the river and had turned the whole area into a shallow lake by building a man-made bank of earth one metre high across the stretch of land not enclosed by the river bank. One could see that, as the flood water subsided to the level of the river bank, a sheet of water would have been trapped in the circle of higher land formed by the curving river bank and the man-made bank of earth which completed the circle.

In this shallow lagoon a huge number of aquatic plants grew, and types of plankton and water moss packed the surface. Assuming that the water evaporated and was also allowed to drain away after a time, this would have left a carpet of lush green vegetation to rot on the dried-out bed of the lagoon, thus making rich fertiliser. In addition to the green vegetation, there would have been thousands of fish and probably millions of water snails, as these still flourished in the area. In other early settlements in Bolivia the indigenous people used to crush the snails' shells to secure a good supply of lime. If the Indians of the Mound culture did the same, they could have built an immense store of balanced fertiliser on the dried-up bed of the lagoon. There would have been lime from the snail shells, plus phosphate, potash, and some nitrogen from the rotted layers of vegetation and dead fish. There is nothing more that these prehistoric people would have needed to guarantee a phenomenal harvest of fruit, maize and vegetables. They obviously had long, hot days during the dry season, an adequate supply of water, and a reasonably rich soil to work with.

When we examined the photographs we had taken from the air, we noticed several quite large areas of wet land or shallow lagoons which had been enclosed by this method. We also realised that most of them were situated between groups of three or four mounds, and that the man-made banks of earth also provided a footpath between the hillocks. This was certainly one piece of evidence to support the suggestion that the location of each of the mounds was carefully planned before construction. They were not pimples of earth thrown up haphazardly simply to provide a haven during the floods of the wet season. More and more it appeared that we were putting together the jigsaw which might paint the picture of a highly-organised, technological empire of enormous proportions.

We marshalled the evidence.

The undamaged artefacts we found (and there was a huge number) included pottery that was both engraved and painted and, according to Dr. Victor, showed many similarities, both in patterning and colours, to the pottery of the Andean cultures. He told me that it would be difficult to deny that there had been a link between the two civilisations. We also found knives and arrowheads made of animal bone and granite. The stone at least must have been gathered and imported from some distant part, since there was none in Beni.

The cemeteries we uncovered on two of the largest mounds contained a vast number of funeral urns; although we assumed that they had contained the bones of the dead, there was nothing but dust remaining. Dr. Victor did suggest, however, that the arrangement of the urns and the particular decoration on them led him to believe that there had been religous life in the prehistoric community.

Two years later I revisited the area, by which time Dr. Victor and his staff had carried out much more scientific investigation, and he told me of his sensational progress.

The National Institute was convinced that they were on the brink of proving that the Rosinda culture (as I have named it) had been an enormous empire of millions of pre-Inca Indians, who were highly-organised, skilled people with a religious and social organisation to compare with the great cultures of more recent times in the Andes.

The social organisation in particular must have been most impressive, apparently with each mound governed and controlled by a unit of engineers in charge of construction, religious leaders, farmers, hunters and labourers. Dr. Victor suggested that each mound had a king serving the king of each group of mounds, with one supreme king over them all.

But if this culture had been so well-organised and so flourishing, why had it disappeared off the face of the earth long before the Spaniards arrived?

Dr. Victor suspected that total crop failure had probably forced the inhabitants to emigrate to other parts of the continent. Such a catastrophe could have been caused by an epoch of great floods, which would have submerged the modest hills of earth on which they lived. The Chilean scientist quickly emphasised that he was talking about a hundred years or more of excessively wet weather, which would have presented the people with problems of such magnitude that even they could not cope.

"Are you talking about the Great Flood which we read about in the Bible?," I asked.

"Yes, indeed," Victor agreed. "There is overwhelming evidence from all over the world that this planet was engulfed in floods, following phenomenal rains, about ten thousand years ago. In my opinion it was not a sudden catastrophe, as many people interpret the Bible story, nor was the water anywhere of sufficient depth to bury cities. Geological evidence suggests that it was a slow, steady process of inundation over many years, but the effects were cumulative. If the flood-waters on these plains, for instance, had risen by an extra metre, it would have ruined the Indians' agriculture and wrecked their ability to produce the enormous harvests essential to support such a mighty nation."

"But that was ten thousand years ago," I said. "Was this Mound culture founded by then?"

Dr. Victor shrugged. "We cannot say yet: not until we have some of the artefacts dated. Maybe there was a culture here that far back in history. It could be that they were driven up into the Andes by the great floods, and that they founded the first Andean cultures thousands of years ago. It is just as likely that some tribes returned here in the centuries after the Great Flood, and it is the remains of the Paititi empire that we are now uncovering."

"But Paititi is a place," I cried in a state of great excitement. "It is the Lost City. They called it El Dorado in Brazil, but Paititi was the name used here in the western half of South America. That's what I'm looking for—well, one of the sites I'm looking for, anyway."

Dr. Victor looked straight at me, his eyes full of scorn and contempt.

"I thought you had given up this senseless search for a lost city," he snapped. "I thought you were now interested only in the momentous story of the history of Bolivia and its people."

"I am," I insisted, "but your talk of Paititi . . ."

Dr. Victor cut me off abruptly. "I was talking of the people called Paititis. They were living here in Beni alongside another group called the Moxos when the first Spanish mission was founded here in 1686. This is a historically known fact, and I only deal in facts. That is why I hesitate to say much about the fascinating culture of the people who lived on the mounds. There is so much scientific work to be done that it will probably be years before we can offer any theories even for discussion. The Smithsonian Institute of Washington is about to embark on a four-year study with us, which will involve several hundred men with a number of aircraft and a cavalcade of machinery and equipment. The Bolivian government is sharing the costs, which will amount to more than a million dollars. At the end of this investigation we may have something important to say."

Dr. Victor softened somewhat when he saw the regret and humiliation that must have flooded across my face.

"Mind you, I think there will be sensational facts to reveal. Dr. Carlo Ponce Sangines has said that afterwards it will probably be necessary to rewrite the history of South America."

Dr. Victor relaxed his attack, and calmed down somewhat; so I dared to remonstrate mildly with him.

"I respect you scientists—I think most people do—for the cautious and very responsible way you tackle every problem; but some of us think this is a colourless approach to life. I agree that I am no scientist—more of an adventurer, perhaps, but more of a typical man in the street. We like to dream, to hope, and to cherish buoyant ambitions. Life does not have to consist solely of a catalogue of proven facts." I was warming to one of my pet subjects. "I understand your point of view, and your principles. I just ask you to appreciate that some other people take a different view of life and I don't believe you have the right to condemn this outlook."

Dr. Victor slowly subsided.

"Yes, you are right," he said, contritely. "All I want to say quite categorically is that you should treat your account of our work together on a scientific basis. Report anything I have told you, but please don't associate me with any wild stories of a lost city of gold."

I assured him that I would not, and I pointed out gently that his part in my documentary and my reports would be wholly scientific, but that I wanted to look for myself, to see if I could unearth any new prehistoric ruins or make a discovery which would fit a further piece into the jigsaw of South American archaeological-anthropological knowledge.

My plea did not fall on deaf ears. Dr. Victor relented and, after a long pause, he turned to me with the glimmer of a friendly smile on his face.

"All right. If that's what you want I might be able to help you," he said gently. Then his expression hardened. "But don't expect me to come with you, or support you in any way."

Suddenly my hopes rose once again, because here was a man who was a mine of information. Whatever he was going to tell me might not be a proven fact, but he would never deal in pure fantasy, and I knew I could give any suggestion of his very serious consideration indeed.

"There are still some Paititi Indians living on the mounds in Beni," Dr. Victor began, "and they have a small council of governors who believe, like you, that there is a lost city called Paititi which was their capital city and seat of government. They think it is somewere in the Yungas (temperate valleys) between the Province of Beni and the High Plateau of the Andes around Lake Titicaca.

"For the last decade ten or twelve of them have made the long and arduous journey every dry season from Beni up to the top of the Andes mountains. They take a different route each year and they comb the area on each side of the path they walk.

"They even plant crops of maize in some of the valleys on the way up and harvest it for their food on the return journey. They have not found their Paititi yet but, when we return, I will introduce you to Professor Gomez in Trinidad who may be able to arrange for you to accompany the Indians on one of their journeys."

My heart leapt at this wonderfully exciting prospect of forsaking scientific study for a time in favour of one more exhilarating adventure.

CHAPTER FIVE

Following the Paititi

PROFESSOR GOMEZ WAS TREMENDOUSLY enthusiastic about the idea of making a film of a journey from the plains of Beni, through the temperate valleys of the Yungas and up to the high plateau. He doubted if any white man had ever seen much of this glorious picturesque wilderness; certainly no one had ever taken film of it to be shown in Europe. The only trouble was that the Paititi Indians had already left a week before on their annual trek into the Andes and so there was no one to guide me. The Professor looked almost as disappointed as I felt: clearly he was not going to let me down if he could possibly avoid it. He dashed out of his room at the college, and returned within a few minutes with a request, that almost amounted to a command, for me to return on the morrow and he would see if he could organise some help.

Next day I was introduced to Carya, a semi-civilised Paititi Indian, and to Darillo, a *mestizo* youth of about twenty. Both these men looked strong, capable and self-sufficient, just the sort of companions I would choose to help me on a hazardous journey through isolated areas of unexplored jungle.

The Professor explained that we could not catch up with the Paititi Indians, because no one ever knew exactly which route they were taking. They did not even know in advance themselves which path they would follow, since they relied on intuition and memory rather than map-reading. But he thought that the best route we could take would be due westwards across the plains through San Ignazio de Moxos to the river Maniqui, then across the river Beni up into the mountains. Professor Gomez was bubbling with excitement by now, but I cut him short and asked to see a map of the journey, explaining that I was no youngster and not fit enough to undertake what was beginning to sound like a formidable journey lasting two or three weeks.

When the map was laid out I was filled with trepidation and my face must have mirrored my dismay at seeing the length of the trek across the plains, into uncharted jungle and hills before reaching Lake Titicaca at least four hundred kilometres to the west. I was just thinking that such a journey was quite beyond my capabilities, when the Professor chipped in. He was not going to let me off the hook. Clapping his hands and hopping up and down with anticipation, he quickly pointed out that, for a very small fee, the two young men would guide me, carry all my equipment, feed me and look after me completely. He made them sound like expert nursemaids who would succour me at every turn and, just to emphasise their usefulness, he pointed out that Carya, the Indian, knew the route well, and was a friend of the people in the villages we would pass through, whilst Darillo was as strong as a mule, and an expert hunter who had his own revolver. What more could I want, the Professor asked.

Gently I explained that, at my age, I could not walk so far even on a straight highway, much less fight through virgin jungle, climb mountains and cross rivers. Professor Gomez hopped around like a weasel with fleas as he searched for answers to all my objections. He was not going to be thwarted.

"I will borrow the Cessna from the government," he said. "Then you can all fly across the plains, which will save you half the journey. The plane can land anywhere on the edge of the flat lands, and then all you have to do is to travel into the hills, where there are some roads."

The way he said the word 'some' left me in no doubt that they were what I call jungle tracks, and that there weren't too many even of those.

"You could hire a mule if you like. No need to walk at all. You *could* hire a mule couldn't you?" he asked Darillo, who nodded in such a nonchalant manner that he imparted no confidence.

Professor Gomez could see that he was shooting down all my objections one by one; so now he decided it was time to dangle the juicy carrot.

"And when you cross the river Beni and follow the river up into the Andes, you will find Paititi," he said triumphantly.

"But Dr. Victor said there is no Paititi. It is just a legend,"

I challenged him.

"If not Paititi, then another lost city on the bank of a river. Is that not so, *amigos*?" he asked Carya and Darillo.

The two young men nodded silent agreement, and then Darillo added a few works of confirmation in a quick, serious tone of voice that gave me the confidence to believe him.

"There are several ruined cities in the Yungas," he said, looking me straight in the eye. "They are mostly forts which used to guard the rivers, but there are two cities which I know, as well."

The Professor could see my mounting interest, and he pressed home the advantage.

"We think the Incas built the fortresses to guard their cities in the Andes against invasion by the Paititis and the Moxos. The only way to get into the mountains in those days, before they had any tracks up the hillsides, was to walk up the river beds in the dry season, and that is why they built the forts on the river banks. We do not know which people built the cities, though; or why. If you take film of them it could tell us what we need to know to identify them."

Surrounded as I was by the irrepressible enthusiasm of Professor Gomez and the quiet strength and confidence of the two young men, I could hardly refuse to go, without appearing to be a spineless coward. I looked at the map again, walked round the room and thought furiously, but I knew what my answer had to be. The rainbow of success was too tantalisingly close for me to turn my back on it now.

"All right," I said to the Professor. "If you can get the aircraft to fly us all to the edge of Beni, and if the boys can hire me a mule, I'll go. But if it doesn't work out exactly like that I shall have to turn back, and then I cannot pay Carya and Darillo; so be quite certain before we set out."

Professor Gomez hesitated for a fleeting second before he came bouncing back to assure me that this was the wisest decision I had ever made, and that I could be sure of taking off the next day. All I had to do was to give Carya and Darillo some money in advance to buy their supplies and a couple of machetes, and we could meet at the airfield next morning. He would confirm the time.

Later that day the Professor duly arrived at my hotel to confirm that the aircraft was organised 'at a special rate' for me of one hundred dollars. This was not exactly in line with the arrangements of the previous day, but at least it made me realise that the whole plan was not a farce or a figment of his imagination. It meant that I had to race round the shops to buy my own supplies. I asked if we were likely to meet any indigenous tribes, who would appreciate small gifts.

"There are only a few Indians left in the hills now," said the Professor. "They are not very friendly, and resent the presence of strangers, but Carya knows who they are and where they live, and so he will avoid their territory. There are no wild Indians, if that's what you mean. I doubt if you'll see anyone at all. It's mostly wide open spaces, the most beautiful, spectacular scenery you will ever find."

During my shopping expedition, I bought packets of soup powder, raisins, powdered stew and any lightweight dried food. Just to be on the safe side, I decided to buy a few packets of razor blades and disposable lighters in case I needed them to give as bribes or presents.

Next morning the three of us met at the airfield, and I was interested to see that Carya, the Paititi Indian, was now wearing a shirt and trousers, whereas on the previous day he had appeared in the cotton cloak of the Indians, which reached down to his bare knees. He still wore Indian sandals on bare feet, and his long hair was tied back with a length of cotton braid, but his first trip by air seemed to represent for him a gigantic step into the western world. I noticed that he hardly ever took his eyes off Darillo, so that he could mimic and copy the *mestizo*'s every move.

Both my companions had their machetes hanging from their belts, but all the rest of their food and equipment was packed into one string bag. not much larger than a schoolboy's satchel. In contrast, I had a haversack crammed full of spare clothing, tent and sleeping-bag, plus my camera case and a large leather shoulder-bag with food, film and medicines. Darillo certainly looked dubious as I packed it all into the aircraft, but he said nothing.

Once we were airborne above the western plains of Beni, my attention was riveted on the scene below: the vast, flat prairie was barren except for occasional groups of three or four mounds covered in grassy scrub and forest. Some of these hillocks were very much larger than those around Trinidad, and two of them appeared to extend over five square kilometres. As far as I could make out, these hills were much more numerous and closer together than those I'd seen before; so this might well have been the focal point of the Mound culture.

This would stand to reason, because the rivers all ran from south-west to north-east, indicating a slight, almost imperceptible slope in that direction. As we approached that part of the plains which ran into the foothills of the Andes, one could see that the flood-waters would not have been quite so deep in the wet season as those in Trinidad. The mounds would not have needed to be so high to remain above the level of the floods, and yet the whole area would have enjoyed the same long hours of tropical sunshine and the same warm climate to make the crops grow throughout the year.

All the visual evidence from the air indicated that there must have been a much higher density of population in this favoured area, and the appearance of the mounds led me to believe that the system of farming and the methods of controlling the inundations were even more advanced, and the way of life more prosperous, than in the area to the east.

The rivers Caripo and Charparini being much wider than the eastern tributaries of the Mamore, the areas of cultivation at the foot of the mounds were twice the size of those at Suarez and Ortiz; both the drainage by man-made canals and the system of cultivation on terraces were much more extensive. Everything was on a grander scale and, since some of the mounds were still inhabited by present-day Indians, the outlines of the original works of the prehistoric Indians could be seen even more clearly.

The pilot attracted my attention by slapping the map on to my lap and pointing meaningfully at a spot on the banks of the river Maniqui. He then pointed to the horizon and mimed an aircraft landing; so I quickly studied the area where we were to land.

We were still in the province of Beni, but right on the border with the province of La Paz, and indeed, gazing far ahead, I could just make out an outline of jungle-covered hills on the horizon. Looking back at the large-scale map, I could see seven black dots which had names printed against them, just as one would indicate a village or town on a map of Europe, but when I searched for any sign of a village below me I could see nothing but gently-rolling hills running into a vast expanse of flat lowland. I turned to the pilot, showed him what I thought were villages marked on the map, and mimed the question 'Where?'

He banked to port, dropped the nose a little, and pointed to what looked like a lonely farmhouse on the bank of the river. Then he pointed to a similar settlement another two kilometres further along. His message was clear. In this wilderness of wide open spaces it seemed that even a farm and a couple of families were worth a name and a dot on the map.

The pilot throttled back, let the aircraft glide to one hundred metres above the land, and pulled down the flaps ready to land. I looked around uneasily to see where on earth the airfield might be, or indeed if there was any stretch of flat, clear land that would do, but saw nothing. We flew low over the river and turned northwards and, as the plane dipped, I was suddenly aware that we were flying over a wide earth road. In the far distance, which must have been ten kilometres to the north, I could just make out a black speck, perhaps a jeep or a wagon enveloped in a cloud of dust.

While the pilot searched this unexpectedly wide track for obstacles, I quickly scanned the map. The road was marked with a thin red line, and the words Carratera Marginal de la Selva (Edge of the Jungle Highway). After a couple of dummy runs we landed safely and, as soon as we'd unloaded our gear, the pilot revved up and was gone with a cheery wave.

For a moment I felt very cut off, but the beautifully warm, dry weather assuaged my apprehension, and cheerfulness came flooding back when Darillo and Carya picked up all the bags and marched off down the mud track to what Darillo assured me was 'the hotel'.

The two youngsters obviously had everything under control, and the way they spoke to me and addressed me as 'Senor Ingles' (Mister Englishman) quickly established the fact that they 'respected my age'. I had the feeling that all was going to be well.

After half an hour's walk we reached a primitive hamlet of six one-roomed adobe huts built around one larger timber house. On the roadside in front of this house was a solitary petrol pump, looking utterly out of place in that wilderness.

At that moment, the station wagon I had seen from the plane drew up at the petrol pump, which must have been one of the main filling-stations on the edge-of-the-jungle highway. Just to make the scene even more absurd, the Indian who came running out of the timber house ignored the dangling lead of the petrol pump and filled the wagon with petrol from a two-gallon can. He filled this petrol can over and over again from a large fifty-gallon drum, into which he stuck a thin rubber tube, sucking the petrol until it began to run, then allowing it to overflow the smaller can while he spat out the mouthful of petrol he got for his trouble. At close quarters the smart-looking, glossy-painted petrol pump turned out to be a wooden dummy resting on a tiny platform of levelled earth.

The so-called hotel was also well-suited to this land of make-believe. A piece of cardboard leaning against the wall, on which was printed the work 'Hotel', announced its function somewhat defiantly. The first door, which was wide open, led into a large square room with worn tiles on the floor, and four wicker chairs tucked into the corner as though they were in hiding.

A middle-aged *mestizo* with a rather care-worn expression came to enquire what we wanted. Darillo took charge and, speaking in Quechua, he indicated that the three of us needed accommodation. The proprietor, who replied in Spanish, merely demanded twenty pesos, then looked me over carefully and changed his price to thirty pesos. He probably thought I didn't understand; so I rattled off my most fluent Spanish to tell him that, for thirty pesos, we would also expect some good food, as well as the exclusive use of a lavatory. He shrugged and held out his hand; so I handed over the thirty pesos, rather than look small in front of my two young companions.

The proprietor waved towards the two corridors which led out through the far wall of the room towards the back of the house. I let Darillo and Carya lead on, because I wasn't quite sure what we were being offered, and I certainly was not prepared to admit that I was not entirely in command of the situation and full of confidence. We had not been together very long, and I had not been given the opportunity to earn their gratitude or respect so far, but they seemed to be looking after me well.

Darillo opened the first door in the larger of the two corridors, looked inside, shut the door quickly and moved on down the corridor. At the third doorway he paused, and then went in. Carya and I followed him into a small, dingy room with the grey light from the high, barred window just bright enough to reveal two piles of bedding. Darillo surveyed the scene in some depth before he plonked my haversack in the middle of the floor, untied the cords, hauled out my sleeping-bag and reverently laid it out in what was obviously the least awful part of the dormitory. He then unceremoniously tossed the heap of bedding into the far corner. Finally he placed my camera case and shoulder-bag on the floor and, in an urgent conference with Carya, proposed that one of them should always stay there to guard my precious belongings.

I blessed them both for their attitude of friendly support and their comradeship, which no money could buy. The only way I could think of expressing my immense gratitude was to plunder my meagre supply of tropical shirts and give them one each. Their absolute delight at this small present instantly washed away any vague regrets I might have had about running down my own supply of clothing at the start of our long journey.

At that point two men, who looked much like any Indian labourers from any village, walked boldly in through the door. The more belligerent-looking of the two pointed to the disturbed heap of bedding and demanded to know who had moved it. My intake of breath was unfortunately audible.

Carya let fly a torrent of Quechua words at too great a speed for me to understand. The square-shouldered Indian turned to look at me challengingly with his blood-flecked eyes, before he bowed his head in acquiescence.

Dinner that evening consisted of a bowl of piping hot soup, large wads of maize bread, and cheese. To judge by the steam rising from the soup it must have been boiled, and this would kill the bacteria. Just to be safe, I put in a couple of my water-purifying tablets and waited ten minutes before I drank the soup out of the side of the bowl. I didn't risk the bread and cheese, but I tucked into the bananas and oranges which Carya fetched at my suggestion.

A reasonable meal and an undisturbed night's sleep put me in the right frame of mind for the start of the long trek into the unknown next morning. I was anxious to get as far as the jungle-covered hills quickly, because I wanted to go to the lavatory. I just hadn't been able to face the sordid, verminous and filthy shed at the back of the hotel, and everywhere else in the village was either someone's property or else a public road. Not for the first time in South America I preferred the clean isolation of the jungle.

To my great satisfaction Darillo and Carya seemed to want nothing more than to prove their usefulness. On his own initiative Darillo went off and negotiated with one man in the hamlet who owned a station wagon. For only one hundred pesos (five dollars) he would drive us along the narrow mud track until it petered out in the hills. This journey covered about twenty kilometres, but it took all the morning to complete. The track was obviously used by mules and Indians travelling to the allotments of cultivated land between the hamlet and the foothills, but it was the station wagon's first trip. Frequently we had to roll large stones off the trail or cut a wider path through the bushes, but it was much easier than walking even if it was not much quicker. Eventually the track led into the clearing occupied by a small timber house with a corrugated iron roof. This isolated, one-roomed dwelling was occupied by an Indian couple with their three small children between five and ten years old. The reason for living in this lonely spot was not obvious. I could see no small areas of cultivation and no animals. Darillo told me that they were 'guarding the road', and that we would have to pay the man ten pesos (one dollar) if we wanted to pass along the narrow, winding footpath which led out of the far side of the clearing.

One did not have to be astute to realise that this was pure chicanery. Probably this Indian family was employed by the inhabitants back in the village to act as look-outs to forewarn them of any invasion by the Indian tribes of the jungle. A white man travelling in the opposite direction was seen as a sucker or a soft touch by this semi-civilised Indian family, who knew the value of money, but not much else about civilisation. I told Darillo I'd pay up if they would also let me hire a mule, 'to carry our equipment,' I said. In truth this was to cover my shame at not being active enough to walk the trail into the hills. It was I who needed the mule, but the impoverished state of this family did not augur well; indeed, they soon made it quite clear that they had no mule, and had never even seen one in that part of the jungle.

The wagon-driver came to the rescue. He told me he could hire a mule back in the village, and made the excellent suggestion that he take Carya back in the vehicle to collect it. Darillo made the point that no one would trust us to take a mule way up into the hills on a long journey and bring it back again. Once we'd gone . . .

The driver was taking his cue from the behaviour of my two young companions, and obviously wanted to be as helpful as possible. He suggested he could do a deal with one of the farmers to hire a mule for about a dollar a day for thirty days plus a deposit of another twenty dollars against its return. That sounded reasonable enough to me until Darillo observed tartly that most of the mules in the village were not worth more than fifty dollars, anyway.

I dipped into my wallet, found that I could just about afford the outlay, and so handed over the money to Carya, asking him to negotiate the best deal he could. Darillo, who was assuming the mantle of my chief lieutenant, told Carya to make sure he got a good working mule, used to carrying heavy loads, and to be back by the next morning . . . even if he had to ride through the dawn.

After the driver and Carya left, Darillo and I pitched my tent in the clearing, to the amazement and curiosity of the whole Indian family, especially the children who, until then, had been too shy to come out from their hiding-place at the side of their house.

Then Darillo set about preparing a meal with the help of the Indian family, whose tunics of beaten bark fitted so tightly round the knees that they could only take little mincing steps as they scurried around to obey Darillo's fusilade of orders. Soon we had a fire burning and an earthenware pot of water on the boil. Surreptitiously I threw a few water-purifying tablets in the pot just to be on the safe side, but without wishing to offend Darillo, who seemed to relish his power to command the Indians. He barked out more orders in Quechua and, although I did not understand some of the words, I soon realised that we were to enjoy their hospitality. Into the cooking-pot went cobs of maize, what looked like a piece of animal meat, some yucca, and two small birds which had been recently plucked. I then sloped off into the trees at the edge of the clearing, and went to the lavatory at last. By taking a very strong anti-diarrhoea tablet early in the day, I had found that the urgency to answer this particular 'call of nature' could be made to vanish for a time. As the journey progressed, I was to find this an excellent method of procrastinating.

On my return Darillo triumphantly handed me an earthenware beaker of maize *chicha*. I told him that I'd seen Indians making *chicha* by chewing maize and spitting it into a bowl and leaving it to ferment. I did not fancy drinking mead made in such a fashion. Darillo was horrified and assured me that this *chicha* was made most hygenically. He explained that they toasted the grains of maize, crushed them into powder, added water and sugar, and boiled the mixture.

"It is the drink of the gods in these parts," he whooped. "We are very lucky to be offered some."

Having made sure that the water had been boiled, I risked taking a sip. It really was deliciously refreshing; so I wrote down the recipe in my notebook, thinking that I might introduce the drink during a hot spell of weather back in England.

The *chicha* was the one isolated gesture of hospitality by the Indian family, who never invited us into their house, but hung on our shirt tails most of the time, consumed with curiosity about our every move.

The cooking-pot produced a splendid stew which tasted all the better for being eaten picnic-style in this excitingly remote setting. Looking back across the plateau and forest-studded earth mounds, I was reminded very much of parts of Salisbury Plain around Stonehenge, and of the level land in Dorset and Wiltshire which is also studded with hillocks surmounted by trees. Thinking of Stonehenge reminded me to ask Darillo if he knew of any ancient ruins in the immediate vicinity, or, if not, if he would ask the Indian family. The man, whose name was Tupaco, knew of a number of large cities which belonged to 'the people of yet before', but these were a long way into the hills; we would have to walk many sundowns to find them.

His vagueness about nearby ruins persuaded me to offer him a bribe of a dollar, which had the effect of refreshing his memory. There was a ruin overlooking the ravine, he told us; people had lived there at one time not so long ago, and they had left some of their belongings behind in a small stone house.

Tupaco offered to show us what he had collected and I followed him over to his house, but Darillo held my arm as we approached the doorway, and shook his head as if to forbid me to go in, if I were invited.

"Chaggers," he whispered, and I realised that he was warning me about the evil insects whose bite raises festering sores which often set up septicaemia before treatment finally brings them under control.

Tupaco returned with an armful of very interesting souvenirs which he spread on the ground for us to examine. Beautifully made out of strong fibres woven together was a helmet in the shape of the headwear shown in ancient Eygptian drawings. There was also a crudely carved small stone figure, a typical funeral urn made of pottery, a stone necklace, a rattle made from what appeared to be a dried fruit shell, a complete figure cast in gold, part of another gold figure, as well as a gold knife in the shape of other knives which have been found in Inca ruins and which archaeologists presume to be surgeons' knives.

The Indians did not speak Spanish; so I was able to tell Darillo to attract Tupaco back into his house and keep him there, while I took a photograph. Darillo entered into the deception with savage delight, as if he wanted to prove his superiority to the indigenous people, and claim his rightful place as 'a superior person from civilisation'.

Having taken my photo, I told Darillo to 'release his prisoner', and I suggested that, in the morning, we might visit this ruin if it were not too far away. My admirable guide discussed such a project with Tupaco as we all sat round the campfire that evening, and eventually the Indian agreed to guide us, after I had given him another dollar. But he would not go right in, he told us, because the place was infested with snakes, and he had faced many dangers when gathering his small collection of artefacts.

Tupaco's expressed fear of snakes surprised me greatly, and I said as much to Darillo. I remember saying, "That's a load of Chinamen's balls," in the colloquial Spanish I had learned as a ranch hand. But Darillo looked a bit doubtful.

"I lived in the jungle for years," I told him, "not very far from here. I saw two or three snakes every day of my life; always they made off as fast as their wriggle would carry them. They never come after you to attack."

"But if you tread on one, or move a stone and there is one underneath?" Darillo protested.

"So you have to be a bit careful, that's all. Anyway, they don't generally inject any poison even when they strike you," I said. "The peons on my ranch were bitten at least once a week when they were chopping down the scrub, but only rarely was one poisoned, and then not badly. One or two were ill for a while, but not one ever died, despite dozens of snake bites."

Darillo still did not seem convinced; so I pressed home my argument. "There's a great deal of nonsense spoken and written about the menace of snakes," I insisted. "Always from people who don't know, who don't have any personal experience, who've never even lived in the jungle. But you chaps are different: you know the jungle, and you've been brought up here. Why the hell are you scared of snakes?"

Darillo was nonplussed for a moment but, strangely, he did not appear resentful that a foreigner should be lecturing him about his own environment.

"You know I never thought about snakes biting you, and not injecting poison," he admitted. "Are you sure it's true?"

I nodded vehemently. "Absolutely certain."

"Well, well," Darillo said, dumbfounded. "I always thought it was the witch doctors who cured the men who were bitten. Mind you, some did die, and when we were children we were always taught to beware of snakes, because they kill."

"Men have always had a great revulsion from snakes," I said, "but I think it is purely psychological. Can you tell me of any man in South America who was ever attacked by a snake, which came after him, pursued him? Doesn't every snake try to escape as soon as it becomes aware of your presence?"

Darillo searched his memories. "You may be right," he agreed at last. "If a man like you, a man who does not come from our jungle, is willing to go to the ruins, I suppose I ought to pluck up courage and come with you."

"Tell Tupaco what I said," I told Darillo. "Perhaps he will come, too."

"He won't come inside the ruins," Darillo replied. "I don't think he's frightened of the snakes, no matter what he says, but he is afraid of the spirits of his ancestors. They still live there. While they won't harm me, they might seek revenge on Tupaco for some evil he has done."

"But he has already been in the ruins," I protested. "He showed us all those artefacts."

"They did not come from inside the ruins," Darillo affirmed. "I think he found them just outside, or perhaps in a tomb near here, which he could have uncovered when he was digging the land for cultivation."

My confidence in Darillo, and my gratitude to him for his whole-hearted assistance to me, was growing day by day. He was indispensable as far as my plans were concerned, but I was immensely gratified to see how much he entered into the spirit of our adventure, fast becoming much more of a true partner than a paid guide. Eventually we decided that Tupaco should take us to the ruins in the morning before Carya returned with the mule, and we would do some investigating, even if Tupaco stayed outside.

As night began to deepen, and the moon rose to bathe the clearing in a subdued and shadowless shimmer, I asked Darillo where he was going to sleep.

"I don't need to sleep. I shall sit here by the fire, near your tent," he replied.

I looked at him questioningly, as if asking him to elaborate.

"I can't go in the house, because of the insects," he admitted. "They don't bother the Indians, but they could attack me. If I sleep out here I don't know what dangers there might be: even snakes," he said with tongue in cheek. "So I'll keep a fire going out here."

Darillo was putting a brave face on what was a difficult situation, made even more of a problem because of the absence of companion Carya. The obvious solution was to invite him to sleep in my tent, which I did. Not only would this ensure a decent night's sleep for Darillo; it would also be a clear demonstration of my gratitude, showing that I regarded him as 'one of us', as a partner in my adventure.

Next morning Darillo breakfasted on maize bread and a sort of Cornish pasty, which Tupaco's woman made for him but, just to be on the safe side, I ate only my own biscuits and raisins. I drank a little of their very strong coffee, after I'd purified it with a tablet, and then the three of us set off to the ruin, which turned out to be only two kilometres away.

Perhaps I had been expecting to see something exciting: not a city, of course, but perhaps a substantial village with the possibility of interesting buildings in an unusual setting. I was very disappointed. When Tupaco stopped and pointed ahead, all I could see was yet another barrier of interwoven scrub and stunted trees. There was no thick jungle, but the bush was lush.

"There are houses in here," Darillo said as he slashed his way through, machete flailing like a scythe. "Here's a stone wall," he cried at last, and I rushed forward to join him. But it was a miserable specimen, less than one metre high and, at first sight, not particularly well made. The stones were quite small compared with those at Incallacta, for example; they did not even appear to be carved or shaped to fit together. Much of the earth that had been used as cement was washed away, so that the joins looked ragged and clumsy.

"It is a house," Darillo told me with just a tremor of excitement in his voice. "I will cut down the *monte* (scrub) to show you."

Half an hour later he had exposed what was left of four walls of a small house, in a pretty untidy state. It was all rather disheartening at a casual glance, and even a more lengthy examination did not expose anything to get enthusiastic about. This was certainly not in the traditional style of Inca workmanship, but it did appear to use the same form of construction as that of the ruins I had seen on my trip to Tablas. That is to say, if this ruin were very ancient, it could have been built in the same style as the other prehistoric ruins—namely a low stone wall to afford solid protection for the first metre or so, with a timber wall built inside the stone perimeter.

I prodded around the ruin while Darillo slashed his way through the surrounding bush to see what other buildings might he hidden there. The floors of the houses near Tablas were laid stone, and had not therefore become overgrown. At this site, however, the mud floors had provided a seed-bed for patches of wild grasses and an odd plant. All I could do was to scrape around with long, sturdy pieces of stick, not forgetting my own words of advice about watching out for snakes. I saw two rattlesnakes, but one of them rattled his tail to give me plenty of warning that he was lying there on a patch of dried mud; they both made off at high speed, straight out through the empty space that had been the doorway. It was as if they knew their way around.

Digging in the clear spaces was hard work, with only a machete and wooden pole; so all that I uncovered was earthenware pots, cups and spoons. But they were all unbroken and lying close to the surface, which suggested to me that the house had been occupied many years ago, but abandoned in a hurry. The pots were crudely modelled, without any patterns chiselled on the surface and without any painted decorations. It seemed most unlikely that this could have been the residence of an Inca or any Indian of similar high culture.

Darillo returned to report. "There are only six houses, all built around a spring of water which flows to the edge of a precipice and then falls straight down to the river." He broke off suddenly, and lunged forward to tread on something at my feet. Having ground it into pulp he announced boldy, *'Aranya'* (spider). "They bite."

We discussed the possible significance of the ruins of this tiny hamlet. Darillo offered the suggestion that it might have been a fort, because it was situated directly above a steep drop down to the river below. We both knew that this was just the sort of place chosen by the Sierra Indians of long ago as a look-out post and defence outpost from which to guard against the incursions of the lowland Indians from the Amazon basin, for in those days the only way an invading force from the lowlands could march on a settlement up in the hills was by walking along the river banks in the dry season.

"Are there many more ruins up-river?" I asked.

"Many, many," Darillo confirmed. "In the next days I can show you ruins, big ruins: places that were cities. Not like this one, which is only a small fort. Big forts are up there," and his eyes widened.

It all sounded very exciting, but, of course, I had to take it with a pinch of salt. Darillo, who desperately wanted to impress me, might be expected to tell me what he thought I wanted to hear, rather than the truth, In his own mind, he would not be lying, merely looking on the bright side in an effort to win my approval.

We made our way back to the Indians' house in the clearing, to find Carya waiting with the mule. He had been riding since before dawn, he revealed, because he was afraid he'd be too heavy for the mule, and would have to walk up some of the steeper hills. This fear had apparently been confirmed, and one look at the mule told the whole story. It was a pathetically skinny and fine-boned animal, and if it had not been for Carya's superhuman efforts to collect it, I might well have expressed my dismay.

Carya must have noted my apprehension.

"It doesn't look so good, Mister, but it is very strong," he assured me, "and it can travel far without food."

That could well be true, I thought, judging by the experiences the creature must have had. Anyway, I bought a bowl of maize from the Indian to feed it and tied it to a tree to rest for the day.

That evening round the camp-fire I asked Darillo to mention the Paititi Indians very casually, in such a way that our Indian host did not get alarmed or think we were chasing them for some reason, but so that we could discover whether or not they had passed this way.

"He says they did," said Darillo at once. "He knows which route they took, and we are following them. We shall only catch up with them if they have stopped to sow a crop of maize, and are searching an area thoroughly. Otherwise they will reach the mountains ahead of us."

We all agreed to set out at first light in the morning, and I paid the Indian our fee to pass along his footpath. I heard my two companions discussing their sleeping-arrangements. It seemed that they intended to lay out one bed, taking it in turns to sleep and keep guard. This developed into the permanent routine every night during the rest of our journey.

Only the first day's trek was really uncomfortable, as we fought our way along the narrow footpath which had become overgrown through lack of use. I soon abandoned the idea of trying to ride the mule, as my head and shoulders were forced through the overhanging vegetation. Also I felt guilty about asking Darillo and Carya to carry my haversack, camera case and tripod, and to hack away at the scrub growing across the trail. So I loaded my equipment on the mule, and I walked.

By late that afternoon, we had only crossed one hill and descended into the next valley, where we set up camp. I noticed that Darillo had unpacked his pistol at the start of the day. Now he took it out of its holster and carried it everywhere in hand—ready.

I asked him why.

"Animals," he replied, shrugging his shoulders philosophically, as if there was no more than a slight chance. "Maybe Mosetenes," he added as an afterthought.

"I thought the Mosetenes lived much further south," I observed.

"Yes they do, but sometimes they come to this area for hunting and fishing."

I had no first-hand knowledge of the Mosetenes. I only knew the name, that of the only tribe of Indians living in the fertile valleys of the Yungas who had never surrendered to the Incas.

"Are they still a hostile people?" I enquired.

"Not if you leave them alone," Darillo replied. "They might not like it if they find us in their hunting area. Soon we will reach the river Beni, and there's a Mosetene village where they know me. We shall be all right there. And that's where the Paititis are heading."

"Do you want to share my food?" I asked as the sun dipped towards the horizon.

"Thanks, Mister," said Darillo, nodding his head in pleasurable surprise."Tonight we lay traps, and tomorrow we have who knows what marvellous food for our breakfast."

Darillo called Carya to show him what he thought would be the best spot to dig a trap. Carya, I was told, was one of the best animal-hunters in the whole of Beni, and Darillo obviously respected his skills. Carya surveyed the scene carefully, turning through a complete circle. Then he suddenly pointed towards the river, and set off without saying a word. Darillo followed obediently and, deciding very quickly that I was not going to be left alone with only my machete for for protection, I followed them closely along a narrow muddy trail. Presently Carya slowed down, pointed out a small earth mound in the bushes, and his eyes followed the tiny track that led from the mound down to the river.

"There," he said to Darillo, pointing to a spot where two tracks crossed. At once the two of them started digging a narrow pit with their machetes about one metre deep; then Carya stepped in it and hacked away at the earth wall like a miner cutting coal. A few minutes' carving, and he had made both sides of the pit slope inwards, so that it was much wider at the bottom than the top. Then he cut a number of small stakes and drove them into the earth walls. A rabbit or a small fox could wriggle down into the bottom of the pit, but would find it very difficult to get up the sloping walls to the narrow entrance, nor could it easily jump past the barrier of stakes.

"What are you going to catch?" I asked.

"Chigwiree, Mister, if you have some bait," said Darillo.

Carya had the answer. "Get me a piece of that maize bread, and that meat which was beginning to go bad."

Darillo shot off at high speed, and I was only too glad to pull Carya out of the pit to keep me company while I waited on the trail.

In a few minutes Darillo returned to find Carya putting the finishing touches to his trap. As Carya threw the bait into the bottom of the pit he explained very briefly, for he was not a great talker, "Chigwiree smells food. Goes in to eat. Cannot get out. We eat chigwiree."

It seemed an ingeniously simple idea, quickly prepared. I

hoped it would work, because my meagre supply of raisins and biscuits would not last long, shared between the three of us. My companions had always said that they would feed all of us on the journey.

Next morning when I got out of my tent it was barely light, and yet there were my two guides making breakfast out of a fruit about the size of a melon. I don't know if they'd found it in the jungle or whether they'd brought it in their small kitbag. At the time I didn't care. I was too hungry, and tempted by the fruit that Darillo was cutting out of one half of the skin. Since it had a skin, I knew it would be safe to eat, and I gratefully accepted a few chunks of what looked like a large juicy pomegranate. We all tucked in until the fruit was gone, and we were left with the two halves of rough skin.

Carya went down to the river and filled both with water. Darillo meantime had spread a deep bed of red-hot ashes at one side of the roaring fire, and Carya carefully placed the two bowls of water on top of the glowing ashes with the help of two machetes, which he used like arms to lower the bowls on to the hot surface. At first they fizzed a bit, and then they settled into the bed of ashes while the water slowly heated. From his kitbag Darillo drew out a few coffee beans, and started to crush them with the blade of his machete on a large stone nearby. I jumped up as soon as I saw what he was doing, and offered to get my small tin of coffee powder.

"You have your American coffee," said Darillo. "We'll have ours."

I handed over a teaspoonful, and Darillo poured it on top of the water in one of the empty fruit shells. Into the other he ladled a larger quantity of his own ground coffee; soon the water began to steam and, with more red-hot ashes placed around the shells, it began to bubble. After a minute or two of stirring the black concoction, the shells were lifted out of the ashes, and mine was placed on the ground in front of me.

"Wait until it cools down, and then you can drink it," I was told.

I've had some rare drinks in some strange places around the world, but I don't think I shall ever forget that first swig of fruity, black coffee on the banks of the river Maniqui. The thrill of survival in that lonely and isolated wilderness, plus the fact that the water was boiled in the inside of a fruit skin and therefore pure enough to drink, persuaded me that I'd enjoyed a quite delicious breakfast.

The fruit skins were by now quite hard, and Darillo packed them away carefully for future use. Then we all went down to the pit, where Carya announced with some regret that we'd caught only one chigwiree, and it was not very big.

The chigwiree, which looked like a very large extremely fat rat, must have been lying doggo. As soon as Carya peered down into the pit with his machete raised, the creature started to leap around. It tried to climb up the walls of the pit which were sloping against it, but it had no more success than a spider trying to scramble up the glossy wet surface of an enamel bath. It kept falling back to the bottom of the pit; so it tried to leap straight out. The wooden stakes in the walls of the pit sent it crashing back time after time until, somewhat dazed and bemused, it finally succeeded in clawing its way up. Carya chopped its head off, picked it up by the tail and carried it back to the camp. While Darillo skinned and gutted the huge rat, Carya walked around, digging small wedges of earth with the blade of his machete. Finally he came to some that was apparently satisfactory, and he dug a bucketful and spread it on the rock they had used for grinding coffee.

He cut a large palm leaf, trotted down to the river and returned with his leaf-bag full of water, which he spread on the clay. Both the Bolivians then worked the wet clay like Plasticine before they slapped the mixture around the body of the dead chigwiree, enclosing it like a joint of beef in tinfoil. Again they made a heap of red-hot ashes at the edge of the fire, dropped the mud parcel into the ashes, and scooped more hot ashes out of the fire to cover it completely. They built the fire on top of the ashes, replenished the blaze with more dry twigs, then packed my tent and equipment. While the mule munched his breakfast of maize bread, the boys loaded him with my camping gear and filming equipment, having apparently decided that my idea of walking was a good one. Finally the hard-baked mud pack was hooked out of the fire, wrapped in layers of palm leaves, tied with the piece of the twine that I always carried, and loaded on the top of everything else on the mule's back.

We waded waist-deep across the river, reached the narrow trail on the other side, and began to ascend the next range of hills along a much easier path. It was easier because it changed from hard-packed mud into stone and shale as we ascended, and the complete absence of growing vegetation on the path itself and of overhanging branches at the side made me think that possibly the trail was not unused. Indeed, Darillo told me that the Mosetene tribe he knew would use this path as far as the river, but the other side of the river where we had camped was territory claimed by the Moxos, and for the Mosetenes to cross the river could lead to dispute.

For two more days we headed westwards into the hills, with no sign of danger. As we marched inexorably forward along the rocky pathway, I thought about the adventure books I used to read, which always described the perils of dangerous reptiles and wild Indians in the steaming humidity of mosquito-infested forests. As far as I was concerned, these accounts in schoolboy thrillers were a long way from the utterly peaceful, and often beautiful, setting of the jungle-covered hills. I found it a challenge to invade this lonely wilderness, as we trekked slowly onwards for the next two days, completely undisturbed by reptiles, animals or so-called wild Indians.

During the afternoon of the third day we climbed another hill, and Carya pointed out a few puffs of fleecy white cloud above the next valley.

"Looks like smoke," said Darillo. "Could be an Indian camp. We'll see from the top of the hill."

Indeed, when the narrow stony trail broke clear of the trees at the summit of the hill, we had a splendid view for miles across rolling green hills which swept gradually up towards the Andes. There in the valley immediately below us was a little oasis of activity that was somehow out of place in the middle of this peaceful countryside.

On the dried-out mud bank on one side of the river, a huge fire was burning, and half a dozen small figures were scurrying along the short path which led from the river to a small clearing, in the middle of which were six crude dwellings. Each one looked as though it consisted of only one room with one doorway, and had been hastily constructed of tree branches, palm leaves and timber supports.

My two guides were undecided what to do next. Carya favoured making a detour, but Darilla thought we might get news of the Paititi Indian group, and that we would be safe if approached carefully. I was dubious about trying to make contact with the isolated group. It might have been interesting to spend a little time studying them, and possibly obtaining some information about any ruins in the area, but against that I had to weigh the disadvantages if they turned out to be unfriendly or even hostile.

Their settlement was, after all, a long way from civilisation, and so I put my doubts and fears to Darillo, emphasising that he was not to take any risks. He nodded agreement, and then put his hands to his mouth and yodelled loud and long. On the river bank below, all activity suddenly froze and, as if at a given signal, the Indians scurried back into their camp and disappeared into their camp and disappeared into their huts.

Darillo pursed his lips and frowned.

"I think we shall not be welcome," he said. "No one is coming to meet us, so I think we had better make a slight detour. They know we are here; so there will be no danger if we just keep walking, and leave them alone."

We continued along the narrow trail which skirted the Indian village, crossed the shallow river and climbed into the next hill.

"There are more ruins," said Darillo, pointing down and along the river we had just crossed. "Only small ruins."

On the top of one steep bank which fell sheer down to the river bed about thirty metres below, I could just make out the remains of several stone walls, built in similar style to that of the many other forts I had seen during all my journeys, in a strategically commanding position looking down on a river.

Once again I got out my large-scale map and marked the exact position of these small forts. It needed no more than a cursory glance at the map to see that all the forts I had charted on my journeys so far formed three sides of a square—from Cochabamba to Santa Cruz, northwards along the foothills of the Andes, and now eastwards to a point north of Lake Titicaca. Some of the forts were built on the top of steep hills giving a commanding view of the countryside for miles, but the vast majority were built on the banks of the rivers situated on the perimeter of this wild area bounded by the three sides of the square.

From my own experiences, and after reading the accounts of some of the Spanish *conquistadores,* I know that the dried-up riverbeds were, and to some extent still are, the main roads through the lower valleys of the Andes; so it seemed reasonable to suppose that the forts on the river banks might have formed a very effective barricade around the almost unknown area of what is now northern Cochabamba, Chapare and as far as San Ignacio. The isolated garrisons on some hilltops would have provided wonderful look-out points covering most of this huge area.

I did not discuss my theories with Darillo and Carya, partly because they showed little interest in the subject, but chiefly because my studies were far from complete. I felt that the hills would yield up a lot more evidence yet and, happily, we were making much better progress once we'd left the jungle behind.

The youngsters insisted that I now ride the mule, because there were three short sharp hills before we reached the river Beni. Actually the stony footpaths, which must have been cut out of the hillside many years or even centuries ago, were quite easy for travelling along. They wound round the hillside with no particularly steep incline, and had not been allowed to become overgrown, which led me to believe that they must have been in regular use by the Indians of that area. Indeed, Darillo confirmed that many Mosetene Indians lived in the hills but, since their agriculture was based on the slash-and-burn method, they moved their camps every few years as the land became sterile.

Halfway up the first hill the poor old mule puffed, panted and stopped continuously, which was not surprising with my fifteen and a half stone on him; so I got off and led him as far as the top, where we stopped for a snack and a drink.

"Where are these ruins, then?" I asked Darillo, perhaps a little unkindly.

"Down in the valley near the next river," he replied. 'We will go straight down, but we will have to turn up river to avoid the Mosetene village on the next hill."

"What Mosetene village," I cried with some alarm. "I can't see any village."

"You see over there, a little way up from the river, where there are no trees?"

"Yes, I can see the clearings, but there's no village there."

"Oh yes, there is," Darillo insisted.

"The houses are under the cover of the trees," Carya chipped in. "And there are Mosetenes living there, for there are crops growing in the open spaces."

I couldn't pick them out, I must admit, but there was no point in discussing it further. The two of them knew exactly what they were talking about, and their nonchalant attitude exuded confidence.

Again they insisted that I rode the mule down the hill into the valley, probably because it enabled them to make more speedy progress than when I was walking.

In an hour we were on the banks of a sluggish, muddy river. In the wet season it was probably a raging torrent at least twice its present width but, when we arrived, I was delighted to see that it had dried out to less than two metres deep, leaving dry banks of flat sandy soil about four metres wide on either side, like a great ribbon highway through the dense jungle. There was a stepping-stone pathway of rocks laid across the river, which led to another trail into the hills on the other side but, since we were avoiding the Mosetene village, we stayed on the same bank, and made good progress. The two Bolivians were looking for the next easy crossing-point because, as they explained, it would certainly lead to a trail into the forests on the other side.

Whenever we approached a bend, one of the Bolivians would run on in front, and, keeping close to the cover of the trees, spy out the land ahead. Happily, there was no sign of another Indian village near enough to baulk our progress. All that we did see, on the other side of the river, was two ruins of stone fortresses built at two bends in the river where the rock-face rose sheer from the bank. The fortresses had been erected on top of the shallow cliff, thus providing a formidable barrier against would-be attackers walking up the river.

Although the river did not look very deep, we dared not risk a casual crossing, because, as Darillo explained, there could be pot-holes or quicksands; so we would have to cross at the recognised sites to be safe.

I was rather disappointed at not being able to visit the ruins on the other side, even if they were only comparatively small forts, but Carya had an encouraging comment.

"We shall see more ruins on this side of the river soon," he said.

"What are they guarding, all these fortresses?" I asked.

"Settlements and small towns where they used to live, further into the hills," Darillo said. "Would you like us to stop on the other side, and look for one of the bigger ruins?" he asked without a great deal of enthusiasm.

"How long will it take to uncover one of these large ruins?" I asked.

"I think we might find one in two weeks if we search," Darillo replied, "but it would take some days to cut down the jungle around it." He looked a bit doubtful, and added a warning. "I'm not sure that we should stay in this area that long."

I knew what he meant: there was the threat of the Mosetenes, if they resented our presence; but I had not travelled thousands of miles, endured some pretty laborious expeditions and spent a lot of money, to be thwarted when I was almost within sight of what could be immensely important, unknown ruins.

However, all these doubts faded into the background as soon as we rounded the next bend. Carya had been a long time returning from his reconnaissance; he then reported that he could see maize, yucca and bananas growing, but no sign of people, no permanent dwellings at all; so we were safe to proceed. This did not prepare me for what lay round the corner, for there, on both steep banks of the river, I could clearly see substantial ruins of stone buildings, with a stone footpath across the river to join what had obviously been two ancient cities. All the surrounding land had been cleared of jungle and, as Carya had told us, was still being used for cultivation, as it probably was in ancient times, when the cities were inhabited.

I heard Darillo double-check with Carya that there were no Indians around and, when he received that assurance, we proceeded up the steep path leading from the river bank to the ruins of the ancient city above. At once I was reminded of an Incallacta overgrown with bushes, long coarse grass, with a great deal of moss and lichen on the remains of the stone walls. The groundcover was thin enough for me to be able to push my way through quite easily in order to walk around the ruins. Inside some of the stone houses, and one larger building which may have been some sort of temple, there was plenty of small, stunted vegetation, but nothing more than waist high.

At first I suspected that the city had been occupied in comparatively recent years, but Darillo pointed out a more likely reason for the lack of trees and dense jungle vegetation. Many of the houses had well-made stone floors, and most of the parade-ground, around which the dwellings had been built, was also made of stone, and also very nearly intact. Only the smallest plants could have taken root in the layers of dirt that collected in the ridges of the beautifully-fitted stones. There were even one or two houses with no more that a fine covering of moss, grass and weeds on the floor.

I suggested that we prepared camp for the night long before darkness fell, and pointed out the suitability of one of the empty, roofless houses. Darillo demurred because of danger from poisonous insects that lived in the stone walls. We would be safer just outside the ruins, he insisted, on a flat area of cultivation where a stream flowed down the hill to join the river below. I was not convinced by this unlikely notion of poisonous insects which lived only in stone walls. It was much more likely that, for all his sophistication, Darillo was apprehensive about sleeping in the ruins and scared of the spirits of his ancestors. But it was of no great consequence to me where we slept, and I had absolutely no desire to shatter the young man's illusions; so I went along with his plan quite willingly and without question. Our camp-site was ready in less than half an hour and, while Carya built up a roaring fire and warmed up the maize bread and meat, Darillo and I walked round the ruins, studying them carefully. Even late in the afternoon the light was quite adequate for filming; so I shot several reels inside the city wall. I hoped this would show the method of construction of the stone walls, which, although not nearly so good as the carved and shaped stones in the walls of Cuzco, was nevertheless good enough, and so carefully put together that stone walls without any cement were still standing, one to two metres high, several hundred years after they were constructed.

Following my promise to Dr. Ponce Sangines, I am not going even to refer to gold. Suffice it to say that over most of this part of South America there is gold in the rivers. There are silver and copper mines as well, and tin mines in the Andes. The Indians of ancient times used all these metals, either on their own or mixed together; so it was no surprise to find a huge quantity of metal objects for tilling the soil, for cutting down the jungle, and for everyday use in preparing and consuming food and drink. It was not a great surprise to find these artefacts in small niches in the walls and just under the surface of many of floors, because it was clear that the city had been evacuated in a great hurry. The place was littered with earthenware cooking-pots of all sizes, many of the larger ones still sticking out above the layer of dust deposited over the years. Many more were exposed by just flicking away the top few centimetres of earth with a machete.

Everything was lying higgledy-piggledy with no attempt at careful storage or preservation, as though the inhabitants of long ago had fled at the sudden appearance of an enemy or the arrival of some natural cataclysm. I am inclined towards the theory of retreat from an enemy, because I think it highly likely that the city was burnt as it was attacked. It would need detailed excavations by archaeologists to prove the point, but I noticed one piece of evidence to support such a theory. In the middle of some of the walls I saw that there were two and sometimes three large stones that were split right through. It is possible that these were the stones supporting the large timbers on which the roofs had been built and, if these timbers had been set ablaze, it would have been possible for enormous and prolonged heat to split the stones, which were rather like chunks of sandstone rock.

Next day we walked another five kilometres up the river, and found two more ruins of settlements whose principal houses were built of stone, and finally we crossed the river to investigate the ruins exactly opposite our camp-site. These three ruins were all a little smaller than the first city where we had camped, and they all consisted of a nucleus of between twenty and twenty-five stone-built houses at the centre, with areas of raised earth nearby, where the jungle grew thick and tall. If this city fell into the same pattern as Incallacta, the raised banks would have been formed by the earth from groups of adobe houses, which would have tumbled down over the years and provided a depth of soil in which trees and tropical vegetation could have taken root. Again, following the prototype of Incallacta, it is possible to surmise that the stone dwellings were for the rulers and upper classes, while the adobe huts were for the rest.

It seemed likely from the general lay-out that the four settlements all formed one cultural and economic unit, and that the first, and larger, city was the centre of administration. I judged this to be the case, since it was the only one of the ruins where there were any large stone buildings. The others were like small rectangular boxes in which no more than one family could live.

In this larger ruin there were more dwellings, as well as three much more substantial stone buildings which might have been a temple, a meeting-place, a palace, a store-room, or a building of substance and value to the whole community. The first of the four ruins also had the advantage of a much larger stretch of level land around it than the others.

I asked Darillo who was growing the crops on this land now, and were they lived.

"Nomadic Indians," he replied. "There are many tribes in all these hills," he added, waving his arms to cover the whole wilderness. "They build a village near a river, and then move on after a few years. They plant their crops in many places, and come back to harvest when it is ready. This is good land for growing food."

"Why don't they settle here, then?"

"They are afraid of the spirits in these ancient cities," said Darillo with the hint of a smile, which did not blot out my recollection that he, too, had been apprehensive.

"Then why don't they take all the metal and earthenware artefacts?" I queried. "They could sell them to unscrupulous dealers."

"Spirits," repeated Darillo gravely. "They don't come into the building even in daylight. Anyway, they don't trade with white men or other Indians. They keep to themselves always. In fact, they do not even know about white men if they have never seen one."

I took this hyperbole with a pinch of salt, but I believed the general picture Darillo was painting of a considerable number of tribes of nomadic, primitive Indians living in this vast area, untouched by civilisation.

During the following three days we ambled steadily along the ancient trails that led westwards; we crossed one more major range of five more gently sloping hills and four more shallow rivers. Sometimes it was easy-going along footpaths which had been trodden into the hillsides many years ago, but occasionally we had to hack our way through overgrown trails, and suffer a continued buffeting and bruising from tree branches and thick scrub. Some trails were obviously in constant use, while others could not have been used for decades. This wilderness of tropical lowland jungle was even more isolated and desolate than the areas of Colombia and Venezuela, where I had worked for years. But it was so calm and peaceful that I almost envied the nomadic tribes who existed in the tranquility of this ecstatic escape from the struggles and hostility of modern life.

During our travels through the more open country I rode the

mule, for I felt safer up on his back. It occurred to me to ask the Bolivians if they were scared of animals, reptiles or Indians.

"Carya is only afraid that you won't give him another toffee," Darillo said, cracking a joke and laughing for almost the first time on the journey. I gave them both a toffee before they answered my question seriously.

"I would be frightened of some Indians," admitted Carya, "but we avoid them."

"What about jaguars and pumas?"

They both hooted with derision at the idea. "Jaguars, upon my mother's life, no! They are everywhere in the jungle, but they don't come near," Darillo scoffed. "Are you afraid of anything, Mister?"

I thought about it for a while. "Not of animals, perhaps," I admitted, "but sometimes I'm very scared at being so isolated. Supposing I had an attack of appendicitis, or fell and broke an ankle. How on earth would I get back to hospital? That frightens me sometimes."

"We could carry you back," said Darillo seriously. Then they both took a good long look, and realised the impossibility. I relieved the tension by suggesting that, when the mule got tired, they would have to take it in turns to put on the saddle and carry me. That thought kept us all in good humour for a long while, and even the normally humourless Carya caught the bug by telling me that 'we three mules must stop for a drink and feed'. Needless to say, we stopped on the banks of a river at night to be near a water supply, and my two guides, although they were showing signs of fatigue, acceded to my request that we should spend a little time exploring along the banks. What we found there surprised even the Bolivians.

On either side we trekked no more than ten kilometres, but we came across a total of eight ruins—mostly small forts which might have accommodated fifty or sixty Indians, but again there was one much larger settlement just as there had been in the previous river valley.

During our long trek across the hills we also found evidence of settlements with half a dozen small stone houses in each, as well as the usual mounds of earth left by the collapse of many adobe huts. Adjoining each village was an area of more level land that appeared to have been used for cultivation.

This much we saw within metres of the track; there's no

knowing how many more settlements there might have been deeper into the jungle, wherever a cool, clear stream came bubbling down the hillsides. I would like to go back, and cover the whole area thoroughly in a helicopter before making any firm statement, but on the strength of what little I saw during that exploration, I should not be surprised to find that there is ample evidence to show that this area was once inhabited by a very large, organised culture, and that the ruins we saw on the river banks were defensive positions guarding the main area of population down-river where the foothills of the Andes roll gently through the tropical and sub-tropical forests. Today there is an area east of Santa Ana, about the size of Britain, which is totally unknown and unexplored. In other parts of Bolivia there are even larger areas still awaiting the first explorers. This whole region I believe to be the location of the lost empire of the Incas.

Next day, when we reached the top of a higher range of hills, we saw the village of Santa Ana. It certainly wasn't civilisation with a capital C, but it was company and safety for three lonely travellers.

Just before we reached Santa Ana we passed through a Mosetene village which had accepted the advance of civilisation. The Indians there looked much the same as the few we had seen on the other side of the hills, but the discipline imposed by the mission in the village, the influence of the *mestizo* traders with their incongruous bottles of beer and Pepsi made me pity these Indians. They lacked the freedom and tranquillity of their brothers in the jungle.

Santa Ana is significant enough to be marked on a large-scale map of Bolivia. It is still as it was in centuries gone by, a trading-post to which the indigenous farmers of the sub-tropical valleys bring their maize, coca, fruit and vegetables to sell to the merchants who come down from the towns in the Upper Andes. For that reason I had expected to find a relatively substantial village at the very least. In fact, it turned out to be a good deal smaller than that.

Across the Beni river was a small timber-built house called the hotel, which boasted one bare room in which the travellers could lay out their own beds, an adjoining room with a couple of wooden benches and a table with a jug of coffee and some tin mugs. Near the river were half a dozen small houses, some made of timber and some of adobe, in which the traders, the owner of the ferry, and two Bolivian soldiers lived. On the hillside I could see four small farms where Indians were growing some crops. There were two Indians fishing from canoes on the river, and that was all.

We crossed to the hotel on a large pontoon which the local Indians pulled backwards and forwards with a rope. Here, on the other side, I reckoned I should find it easy to hire a good mule and a guide for the rest of the journey back to the nearest town, and as it happened I was in luck. They told me to wait one more night, because a wagon was expected next day to fetch a load of bananas.

Next day the wagon turned up, and the driver agreed to take me right back to La Paz. So I said farewell to my two loyal and hard-working companions and their mule. I paid them more than the agreed fee and, with just a touch of nostalgia and regret, watched them return with the mule across the river on the pontoon.

The first twenty kilometres of the return journey in the wagon were a pretty hair-raising experience. The narrow stone track wound round the hill-sides and, if by chance we had met another vehicle careering down the hill, one of us would have gone over the sheer drop to the valley a hundred metres below.

On arrival in La Paz I went to see my friends at the National Institute of Archaeology to discuss with them what I thought was my very exciting news. I'd hardly got inside the door before they greeted me with bubbling enthusiasm about their own latest discovery at a site called Iscanwaya to the east of Lake Titicaca. They were so thrilled about the filming they wanted me to do that they brushed aside my attempts to relate the momentous events in Beni.

"We know about Beni. It's interesting, but nowhere near so exhilarating as these ruins near Aucapata, on the river Llika. Jorge Arellano is the archaeologist in charge. He'll tell you."

Jorge needed no second bidding, although his was a more sober approach than that of some of his exuberant colleagues.

"Yes, it is interesting, Ross," he affirmed. "Probably the most important ruins we have discovered in Bolivia this century. Iscanwaya covers about twenty-five hectares—five times the famous Inca city of Machu Picchu in Peru. And down the river Llika there are many more ruins. It is a most important prehistoric area of Bolivia, that's certain."

Dr. Carlos Ponce Sangines joined in.

"We know you will want to film this very important site," he said. "Jorge will go with you. It will take about ten hours in the jeep, and then you have to walk a bit. But we have taken a house in the village of Aucapata, so you can sleep there, and get a mule to take you on to the ruins."

The manner in which the proposition was put to me left little room for discussion. I was being told that I wanted to go, whatever I felt about it, and whatever plans I had hoped to fulfil by leading a party of experts back to Beni. I hid my disappointment, and tried to enter into their world of intense enthusiasm about their new discovery.

"You are now our official documentary maker," they said encouragingly, and of course I took pride in accepting their invitation to go to Iscanwaya. It was one of the wisest decisions I have ever made, because Iscanwaya turned out to be another gateway to the lost empire of the Incas.

CHAPTER SIX

Iscanwaya

DR. CARLOS CALLED ME into his study for a conference.

"What is so important about the ruins of this city called Iscanwaya is that it is by far the biggest of the Mollo culture yet discovered," he said earnestly. "And we are now convinced that the roots of the Inca culture are to be found here among the Mollos."

He must have seen that I was somewhat perplexed.

"If you insist on working on this theory of the lost cities or the lost empire of the Incas, you must first study the available material on the foundation of the culture and its development, before you can possibly say what happened to them after the conquest. In this I can help you. Later on I will let you read my papers on the prehistory of Bolivia, thousands of years ago, long before the Incas. For the moment we only need to go back one thousand years."

I took out pen and paper and wrote copious notes as Dr. Carlos talked. He told me that in the year A.D. 900 the great Aymara culture reached its zenith as an empire; based at Tiwanaku on the southern shores of Lake Titicaca, it controlled all tribes and settlements throughout the Andes. According to Dr. Carlos, the Aymara empire was probably larger, more powerful, and covered a greater area than either the Greek or the Roman empires. For some reason it slowly disintegrated. There is no evidence of conquest by another culture, nor of any natural cataclysm, only a slow migration of the population from the high plateau to the temperate valleys to the east.

In these areas new leaders emerged, and new cultures developed, with their own social systems, languages and traditions, but based on the original Aymara culture from which these people came.

Dr. Carlos went on to tell me that, in his opinion, not enough has been found of these new cultures for us to be able to identify them positively. The Mollo culture is the exception because, in the valleys to the east of Lake Titicaca, there are the remains of many stone-built settlements which are all connected by stone highways, and all of which appear to have had a common way of life.

The method of construction of all the houses and other buildings is exactly the same. The system of introducing running water, the style of pottery, the engraving, painting, ceramics, and the design of the settlements are all very similar. Most significant of all, perhaps, is that each settlement centres on the same system of agriculture on man-made terraces with sophisticated systems of irrigation.

Of all the Mollo settlements so far discovered, Iscanwaya is by far the largest and, because of its position in the centre of an area of stone villages, it might have been a capital city and a centre of government.

Dr. Carlos went on to suggest very tentatively that, because the methods of construction in stone as well as the terraces for cultivation and the irrigation systems used were all so similar to Inca methods, it is just possible that this is where the Inca culture was founded, and that it developed from these more simple beginnings. The Mollos also spoke Quechua, the language of the Incas. (Quechua has a common ancestry with Aymara in much the same way as French, Italian and Spanish share a common foundation in Latin.)

Carbon dating of ceramics shows that the Mollo culture flourished from A.D. 1100 to A.D. 1400, just before the Incas took over power and control of this whole area.

Dr. Carlos got up to signify that our most interesting conference was at an end.

"I will send Jorge Arellano to guide you," he said. "Jorge is one of my best young scientists, and he is the one I am going to put in charge of our long-term excavations at Iscanwaya. You will make an interesting film there."

Next day Jorge and I took the Institute's jeep on a five-hour drive to Lake Titicaca and then eastwards to a tiny Spanish hamlet called Aucapata. After a night's sleep in this isolated outpost in the Andes, just above the insect line, we set out on foot along the narrow trail on the banks of the river Llika, heading down below the insect line towards the lower hills.

With Indian porters to carry my camping and filming equipment it was less than a day's walk to reach the impressive ruins of Iscanwaya, clinging to the hillside that fell away steeply into the valley of the river Llika. A small band of about ten peons was clearing the vegetation so that many stone walls, two to two and a half metres high, were clearly visible.

So that I could appreciate the skill, the expertise and the advance planning that had gone into the construction of Iscanwaya, Jorge took me along the narrow stone pathway that wound round the precipitous hillside at the northern edge of the city. From the top of this hill we had a splendid view right down the valley of the Llika, especially of the hillside on which Iscanwaya had been built. Taking advantage of the superb panoramic view, one's first impression was still of the incredible size and scope of the undertaking by primitive people who, with their bare hands, had reshaped a hillside.

The hill on which Iscanwaya had been built was terraced almost as neatly and precisely as the flight of steps at the entrance to a cathedral. The surrounding hillsides gave a direct point of comparison, inasmuch as they had never been touched by human hand, so that one could see exactly the environment into which these early Indians had walked.

Obviously they had first built the curved stone walls about seventy-five to a hundred metres long, and had then back-filled the terraces with earth to make large, level areas on which to build their houses and grow their crops. Jorge told me that most of the stones, especially the larger ones, had been carried down the hillside from a quarry three kilometres away on the summit and, according to information from qualified engineers, it called for building knowledge and intelligence of the highest calibre to calculate exactly the size of stone and the thickness and height of such a wall to contain that amount of earth. It was no haphazard construction.

In the pre-Inca era the dried-up river beds were the main line of communication for an invading force. That is probably why Incanwaya was built overlooking a gentle curve in the river Llika at a point where the sheer rock-face would have made it very difficult to launch an assault. At the top of this cliff-face the Indians had constructed a fortress wall with pill-boxes at regular intervals to make their river line of defence impregnable.

The engineers who planned Iscanwaya had also taken full

advantage of another natural feature. The volcanic eruption that gave birth to the Andes mountain range had carved out three narrow canyons running from the top of the hill to the bottom, and the city of Iscanwaya had been built on the two fingers of land, so that the three chasms formed another defensive barrier. The only way to approach the city would have been from the top of the hill by the one steep stone path bounded by undergrowth. A narrow column of invaders on foot would have been cut down without difficulty by armed defenders.

It seems reasonable to suggest that the leaders of this intelligent community would have appreciated the defensive potential of the site before they constructed their city, which must have been planned in great detail before a stone was laid. Since there is absolutely no written record of any kind, a great deal of my account must be supposition, backed up with evidence uncovered by experienced archaeological excavators such as Jorge Arellano.

The basic method of construction was easy to see, and did not call for any deep scientific knowledge. Having built a massive stone wall, and then filled in the loose earth to form a relatively level area of about five acres, the future inhabitants would have built the main part of their city with stones from the quarry on top of the hill.

At the centre of the city was a small plaza, a piece of level land twenty by fifteen metres, around which they had built fifteen large, two-roomed houses as well as twelve smaller, one-roomed dwellings. All were built of slabs of stone which had been cut and fitted together, but which still needed a quantity of earth to fill in the cracks and to cement them together, because they were not shaped and fitted with quite the same precision and skill as in the principal Inca cities of Peru. Each of the houses, whether large or small, was built on top of a specially-constructed bank of earth one metre above the ground level, and in every case one had to step up on to a small patio before entering the house. Nobody knows why the houses all had this sharp step up at the entrance, but local Indians living in the surrounding area told us that they build their houses in a similar fashion above ground level to keep out snakes and other reptiles, and to prevent rain water washing into the houses in the wet season.

In the larger houses there was a low doorway leading from the narrow patio into the living-room; this measured three by two metres, and an internal stone wall divided the living-room from the sleeping-area, which also measured three by two metres. There was no doorway through this wall, only a small hole one metre by fifty centimetres, at a height of one metre above the level of the floor. One had to climb through this narrow gap to get from the living-room into the bedroom. The only obvious reason for such an awkward entry would be that it offered further protection during the night against snakes or other marauding creatures from the surrounding jungle.

There were plenty of stone shelves built into the walls of all the houses, and in the centre of each living-room a hole had been dug into the floor and covered with a flat stone. When Jorge and his Indian workers had lifted the stone covers, they found tombs underneath, filled with the dust of skeletons plus a small number of artefacts like drinking-vessels, metal knives and personal tokens, which would have been buried with the dead to accompany them on their journey. The human remains had disintegrated into dust, and there is now no way of knowing who was buried in each tomb beneath the floor. It may have been every member of the household, or it may have been only the head of the family. The latter seems the more likely, because the holes were only one and a half metres deep.

Day-to-day life in the city seems to have been communally organised in a pattern similar to that of the Incas, because everyone must have used the facilities provided in the central square.

Running water from a spring near the top of the hill was channeled into a large stone ditch alongside the square. A much smaller stone culvert siphoned off this running water from the main supply into a large stone-lined water tank in the middle of the city square. This tank was two metres square and one metre deep, and could have been filled time and again by untapping the stone culvert where it joined the main supply channel. The inhabitants must have helped themselves to this supply of fresh water, carrying it to their houses in earthenware pots, of which there were many lying around, half-buried in the ruins.

Apart from the communal supply of running water there was also a group of large stone ovens, presumably for cooking maize bread, as well as another group of stone basins which must have been used for crushing maize into powder. On the outskirts of the city, just inside the boundary walls, were clusters of stone-lined silos for storing grain, and several large underground food cellars. The houses themselves appear to have been solely for accommodation. It seems that the collection of food, the preparation and the cooking must have been carried out on a community basis.

On the other two smaller areas of terraced land, separated from the main centre by two narrow canyons, there were fewer stone buildings of a different character; no doubt in ancient times they were joined to the main city by swaying creeper footbridges across the yawning chasms.

On the level land to the east of the main city, Jorge was clearing the bushes and trees which had overgrown three larger two-storeyed buildings. The bigger house at the lower level was divided into four square rooms downstairs and three more rooms above a flight of stone steps built on the outside of the house. The local Indians called this building 'the palace of the Inca', because, so they told me, this is where the Inca (or the chief of the tribe), used to live. When I pressed them for evidence to support this theory, they had none to offer. "We have always said so," was sufficient explanation for them. They also told me that the stone cross, two metres high, in front of this 'palace of the Inca' was used in ceremonial punishment. The unfortunate criminal was tied to the cross and whipped until he nearly died. The Indians also claimed that a deep pit dug around the base of the cross was filled with poisonous snakes, so that, if the victim struggled loose during the whipping, he would perish in the pit of snakes. Again I asked then for proof or supporting evidence, but, frustratingly, all they would say was, "We have always known that this is what happened." My attempts to bribe a little information from them with toffees drew a blank, except that one of the Indians volunteered that they still carried out this form of punishment in the communities further down the valley. I cannot deny that the account given to me could have been entirely fanciful, and yet there is no obvious reason why these Indians should deliberately lie.

Just above the so-called palace of the Inca, on another terrace, was an even more substantial stone building, which was subdivided into two very large rooms at ground level, but since this building was in a particularly exposed position, the second storey had almost collapsed and it was not possible to tell what divisions it had contained. Jorge would not even speculate as to the purpose of this building until he had completed his excavations, but he did not rule out my theory that it might well have been the city's garrison, since it was obviously built for communal occupation, and the site overlooked and controlled the one footpath leading into the city from the hills.

Across the other canyon the buildings were of similar construction to that of the dwelling-houses around the main city square, but were much more spread out. Two or three were built on each of the ten terraces, and there was one small cluster of six houses overlooking an area of ten much smaller terraces. Practically the whole of this area to the west of the main city was devoted to growing crops; so one presumes that these houses were dwellings for the farmers.

After Jorge had conducted me round the whole of Iscanwaya with its ninety-eight dwellings and its two much more substantial buildings, we sat down to draw sketch maps and correlate our facts and theories. Jorge was particularly anxious to impress upon me that his archaeological findings suggested that the whole city had been carefully planned and built in one short period of time. There was no question of the city growing slowly from small beginnings. Each section was vital to the well-being of the whole community, so that the inhabitants of the main city centre would not have occupied it without the garrison and seat of government across the chasm to the east, or the area of large-scale cultivation to the west. Running water would have been essential for fortress and farmland alike.

I put it to Jorge that it was clearly not an Incan city, for it had no temple, apparently no astronomic significance in the placing of the houses, nor did it follow the traditional pattern of virgins' houses, near a waterfall for purification, and soldiers' houses near a parade-ground alongside the temple. Jorge agreed with all these observations and explained that Dr. Carlos Ponce Sangines would soon publish a document outlining all the evidence to show that Iscanwaya was a city built by the Mollos, a pre-Inca culture which carbon dating of their ceramics suggested, flourished around A.D. 1200, two hundred years before the Incas rose to full power.

Mollo pots were generally larger than those of the Incas; they were much thicker and more crudely manufactured. There was very little engraving on the Mollo pottery and, where the Incas painted lavishly and skilfully, using predominently red and yellow paint, the Mollo used only black and white paint on a few of their earthenware containers.

As Dr. Carlos pointed out, there was ample evidence to support the hypothesis that the cultures of the Mollo and the Inca were quite distinct, and he went on to suggest very tentatively that the Inca empire might have had its roots in the Mollo culture. Perhaps this was not so sophisticated as that of the brilliant Incas, but the planning and construction of Iscanwaya showed perfect judgment in selecting a location so well suited to the needs of the people of that era.

As Dr. Carlos emphasised, the building of the city, starting with the complete re-shaping of the hillside, must have been the work of an enterprising and industrious people. The elaborately prepared areas for cultivation or for house building, and the provisions of a common water supply, kitchens, and stones for grinding maize inside a heavily-fortified boundary wall must all have been the work of a socially efficient state with a supremely strong and respected government, capable of organising such a large-scale co-operative undertaking.

They possessed skilful engineers with excellent mathematical knowledge, for the height of the city from the lowest up to the highest point measured exactly 100 metres, from 1,622 metres above sea level to 1,722 metres. All the two-roomed houses were identical in style and measurement, and all the dwellings were trapezoidal in construction.

Jorge also told me that all these skills were demonstrated in the magnificient building of Tiwanaku and, although there was no positive proof, it was reasonable to suppose that Iscanwaya had been built by a significant group of Aymara Indians after the mysterious dissolution of their empire on the High Plateau.

Having spent a week at Iscanwaya, I decided to explore the other Mollo ruins on the banks of the Llika, both up-river and down-river from Iscanwaya. On the long slow trek back uphill to Aucapata I questioned Dr. Carlos and Jorge closely, to glean every snippet of information I could. They told me that the word *iscanwaya* means 'Two Winds' in the Quechua language and, indeed, I noticed that the wind blew down-river in the morning and back upriver in the afternoon. Did the fact that the Mollo inhabitants spoke Quechua, the language of the Incas, mean that they had been conquered by the Inca nation? Jorge Arellano would not be persuaded to give a direct answer. He would only hint at the possible outcome of the present work being carried out by Bolivian anthropologists. They are gathering fresh evidence that may support the theory that the Mollos, after flourishing for about two hundred years after the downfall of the Aymara, may have sent large groups of their Quechua-speaking people back to Lake Titicaca and the mountains of Peru when the climate improved. They may have joined up with another even more intelligent culture, and so, with this merger, founded the Inca culture. The Incas only flourished for about eighty-three years. During this short time they produced such magnificent feats of engineering that their origins must have been amongst people who were already highly sophisticated.

Dr. Carlos was certainly convinced that the Mollos had founded the Inca culture, and then developed an even more skilful and progressive society with new and improved techniques. After two or three generations, the warriors of this powerful, well-organised Inca culture probably returned to the fertile valleys around Iscanwaya, and conquered the people they left behind them.

Jorge told me that there are many other stone ruins in the valley of the Llika and that when we returned to Aucapata he would arrange for a young Indian of the village to take me on a journey of about two weeks to show me some of these other ruins. I asked him what kind of ruins I might expect to see, and he told me that up and down the valley of the river Llika there were many forts which had obviously been part of a sophisticated defensive system. Since the ruins had been discovered only recently it was too early to state dogmatically what they were defending, but it seemed likely that the protected area centred on the pleasant and fertile upper valleys of the Llika, where the Mollos and then the Incas had established important settlements at Aucapata, Iscanwaya, Karrie and Maukallacta, and, of course, there were in those days more than one hundred small gold mines in the area, which had to be protected from the Spaniards who invaded the area after the conquest of Peru.

Even before the conquest the Mollos were always in conflict with the Chuncho tribes from the Amazon lowlands, who believed that their gods lived in the highest mountain peaks. The Chunchos made regular pilgrimages to worship their gods and their ancestors, and on the long, long journeys from the jungles and the plains they used to set up temporary camps in the temperate valleys in order to sow crops, so that they would have enough to eat on the rest of the journey and an assured food supply for the journey back. The valleys, therefore, were continually in dispute, and the Mollos built strong fortifications to protect those areas where they had established permanent settlements. Dr. Carlos told me that it seemed likely that, when the Incas returned to conquer the Mollos shortly before the Spanish conquest, they took over this admirable defensive system and added to it.

For the fifteen kilometre journey back to Aucapata, the Bolivian scientists managed to hire a mule for me, but so gruelling was the climb up the precipitous rocky path that the mule continually stopped and panted desperately. I let him rest awhile before urging him forward again for another few hundred metres, but by the time we were halfway up the hill it was clear he could manage no more. I dismounted and walked the rest of the journey, to the amazement of the Bolivians, and the very gentle pace of my ascent delayed our arrival at Aucapata until late in the afternoon. After a much-needed meal of soup and stew, I started to plan the next stage of the expedition to see some of the other ruins in the area called the hills of Munecas.

I was in luck. Two men who had just arrived in the village were to render me invaluable assistance.

Antonio Molino, who appeared to be an almost direct descendant of the Spanish invaders, was born and brought up in Aucapata, but had moved to La Paz as a young man, to be educated and to work in his family business there. In retrospect, it is possible that word of my arrival with my filming equipment had encouraged him to return, because he was passionately keen that the world should know of the momentous discoveries in the hills of the Munecas, and that tourists should be encouraged to visit the area. His Spanish-colonial house was by far the largest in Aucapata, and could be converted into a hotel, Antonio suggested. He was also the organiser of a group of folk-lore musicians and dancers who could entertain tourists with genuine local music. The other recent arrival was Hugo Boero Rojo, arguably the best-known and most respected modern author writing about Bolivia. *Bolivia Magica,* one of his many books, is a world-wide best seller, and he was named Writer of the Year 1977 by South American publishers and academic institutions. Both men knew a great deal of the history of the area, and they told me what the written records had to say about Aucapata and Iscanwaya after the three hundred years of occupation by the

Mollos, and then the shorter period of Inca rule.

Apparently the Spanish *conquistatores* did not settle in the area until 1700. They built a garrison at Aucapata and enslaved the local Indians, forcing them to work the gold-mines in the hills. On the 5th August, 1700, according to Hugo Boero's official history, the Inca leader Tupac Amaru enlisted a huge army of 18,000 Indians, and swept through the hills of Munecas, defeating the 2,000 Spanish soldiers in a series of bloody battles all around Aucapata, which the Inca army then occupied after the rout of General Sorata and his Spanish army.

The Bolivians were dumbfounded when I doubted their statements: according to the history books I had studied, the Inca nation had been wiped out long before the seventeen hundreds.

"That is what all you Europeans and Americans think," Antonio Molina protested angrily. "Peru had been completely conquered, and the Inca empire had fallen—that is true. But there were thousands of Incas left in Bolivia and, in fact, the last of many revolts was led by the Incas of the Cochabamba area less than one hundred years ago."

"When was the present-day Aucapata founded?" I asked.

"In 1824," Antonio told me. "The Spanish army returned, conquered and rebuilt Aucapata as it is today and, of course, they continued to work the gold mines. After the revolution leading to liberation and independence for all the South American people, the *m'ta maes,* or Indian slaves, were given their own houses and parcels of land. They stopped chiselling gold ore from the mines, but it is quite possible that they panned some gold from the rivers and, by growing ample quantities of food on the fertile slopes, they lived a calm and undemanding existence in almost total isolation from the rest of the world, simply trading gold for bare household necessities like knives, machetes, shovels, clothing, lamps, and a minimum of furniture.

Both Hugo, who was writing a book about Iscanwaya, and Antonio, who wanted to promote tourism in the area, put all their considerable efforts and influence into helping me to organise my own little exploration to the other ruins. Antonio, having been brought up in the area, knew the exact location of many rivers, and Hugo, drawing on his vast experience as a writer, was an authority on what would be useful to my own work, and what might well be a waste of time. Together they organised a strong young man, Wanaku, to guide me and carry the bare minimum of filming equipment. The word Wanaku means 'noble' in the Quechua language, and I only hoped that this amiable young man was strong as well.

Antonio drew me a sketch map of the ruins we were to visit, all of which were quite familiar to Wanaku, who nodded his agreement to all the instructions that were given to him by Hugo and Antonio.

Early next morning I packed my tent, a few items of clothing, a large parcel of food, my water-purifying tablets and medicine chest, and followed Wanaku out of the village and straight down the steep hillside. I knew that our first stop was to be the ancient small city of Karrie, on the river bank directly below Aucapata. Since this was below the insect line, I had already sprayed myself liberally with insect repellant and started taking a daily dose of Vitamin B tablets to ward off attacks by the millions of mosquitoes that swarmed on the river bank. The exercise of the previous weeks had markedly improved by my physical condition and, since the essential equipment in my haversack did not weigh very much, I kept pace with Wanaku down the rocky slope, and we reached Karrie soon after midday. The sizeable city, covering twelve hectares (twenty-eight acres), had been built on and around a small hillock which jutted out of the very steep hillside below Aucapata.

The ruins were totally overgrown by a few large mature trees, many smaller trees, and a mass of scrub and undergrowth. Clearly the area had been left unmolested for many years, for there were not even narrow tracks cut through the city and, to my great disappointment, it would have taken several days of felling trees and cutting away bushes to have made even a modest inspection. This was a savage blow to my plans but, since I had come so far, it would be folly to give up without a fight. Dejectedly I turned to Wanaku to ask him how we might cope and if perchance there were hidden tracks we could follow.

"I would not go in there," he announced coldly. "We are not supposed to go into the ruins."

What he did not want to admit was that, in common with most Indians, he was afraid. All the indigenous people of practically the whole of South America respect and fear the spirits of their ancestors. Wanaku was no exception, but he must have appreciated that perhaps he was letting me down just a little, for he offered to take me to a point just above the city from where we could get a view of the ruins.

It was all very frustrating and I stood there mulling it over. As it was so near Aucapata, this was not an unknown city, and certainly it would be a monumental task for me to clear even a small section of the undergrowth by myself. Against that was the overpowering realisation that it would be foolish to abandon my study after spending so much time and money in reaching this isolated place which few white men had ever seen. Nobody had visited this particular ruin for a very long time, to judge by the lack of the means of entry. It could well be that there were discoveries to be made. Was I to turn my back on this golden opportunity? It was an agonising decision to make, and what tipped the balance eventually was fear. I knew then that, deep down, I was afraid to go right into the ruins completely alone, amd I cannot deny it now. It was not fear of spirits or ghosts, of course; it was the apprehension of not knowing what reptiles or wild animals I might meet in there, plus the knowledge that if anything went wrong I would never get back to civilisation alive.

Reluctantly I decided to take the cowardly way out and accompany Wanaku to a high point, and so view the ruins from a safe distance. This turned out to be a reasonable compromise, as it happened, because it was only necessary to go two hundred metres up the hillside. I could not make out the panorama of the whole city because of the clinging vegetation, but I could certainly see the outline of some of the more significant buildings.

In spite of his denial, Wanaku had obviously been into the ruins at some time in years gone by, because he was able to describe them in some detail. It's true that I only have his word for it but, if his observations were correct, Karrie was a fortified city, not merely a fort as was Iscanwaya. To start with, there was a temple, and, as in most Inca cities, this was the largest building, around which the rest of the city had been built. I estimate that it was about twenty metres long and about ten metres wide. At one end of the temple there was an impressive stone archway, which presumably was the entrance, and in front of this end of the building were two parallel lines of much smaller ruins which, if they followed the pattern of Incallacta, would have been the dwellings of the priests and the chosen virgins. The fact that there was a waterfall crashing down the rock-face alongside these dwellings adds weight to this supposition.

On the other side of the temple there was a large area, about thirty metres by ten metres, with no visible ruins; so this could have been the parade-ground. Beyond this area there appeared to be a considerable number of small stone dwellings which, surprisingly, were built close together in no apparent order. They were not built around small squares as at Iscanwaya, and not even in straight lines, but the priests' and the virgins' houses did face the rising sun. Otherwise there appeared to be no symmetry or astrological significance in the manner of construction.

According to Wanaku—and I have only his word for it—there was a boundary wall encircling the city, and there were turrets facing the river, which would suggest limited fortification. It was obvious that this was not merely a fort; it was a city built for a community to inhabit.

We lit a fire and cooked a simple meal on that ridge overlooking Karrie, and I deliberately spent the time trying to make friends with Wanaku, to persuade him to co-operate and help as much as my two Indian guides at Beni had done. I enquired about his own life and his family. I explained that my interest in studying the pre-history of Bolivia would enable me to show the advances made by his ancestors in Munecas, and, of course, I kept him supplied with toffees. Gradually he entered into the spirit of my exploration and, looking out across the valley of the Llika, he told me that the people on the other side of the river were not the same people as his ancestors. Interestingly, he pointed out that his people in Aucapata and the nearby hills spoke Quechua (the language of the Incas) while on the other side of the river they spoke Aymara, the language of the Tiwanakotas. He also volunteered his belief that, at one time, before the invasion from Tiwanaku, all the valleys in the area belonged to his people and indeed, many of his ancestors were buried in the stone graves, which he pointed out on the hillside just above the river bank on the far side.

I could see at least twenty of these large stone chambers, and Wanaku told me there were many, many more up and down the river. Since there was gold in the nearby mines and in the river, it is likely that these communal graves were filled with gold artefacts at one time, and this sort of treasure trove was what had attracted the Spanish *conquistadores* and subsequent *huaceros* (grave robbers) to the area.

On the grassy slopes of the hills across the valley I could see large terraces with irrigation ditches, just like the Inca camps of cultivation in the Cochabamba valley and around Lake Titicaca, but Wanaku told me there were no cities in those hills, only isolated houses of small kinship groups. The large ruins we were to visit were all on this northern bank of the river, and as much as thirty kilometres down river.

I had half expected the river bed to be smooth, hard sand like those around Cochabamba but, although there were some nice even stretches, there were huge lengths of river bed that were pure rock and looked almost impossible to walk along. When I questioned Wanaku, he told me that there was a footpath from Karrie, which was about one hundred metres above the river, right down to Iscanwaya and beyond. This was the ancient llama path, which was still used by the mule trains bringing coca, peppers and fruit from the lowlands up to La Paz and other towns in the mountains.

"If you pay for mules I will get them in Aucapata," he volunteered, and at once I accepted. He strode off up the hills and was back within two hours, leading a couple of rather thin, seedy-looking mules. One carried a wooden frame for cargo, and the other, which was obviously for me to ride, had a padded sack with stirrups strapped on its back. As Wanaku tied my haversack and camera cases on the cargo mule, he suggested that we could get as far as Iscanwaya before nightfall, and camp at the site used by the archaeologists. We made steady progress along the llama path. A couple of mosquito bites on my neck reminded me to reinforce my protection with another covering of the insect repellant that worked so efficiently.

We halted a couple of times to drink water from the clear, cool streams that tumbled down the slopes every two or three kilometres, and I stopped once to film the beautiful empty countryside across the river. I saw only one lonely homestead in the centre of a small green area of cultivated land; I marvelled at the hermit-like existence of the family group living there, surrounded by the wild green hills of Munecas.

As we rounded a curve in the hillside I saw the fragmented ruins of two small stone buildings, whose tumbledown walls stood no more than one metre high, with piles of fallen stones lying around. I guessed that, since this was a strategic point with a view of the river in both directions, the buildings had been look-out points. Wanaku told me merely that they were houses of 'the people yet before'.

Looking at this particular journey objectively, it was a relatively hazardous undertaking. Apart from the village of Aucapata we were miles from anywhere, in a part of South America known to very few men, and yet I do not remember experiencing either the thrill or the fear that I might have anticipated. I remember only a unique sense of tranquil contentment in that sequestered haven of sleepy valleys, resting so peacefully beneath the serene sunshine and the impassive blue sky. Somehow it was not the environment to generate danger, and indeed we did not see a single reptile or wild animal all day.

That evening at Iscanwaya I gave Wanaku the packet of cigarettes he required to buy some maize for the mules from an isolated family living two kilometres away on the hillside. While he was away, I brewed up a large dish of soup from the packets of powder I'd brought with me. I put some of the meat to stew in the soup, and this, together with chunks of maize bread, made a satisfying evening meal; then we both crawled into my tent to escape the vicious mosquitoes.

Next morning, after more delicious soup and bread, we set off down the gentle slope that led to the fortress they called Pucanwaya (Little Wind) three kilometres down-river from Iscanwaya, and built almost at river level on a small courtyard of stone that rose direct from the bed of the river.

Pucanwaya was not so overgrown as most of the other ruins, chiefly because the outcrop of rock on which it had been built had no depth of soil in which trees or bushes could take root. There was no more than a thin layer of dust in which grasses and some cactus grew; so, even though Wanaku waited with the mules at the entrance to the boundary wall, I was free to walk around without difficulty.

In my opinion, Pucanwaya, which has never been visited or written about by modern scientists, was built as a small fort or an elaborate look-out point. Its boundary wall, overlooking the sheer drop of twenty metres to the river, was constructed of large flat stones cemented together with thin layers of mud. The stones had been carefully selected to fit one on top of the other, so it seemed, but they were not carved or shaped with the superb craftsmanship of the stones in the walls of Incallacta, although they were efficient enough to withstand the wind and rain of several hundred years. As in many other fortress walls I had seen, there were turrets and peep-holes and, in several places, stone steps had been let into the wall on the inside so that defenders could have climbed easily and quickly to the top to hurl missiles or fire arrows on an enemy approaching from below. Inside the boundary were tumbledown stone walls that might have enclosed eight or ten dwellings, but there was no cultivated land, no terracing, no irrigation channels, and this leads me to suggest that this was almost certainly a pure port manned and supplied by the people of Iscanwaya.

Looking down-river from Pucanwaya, I could see another small plateau of pure rock on which there were more ruins, and there seemed to be another most interesting site on a steep outcrop that jutted out of the hillside like a hugh pimple several hundred metres above the river.

"We can reach Pukarilla and camp there tonight," Wanaku said, pointing to the ruin I had seen down-river where the shallow waters flowed gently round another sharp curve in the hills. "You can look at Pukarilla, and then we will return to Iscanwaya and take the higher pathway to the city of Mamakoro."

"Are there many more ruins?" I asked Wanaku.

"There are a few more down the river," he replied, "as far as the one they call Payapaya."

I tried to find out what these Quechua names—Mamakoro and Payapaya—meant, but unfortunately Wanaku's Spanish was not very fluent. By a mixture of Quechua, Spanish and mime I gathered that Mamakoro means 'Bad Mother' and Payapaya means 'Night Dance' or 'Night Festival'. The more I shared my food with Wanaku and showed concern for his welfare and genuine interest in the history of his country and his ancestors, the more eager he became to guide me and to help make my trip a success. He set quite a pace along the relatively easy level path to Pukarilla and, when we arrived at the plateau of rock on which the fortress had been built, he began to show much more interest and enthusiasm than ever before as we put up the tent and prepared our camp-fire.

By the time darkness fell we had fed and watered the mules and were ready to tuck in to our own supper of soup, stew and maize bread. Since things were going so well, I broke into my emergency rations and shared a packet of biscuits with my young Indian friend, to his great delight.

There had not been the slightest hint of danger during our entire trip but, because of my niggling doubts as we travelled further and further from civilisation, I broached the subject with Wanaku. I asked him point blank if there might be unfriendly or even hostile natives anywhere in the area.

He laughed heartily for the first time since I'd known him, as he assured me that there were no Indian 'soldiers' left to make war or attack us. Then he admitted reluctantly that there were still a few 'bad people' around who might rob a lone traveller, but he left me in no doubt that it was his intention to fight them off. And the frenzied abandon with which he wielded his machete against make-believe opponents was enough to frighten anyone.

Apparently there were very few animals in the hills. As far as I could gather from the Quechua names he gave, he had seen only one puma, a few foxes and a herd of wild deer in his whole life. His lack of concern gave me confidence as we retreated inside the tent once again to escape the mosquitoes. I could not resist the temptation to take one deep draught of the warm still air, and one last look at the gloriously lonely grandeur of the majestic hills bathed in bright moonlight. It was an idyllic setting, the ultimate escape from the world into a magical environment of calm serenity.

Next morning, as soon as we had fed and watered ourselves and the mules, we walked a hundred metres to the ruins of Pukarilla. From a distance they appeared to have been built on terraces cut into the sides of a small, steep hill like an enormous natural pyramid. On closer inspection, however, the entire pyramid structure seemed to have been man-made, by building enormous steps out of very large stones. The bottom step was four metres wide, and there were the remains of the stone walls of many small houses covering most of its area. Surprisingly, Wanaku did not seem to be afraid of this ruined city, and he strolled around with me quite unconcerned.

There was a narrow stone staircase leading up to four more platforms reaching to the very top of the pyramid. Near the summit the steps were less wide, and there were fewer ruined houses to be seen on each one. At the very top were three stone pillars standing close together and in the middle of the circle was a large black stone like the altar stone at Incallacta. The surface of the stone had more of a sheen, more of a marbled appearance than any of the stones used in the construction of any of the houses in the area. It was quite distinctive and, since it had been placed on a bed of earth, I dug around it with my machete in case there were any artefacts.

At once I found several fragments of pottery, and two remarkable gold objects. One was just like the Inca surgeons' knives I had seen during previous excavations. It had a flat blade in the shape of a crescent moon, with a handle attached to the centre point of the curve, and a large gold button on the end of the handle. The other gold object looked like a small, thin breastplate about the size of the cover of a paperback book. A pattern of straight lines had been chiselled on one side of the plate, rather like a game of noughts and crosses. There were four squares across and four squares down, and in each square a hieroglyphic had been carved into the gold surface. The surgeon's knife seemed to be a more noteworthy find, and I suggested to Wanaku that this stone on the summit of the pyramid must have been used to make sacrifices in ancient times: hence the knife. He looked a little nonplussed as he handled it.

"This is a knife of the days of yet before," he agreed, "but I do not understand the other things you speak of."

I started to try to explain a sacrificial ceremony to him, but my lack of knowledge of Quechua and his inadequate Spanish proved an insurmountable barrier.

"This other piece must have been something to do with a festival," I said, using the Quechua word for 'festival' as the nearest I could think of to 'ceremony'.

I handed the breastplate to Wanaku. He looked at it for only a brief moment before he told me that he knew exactly what it was. He had seen two others just like it, which had been found in Maukallacta and in Iscanwaya.

"This is the language of my ancestors," he explained casually. "They understood what these marks say, and this is how they sent their messages to other cities. We have forgotten, and we do not understand now."

This simple statement delivered with such off-hand sincerity was stunning in its implications. Could this possibly be a written language, or the key to it? The *conquistadores* always said that neither the Incas nor any other indigenous people of South America had a written language, but the more I studied the hieroglyphics the more I was convinced that they might contain symbolic meaning. They were far too precisely engraved and shaped to be doodles, and they were not, by the wildest stretch of imagination picture drawings.

I brought the plate away with me, and since that day I have spent countless hours studying it, to no avail. I announced my find one day on a B.B.C. programme and, as a result of my description and my plea for help, many people asked for copies of the hieroglyphics. One of them, Noel Billings of Portreath in Cornwall, has come up with a possible solution. He noted that there were four squares across and four down, an obvious geometric pattern, He puzzled over the problem for months, and then, so he told me, the solution came to him in a dream. I am no mathematician, and I confess that I cannot appreciate Noel Billing's theories, but this is his solution.

It is a mathematical language. He numbers each square from one to four, as shown in the diagram:

1	2	3	4
2	4	1	3
3	1	4	2
4	3	2	1

In this way the sum of the four numbers across or down or diagonally always adds up to ten. He then superimposed the hieroglyphics on the numbered copy, and came up with some surprising results. For example, the lines in the top left-hand square cut through numbers which add up to ten. Applying the same pattern, the square directly beneath the first one represents the number twenty; the square next to the first one represents forty; and the square beneath that one represents thirty.

It seemed to Noel Billings too much of a coincidence that the four squares at the top left of the shield should represent forty (or four times ten) as well as one quarter, one half and three-quarters of that number. He then spent the next two years attempting to use his findings to unravel the messages contained in hundreds of steles found all over South America. He is convinced that the people who drew the hieroglyphics on the gold plate were brilliant mathematicians, surveyors and builders. He claims that, even with his modest education, he can now understand the

The ruins of Incallacta, the largest Inca temple ever discovered, and gateway to the lost world of the Incas.

Victims sacrificed to Inti, the Sun God, were gripped in this cylindrical stone altar.

The fortress city of Iscanwaya, built by a pre-Inca culture to protect the Higher Andes against invasion.

Callawaya women in their bright hand-woven garments. The downward position of the spoons on the silver necklace indicates their material status.

The author filming a group of Mosetene Indians as they begin a ceremonial dance.

Above: The Callawaya council of leaders, the Amautas, whose special hats show their status as medicine men, confer about calling the Condor. *Left:* Wakchu, the 'sacrificial victim', bound hand and foot, awaits her fate. *Below:* The great Condor surveys his prize.

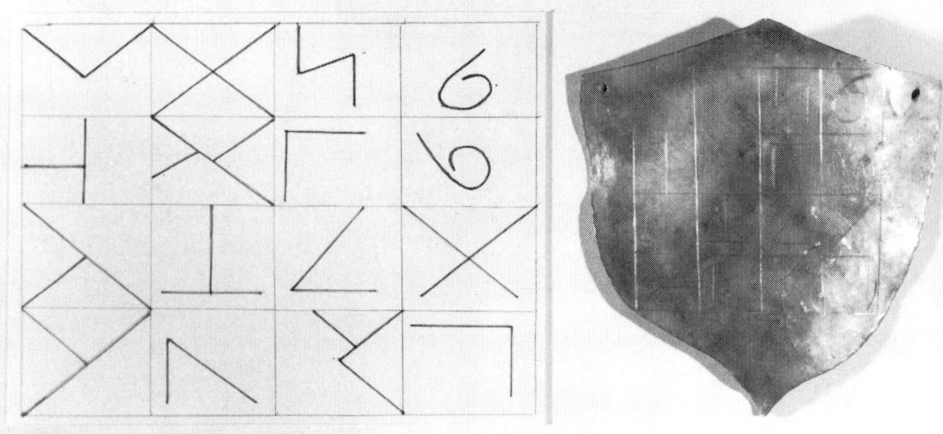

The gold 'language plate' found by the author in the Palace of the Incas. The hieroglyphics *(see left)* provide a possible key to a mathematical Inca language.

The stalwart fortress wall protecting the Inca city near the Moxos, discovered by the author on his last journey.

mathematics involved in building the Giza pyramid, and these the prehistoric people of South America must have understood, he claims.

Modestly the Cornishman reckons that he has only started to scratch the surface, but he hopes that, by the time he has deciphered the messages contained in many more steles—all of which use the same hieroglyphics—he may have a lot of invaluable information.

According to Billings, part of one stele precisely locates a line of latitude. If he can solve the mystery of the longtitude equally precisely, he will have pinpointed an exact location in the wilds of Bolivia, and such a site might well be worth scientific investigation. He will sit down with a skilled mathematician, explain his system in detail, and challenge the scientist to disprove the theory. Two highly-qualified mathematics experts have so far tried and failed. The only problem at the moment, the only stumbling block to a satisfactory conclusion, is getting enough pictures or charts of the steles which have been drawn on rocks and on metal sheets all over South America. It may be years before Billings can decide whether or not this is a very advanced mathematical language used by the Incas.

Surely it is inconceivable that one of the largest, most organised and powerful nations in the world could have flourished in such a huge area without any form of written communication? The Aymaras, who ruled the vast area of the Andes before the Incas, certainly had writing which they called Kelkanya, and it would be difficult to imagine that all this was completely lost during the Inca conquest of the Aymara nation.

At the time I found the plate, I did not realise just how important a discovery this might turn out to be, but even the hint of written communication in pre-Spanish days was exciting. Stimulated, I made detailed notes about the ruins of Pukarilla, and about its possible role in pre-Inca times.

First of all there was no boundary wall with turrets and defensive positions. It was a man-made pyramid of dwellings only, with no temple, no meeting-place, no communal buildings, and no area of cultivation within the immediate area of the city. It did not, therefore, follow the traditional pattern of either a fortress or a purely residential city. Possibly it was a ceremonial centre inhabited by priests who were supplied by other towns in the area.

Secondly, the manner of construction showed more expertise and engineering skill than did the other ruins I had seen in the area. The stones were not carved and fitted like the jigsaw constructions of major Inca cities, but at least the largest foundation stones appeared to have been squared off before they were laid carefully one on top of the other, so that very little mud had been used to cement them together. Pukarilla might be described, therefore, as a Mollo construction, demonstrating a considerable technological advance, or perhaps, a Mollo construction coming under the influence of Inca occupation. When Pukarilla eventually comes under the microscope of qualified archaeologists, I am sure they will find interesting comparisons with the Mayan and Aztec pyramid cities of ancient Mexico.

The rocky terrain leading from the river uphill to Mamakoro presented a formidable barrier to the two of us on foot, and quite impossible for a mule with a passenger or cargo; so, at Wanaku's suggestion, we returned to Iscanwaya to take the more level path to Mamakoro next day. This plan also allowed Wanaku to go back to that lonely homestead above Iscanwaya to barter for a fresh supply of maize for the mules, and perhaps more fresh bread and meat for ourselves. I enjoyed a feeling of euphoria quite unexpected on a so-called journey of adventure to unexplored regions in the wilds of South America. To claim that this was anything but a thoroughly pleasant, comfortable and exhilarating experience would be quite untrue.

Towards the end of the afternoon's ride deeper into this idyllic haven of lonely countryside, we reached the crest of a rolling hill and saw the spectacular ruin of Mamakoro towering above us. The valley ahead swept gently into the slopes of a rugged isolated hill, which rose sheer, like a whipped ice cream from its cornet.

The severity of the craggy contours was in sharp contrast to the serenity of the gently undulating slopes all around. If the rolling hills of Munecas had been pushed up from below at the time of a great cataclysm, the hill of Mamakoro must have been punched out of the surface by an unsympathetic hand. Even the unemotional Wanaku was overpowered with admiration as we stood there, surveying the minor miracle of the ruins of Mamakoro, built on the precipitous slopes of this isolated column of a hill. From a distance the buildings looked magnificent, even as they clung desperately to the sheer slopes.

The superhuman effort of terracing such steep land and then

carrying what looked like large squared rocks of granite up to near the top to construct the formidable-looking walls was almost beyond belief. The ingenuity, the skill and the technology of such men place them on a level with the engineers of today, and made a complete mockery of any suggestion that they were primitive or backward.

As soon as I could take my eyes away from this spectacular city, my attention was attracted to another demonstration of engineering skill that left me breathless with respect once again. From a point just a little below the crest of the hill on which we stood, a gigantic man-made stone causeway led out across the valley to the hill of Mamakoro. It was about fifty metres long, and in the centre it was at least ten metres high. Many hundreds of thousands of stones had been carefully cut, shaped and fitted together to build this level footpath from the hillside, across the shallow chasm into the heart of the city. It was an awe-inspiring feat of construction and one that must have taken hundreds of labourers several years to construct. I was puzzled at first, because to walk down into the depression and up the other side to the city buildings would not have been so difficult for fit men. Wanaku may have realised my uncertainty, because he volunteered a piece of information which made it all quite clear.

"It is for carrying water," he told me. "There is no water on the hill of Mamakoro, but this stone wall carries water from the stream on this hillside. Come, and I will show you."

We walked to the point where the aqueduct joined the hill we were on. A shallow stream, fed by a group of three springs, came tumbling diagonally across the hill; the prehistoric people could have diverted some of the water quite easily so that it flowed into the channel, which was constructed with absolute precision on the top of the stone aqueduct. The stones used to form the channel were shaped and fitted as closely as pieces of a jigsaw and, although the ravages of time had taken their toll, it was clear that, with regular maintenance, the channel would have provided running water for the city of Mamakoro.

Having seen this outstanding piece of engineering skill, and judging by what I could see of the superbly-constructed fortress walls and dwellings of Mamakoro, I came to the conclusion that it had all been built to a much higher standard than the other cities of Munecas, which were impressive enough. It seemed to me that it might have been built by the Incas after they had conquered these valleys. Certainly it had been constructed in the supreme position to control the cities and villages in all the surrounding area. Clearly a garrison of soldiers could have been based there to control by force of arms, but Mamakoro itself was absolutely unassailable, and could have been defended by a handful of men.

We camped that night alongside the tumbling stream which would have fed the channel on top of the aqueduct. Next day Wanaku was going to get more maize for the mules and more food for us before we crossed into the city by the causeway.

Shortly before dawn the next morning I was awake and, since I slept in my clothes, I only needed to pull on my walking-boots to go out and relieve myself. It was almost totally dark as I came out of the tent. I did not bother to look for my torch, because I would be gone for only a minute or so and, most stupidly of all, I did not pay any attention to where I was walking. It did not seem to matter in my somnolent state, but soon I learned my mistake. I had just started to urinate on top of a scattering of brushwood when one of 'branches' flew at my leg and struck me a sharp, stinging blow that made me cry out in horrified amazement. I looked down and saw that the snake that had bitten me in the leg was still hanging on to my trousers. The shock was so great and the reaction so instinctive and swift that I cannot be absolutely certain of what followed. In my terror I shook my leg violently to get rid of the snake, and my impression is that its fangs came out of my trouser leg, but that it struck again even as it was falling and caught its fangs in my trousers again just above the ankle. Once more I shook my leg furiously, and the snake fell to the ground, and I trod it into the earth in a squashed heap.

I had never been bitten by a snake before, but I had seen others bitten many times during my days as a cattle-rancher in Colombia; so I knew what I had to do. I got back into the tent and lay down. Then, while Wanaku held the torch, I tied a tourniquet just above the knee. The snake had bitten me in the fleshy part of my left calf and so, with my very sharp knife, I cut two crosses into my flesh where the snake's fangs had left their two holes. Finally I squeezed all around the fang marks to get out some of the poison he might have injected.

Wanaku asked me if I had any anti-snake-bite serum. At least I think that's what he meant. He called it 'snake remedy'. I had no serum, but I did have a tube of strong antibiotics and took one of these. Wanaku was not satisfied and, with appropriate mime, he made it quite clear that he wanted me to have an injection. I had a hypodermic syringe, but that was all. The young Indian began to get very agitated, but I insisted on remaining motionless. I knew that if the snake had actually inserted any poison—and this was highly unlikely—then it was essential not to get agitated and pump the blood round the body.

Wanaku, however, was jumping around like a flea, and in desperation he suddenly announced that there would be 'snake remedy' in Aucapata, and he would go and get some quickly. I agreed that this could do no harm, and as soon as he had gone, I lay back to await developments.

I took another strong dose of antibiotics just to be on the safe side, but I was genuinely unconcerned at first. In my considerable experience in the jungle of Colombia and Venezuela, I have seen many peons bitten by snakes when they were cutting down scrub and jungle, but only rarely was one poisoned. In nine cases out of ten the snake struck just to warn the offending person to get out of the way. And if this bushmaster had injected a small amount of poison, I reckoned that the incisions, the squeezing, the tourniquet and the antibiotics would deal effectively with it.

My foot felt rather numb, so I slackened the tourniquet for a while, and tightened it again as my ankle joint began to swell and to hurt. So some poison had gone in, I supposed, but it was confined to my ankle and my left foot.

Then the pain began to reach my left knee, which also puffed up.

The first time I really began to feel disquiet was when my groin also started aching at the junction of my leg and torso. This meant that some of the poison had got past the tourniquet, and that was worrying.

Again I released the tourniquet, but not for very long, as the pain began to grip my stomach. I took yet another dose of antibiotics, and prepared to suffer some discomfort and pain for a while until the effect wore off, or until the poison was neutralised by the antibiotics.

The pain in my leg joints was not very severe, but my stomach felt as if it were full of red-coals. It was excruciating; so I took a strong dose of the pain-killing tablets I carried in my medicine chest. I am not sure if they eased the pain, but I suppose they must have done, because I remember drawing comfort from the fact that no more joints were aching. So the poison was not spreading, I thought.

I felt physically very sick, and psychologically I was in a bad way, conscious of the fact that I was very much alone and helpless.

I lost all track of time: so I do not know how much later the real crisis came. I thought I was going blind. Certainly my eyeballs began to burn, and I had the horrifying sensation that they were about to burst from their sockets. The world dissolved into a misty cloud, as my eyes refused to focus on my surroundings.

All the while I had been telling myself not to panic, and not to send the blood coursing through my veins, but now I was trembling with fear, especially when I realised that I could no longer see my medicine chest, even if I wanted to risk any more antibiotics or pain killers.

During the next few hours I lived a nightmare, and now in retrospect it would be easy to overdramatise and to overstress the sheer horror I think I remember. It would be safer, perhaps, to draw a veil over the panic and despair I endured until Wanaku and another Indian returned with some 'snake remedy', which they injected into my buttocks.

During the diabolical trip back to civilisation, I suffered excruciating pain in my stomach to begin with, but mercifully my sight returned and the infected joints slowly improved. Next day I took more antibiotics, and almost all the symptoms eased off completely by the end of another day. All that I was left with was a sore and swollen left foot and ankle.

I could not put a shoe on this foot, but this did not stop me catching the first plane back to England, where my own doctor rushed me to hospital. Two weeks' intensive treatment certainly improved my condition, but left me with a swollen foot which persisted for some months.

Dr. Alistair Reid of the Liverpool School of Tropical Medicine is one of Britain's few experts on the subject of snakes bites, and he gave me his opinion that I must have received a fairly heavy dose of poison, and that some effects could well last for a long time. He also said that, in his experience, this happened only rarely and, like me, he knew of many cases when little or no poison had been injected. In his last letter to me, Dr. Reid intimated that, in his opinion, the danger from snake bites in the tropics is much exaggerated, but he also suggested that my 'do-it-yourself' treatment of cutting through fang marks and applying a tourniquet was not to be recommended. I would reinforce his argument by saying that, in my considerable experience in the so-called snake-infested tropical jungles, you rarely come across a poisonous reptile, and even then you have to behave stupidly to get bitten. That is why I am now persuaded to tell my own story, after pleading with rescuers to say nothing at the time. I knew that the very helpful Bolivian authorities had high hopes of eventually promoting the Aucapata area as a significant tourist attraction, worthy of the discovery of some of the biggest and best ruins in South America. For me to splash the story of my own snake bite, which was entirely due to my carelessness and incompetence, could do the tourist proposition an immense amount of harm, of course. So, once I knew I was on the road to recovery, I kept quiet about it. My Bolivian friends knew that I was very ill, of course, because I could not disguise that, but they thought it was an attack of dysentery that pulled me down.

My enforced return to England was a bitter blow, just when I was beginning to fit the jigsaw together with the invaluable assistance of the National Institute of Archaeology in Bolivia. I had established an elaborate and large-scale circle of fortification surrounding the area north of Cochabamba, a space unknown, unexplored and uninhabited by modern civilisation. Might this area be Paititi and contain the lost empire of the Incas?

Perhaps my theories were not attracting much attention among the academics in England, but things were certainly moving in Bolivia. The government and the National Institute of Archaeology were in a frenzy of excitement about the importance of Iscanwaya to students of South American history, as well as the possibility of making it a tourist attraction to match the famous Peruvian ruins of Macchu Pichu. In fact, just before I left they started to bulldoze a level track from Lake Titicaca, about twenty miles to the west. The road is now completed and you can drive in a jeep right up to the ruin of Iscanwaya, and the Bolivians hope to build a tourist hotel in Aucapata for the thousands of visitors who are expected in the years to come. Soon there will be guided tours, probably with a restaurant, souvenir shop and all the sophistication of a modern package tour. By the time the Bolivians have completed their work they will have uncovered a magnificent city to delight the tourists, but my greatest satisfaction will be that I saw Iscanwaya before all that happened.

CHAPTER SEVEN

Towards Chapare

I HAD LEFT THE tourniquet on too long, so that my ankle and the last two toes of my left foot were still painful and swollen six months later. The Butanan Institute of Brazil thought they might be able to help, but that would mean paying for a long stay in South America which I could ill afford.

Whilst I was still debating what to do, I received a letter from Bolivia telling me about the discovery of many unknown ruins on the banks of the river Cotacajes, north and north-east of Cochabamba, in and around Paititi. The National Institute of Archaeology did not have the personnel or funds to mount a full-scale expedition. Would I like to carry out a preliminary investigation for them?

This was an offer I could not refuse. It might advance my own personal attempts to find the lost empire of the Incas, and it showed a major break-through in acceptance by the scientists of Bolivia. At once I began to work on my plans to return to South America at the start of the dry season in May.

By this time finance was a growing problem. I had paid for Dr. Davies and myself on the first trip, as well as my own second trip, together with a great deal of film, processing and printing costs, and all my savings were now gone; in fact, I was in debt to my bank. The only way I could raise the minimum of £2,000 to cover the air fare, travel in Bolivia, and more colour film was to take out a second mortgage on my house. It was gamble I took and, by the time the money was forthcoming, the organisation of my next trip had become a matter of some urgency.

The letter detailing plans for my return, however, did not turn up in Bolivia before I did; so I arrived unannounced—in August

1976—but still received the friendliest possible welcome from Dr. Carlos Ponce Sangines. Almost at once he summoned the young Bolivian who had found the new ruins. His name was Jorge Ger. At that first meeting I judged him to be a likeable, strong and capable young man, probably a *mestizo* of European extraction. Indeed, he volunteered the information that his father was a Spaniard, who had explored Bolivia before he finally settled on a piece of land on the banks of the river Cotacajes, which had been an Indian area of cultivation since ancient times. Jorge did not volunteer any information about his mother, but merely added that his father had brought up two sons on this isolated farmstead in an area where there were many prehistoric ruins as well as little-known tribes of Indians who rarely made contact with modern man.

Dr. Carlos spread out his large-scale map, and showed me the exact location. He explained that it would mean flying from La Paz to Cochabamba, hiring a jeep for the twelve-hour drive along the rough track to the village of Independencia, and then going by mule or on foot to Pocanche and so into the interior.

Young Jorge, who was obviously very enthusiastic about the projected trip, assured me that he could hire mules for much of the journey from Independencia, and that he would certainly get local Indians to carry my equipment when we had to travel on foot. His bubbling enthusiasm plus his confidence and personal knowledge of the area made my decision easy to reach. We would depart next day on the regular flight from La Paz to Cochabamba. My dislike of living at altitude in La Paz, my happy memories of delightful Cochabamba, and the prospect of more exciting discoveries all added to the glow of anticipation.

Once settled in the hotel in Cochabamba, we set about trying to hire a good jeep. The proprietor of the first garage we called at kept us hanging around for fifteen minutes. He must have put in a quick phone call during this time for, while we were still negotiating with him, an official of the military government arrived, wanting to know all about our projected trip. My B.B.C. identity card helped to allay suspicion. Finally a telephone call to Dr. Carlos proved that we were engaged upon a genuine scientific project. Nevertheless, the army decided not to let us go alone but to send a driver with us to check our every move. The disadvantage would be that we would not be free to do exactly what we liked, but against that was the decided advantage of being allocated an official jeep with an armed escort.

For three days we jolted and bumped our way over tough mule-tracks in our army jeep. At last we arrived at the top of a bleak, windswept ridge from which a barren hillside dropped vertically for two thousand feet down into a narrow valley through which a river cascaded. Jorge pointed proudly down to a stretch of sheltered flat land on the far bank.

"There is my farm," he declared with excitement.

Peering into the distance I could just make out a timber house, eight small mud huts and some tiny patches of green. Jorge explained that one of these patches was his *huerta,* where we could spend a comfortable night. It didn't look exactly inviting to me—more like dense sub-tropical jungle within the insect line. My thoughts turned to mosquitoes, snakes, jaguars and pumas. But that was not all that was worrying me. If we were going to descend into sub-tropical jungle, I should need plenty to drink, and I knew it could be fatal to drink direct from pools of water or sluggish tropical streams; so I would have to buy a bottle of Coke from the Indians living in this small hamlet called Pocanche on the top of the hill.

I should also need help to carry all my camping and filming equipment on what looked like being a particularly arduous and difficult descent down the steep rocky hillside.

The army driver refused to come with us. Apparently he had not been told that our expedition involved tortuous journeys on foot through the jungle, and he was not ashamed to admit that he had no intention of risking his life. Jorge derided the idea that there was any danger, but the driver shook his head firmly, and announced his intention of driving back to Independencia to wait for us.

Jorge demonstrated that he was as resourceful as he was fit and strong. Within an hour he had hired an Indian youth to help carry all my camping and filming equipment, and bought me a bottle of Coca Cola, then we set out.

I poured the Coke into my thermos flask to keep it cool and, since the flask was suspended from a thin metal handle, I was able to carry this one small item as easily as a brief-case. Jorge and the Indian porter were weighed down with pieces of my equipment, and so they did not set a brisk pace, and since it was all downhill I was able to keep up with them after occasional rest periods following a particularly steep patch. As we reached the halfway mark, the midday sun began to beat down out of a cloudless sky and the temperature rose significantly. I took a couple of swigs from my thermos flask and began to sweat profusely. I realised that I'd have to ration my drinks for the second half of the journey into the steamy jungle. In a clearing I put my thermos down on the rocks for a moment while I took off my windcheater and sprayed myself with insect repellant. When I picked up the flask I noticed that the rock was hot to the touch. I thought no more about it until I was swinging my way down the slope, and suddenly the thermos flask exploded in my hand. The cork must have shot out with the velocity of a bullet, because it burst through the plastic cup which was screwed on the top of it, and hit me an agonising blow on the fingers which were holding the metal handle. Such was the shock that I threw the flask sideways, and tucked my hand under my armpit in agony. The explosion sounded like gunshot. It brought Jorge scurrying back to my assistance, but when we looked at my hand there were no cuts, no broken bones, only severe bruising.

As the initial pain subsided a little I could share my companions' amusement at the incident. The two Indians from Pocanche, who'd never seen or heard of a thermos flask, were at first apprehensive and then slightly amused when Jorge explained all about the 'magic' container. They collapsed into hysterics when I told them that it was also a secret weapon as a protection against wild Indians, but I had not meant to shoot myself.

This was all very amusing until I realised that my thermos was lying shattered at the foot of a tree. Almost at one I felt thirsty, and there was still a long way to go in the ever-increasing heat of lower slopes. Soon my mouth became dry as I stumbled down the hillside. On the steeper slopes I had to walk sideways like a crab to retain my balance, and all the time I was becoming more and more desperate for a drink. An hour later I thought we must have covered a great deal of ground, but we were still tantalisingly distant from the clear, cool water of the stream as it crashed between the rocks on the floor of the valley.

At the end of another hour I knew what it was like, for the first time in my life, to suffer from real thirst. The more I hurried, the more the sweat poured off me, and my mouth ran so dry that it was agony to breathe. Perhaps it was just as well that there were no swampy pools of water at the side of the trail, because my desperation would have driven me to drink any brackish liquid, however filthy.

It is difficult to believe in retrospect, but the moment came when I could stumble no further. Admitting ignominious defeat, I collapsed in a heap on the ground. I unpacked a small cooking-pot and begged one of the Indians to go down to the river and bring me back some water. I must have looked a pretty sorry sight, because, without a word, he put his load of equipment beside me, and strode off. The thirty minutes he was gone seemed like an age, as I suffered a swollen tongue and the ill effects of dehydration. When he did return eventually, I grabbed the pot of water and drank the lot. In spite of the possible consequences, I just couldn't wait for water-purifying tablets to dissolve slowly. As a compromise I took an antibiotic tablet with the last mouthful of that beautiful water, and hoped for the best.

With the sun sinking fast Jorge looked anxious, and reminded me that we still had to reach the river, cross it, and climb the steep footpath to his farm on the plateau. I got up slowly and plodded on down the hill, cursing myself for my own stupidity.

At long last we reached the river, walked along the bank for half an hour until we came to the pathway of stepping-stones and crossed over. By the time we had struggled halfway up the narrow ledge used as a footpath up to the plateau, darkness fell; so I took out my torch and stumbled up those last agonising yards to reach the level land. I thanked heaven that Jorge's mud hat was the first house we reached.

We were greeted by an Indian, his woman and their three young children. Jorge explained that they looked after his *huerta* while he was away, and that they would look after us until I was ready to move on. I paid off the two Indian porters, who just disappeared into the night as Jorge and I crept into one small room of the hut, where I collapsed on to one of the two beds made out of animal skins. At once I pleaded for a supply of water, so that there would be time for the purifying tablets to take effect. But Jorge, who still had plenty of energy left, had a better idea. He dashed out, and was back within minutes with a huge jar of pure orange juice which, he claimed, I could drink at once without any fear.

This turned out to be typical of the splendid hospitality I received from Jorge and his workers next day as I rested. The woman washed my clothes, the children brought me bowls of water from the nearby stream, and I soaked my aching feet. Plates of food kept arriving as Jorge busied himself organising the Indian family. There were dishes of stewed meat, corn on the cob, potatoes, and a never-ending supply of bananas and oranges and cups of steaming coffee. I sat on a tree trunk in the yard in front of the mud hut and luxuriated.

As I looked out across the wide green valley and the lowland forest to the stark hills which towered above on the other side of the river, the thought did cross my mind that sooner or later I would face the daunting prospect of having to climb back to the top on the return journey. Just for a moment I caught my breath in panic at the realisation that, if I were struck by something comparatively uncomplicated like appendicitis, or if I broke an ankle, there would be no chance of reaching medical help by the next day, much less in hours. Knowing that Jorge's farm was still only halfway to Paititi made me uncertain whether to continue, but then, as I wallowed in the warm sunshine and surveyed the glorious isolation and the spectacular grandeur of the surrounding hills, my confidence and my love of adventure and achievement returned. I was in no doubt that my heart was in the exploration, and to hell with the consequences.

Jorge went to see his mother at the other end of the farm, but at last he returned, and I persuaded him to sit down for a serious conference. Certainly he was a reasonably intelligent, capable and immensely strong young man, but he had a slightly happy-go-lucky temperament. I know I would have to draw up a very detailed plan for the next few days and hold him to it. He agreed that it would be a good idea to pay one of his farm workers to accompany us, to help carry the equipment. We would hire three mules for the first half of the journey, and then our Indian companion, a middle-aged man called Tjara, could bring back the mules when we reached the steep, jungle-covered hills deep into Paititi.

Next day Jorge loaded two mules with my camping equipment, cameras, film and a supply of food, and prepared the other mule for me to ride. We set out, heading eastwards along the northern bank of the river Cotacajes. On this northern side of the river, the great range of hills plunged down some two thousand feet from the sky and levelled out into a curving shelf of flat land, which then dropped away another hundred feet to the river. This ledge was anything between one hundred and four hundred metres wide, and the footpath which followed the edge near the river was made of fitted stone blocks like the Inca roads of long ago, if not so wide. It had not been maintained or frequently used, and was somewhat overgrown in places, although it did not take us long to brush aside the branches or the low bushes where they were sprawling across the path. Jorge was a bit of a menace with his gun, which he treated rather like a new toy. He pulled it out on several occasions to shoot a couple of snakes and a toad, and to fire at and miss a jungle cat. I had to caution him that we might need that ammunition later on, and eventually I dissuaded him from taking pot-shots at any thing that moved.

As well as occasional areas of relatively thick undergrowth, there were parts of this shelf of flat land where we could easily see the signs of a previous occupation, probably within the last thirty or forty years. Every mile or so we came across the stone ruins of groups of five or six small houses in much less overgrown areas. As Jorge pointed out, the settlers there had been farmers and, according to his father, they were small *ayllus* (kinship groups) of indigenous people who had fled further into the jungle when settlers came to populate Independencia on the top of the range of hills opposite. Jorge also said that, in his opinion, a few Americans had ventured this far, looking for gold, and, since the Indians on the banks of the Cotacajes did pan gold from the river to make ornaments and utensils, the American adventurers would have killed and tortured to get the gold. This is what his father had told him, and this was why the Indians had retreated deeper into the jungle.

He pointed out the small gardens adjoining each house, surrounded by low stone walls. Possibly the walls were built as divisions of territory to show ownership, but I noticed that the gardens were pure earth with no stones at all; so it is quite possible that the stone walls were not boundaries so much as convenient parking-places for all the stones that were lifted to clear a small area for cultivation.

These camps of cultivation, as Jorge called them, sloped gently down towards the river, and all of them had well-preserved stone channels running in parallel, which would have drained the surface water in the wet season. They would also have provided irrigation in the dry season, because they were all connected to a wider stone channel which ran back across the flat land to join up with a stream which led away from the waterfall on the hillside.

What appeared to be an efficient and well-organised system of food production would have yielded harvests all the year round. The temperature was hot enough to encourage growth right through the year, and there would be water from the rains in the wet season, and from irrigation and the mountain streams in the dry season. The inhabitants could have grown large quantities of maize, potatoes and coca, and there would have been meat from the deer, wild pigs and small rodents living in the forest and on the hillside around.

After passing through eleven of these tiny settlements, we reached a point were another rushing river joined the Cotacajes. Again it was little more than a wide mountain stream which sliced through a narrow valley on the right. The hills towered at least three hundred metres above, and the floor of the valley was so narrow that it could be described as a canyon, no more than twenty metres wide with rocks as steep as the side of a bath on either side.

The two mountain streams joined to form a much more substantial and wider river, which in the wet season would have been fifty or sixty metres wide, although now in the dry season it was no more than half that width.

At the point of the V-shape were the two torrents met, the hillside was absolutely sheer. Jorge directed my gaze to a point about two hundred metres above the level of the rivers, where I could clearly see the ruins of fortress walls made of stone.

"We don't know the Indian name for this fort," Jorge admitted, "but we call it the Creston. There is a wall overlooking both the rivers, and about forty houses behind the wall," he told me and, not for the first time, I marvelled at the superb positioning of a fortress guarding a valley pass.

At once I accepted Jorge's offer to visit and examine the ruin, and we started up the one narrow pathway leading from the river. This soon dissolved into a narrow stone ledge cut out of the hillside. It was no more than a foot wide, with a sheer drop to the rocky bed of the river. This one precipitous entrance to the fortress must have made it absolutely unassailable. Long before I reached the top, I was quite overcome by vertigo, and reluctantly I turned away from the sight of the sheer drop to walk sideways like a crab with my back to the precipice, as I retreated hurriedly down to the river once again. Jorge followed without a word of recrimination.

"The Creston is one of the biggest forts guarding Paititi," he said. "Some people say Paititi is to the east in the hills of Chapare but, from what I have told Dr. Carlos, he thinks it could be this area." He waved his arm in the direction of the hills to our left and right, as we walked down the river Cotacajes. "Perhaps it is both here and in Chapare," he ventured. "You can join them together to make one great area. Do you think you can travel another six days to see the ruins on the banks of the Kechuamayo, and visit the Indians in the hills there?"

I hesitated a moment. Six days for him might be eight or ten days for me, and that could mean twenty days before we returned to his farm.

"I haven't got enough food," I admitted with some regret. "Certainly I haven't got enough for all of us."

"You don't have to worry about Tjara and me," Jorge laughed. "We shall eat. There is plenty of food here in the jungle. It is only you we have to feed. Enough food for six days is all you will need," he said earnestly. "When we reach the Indians, I can get you plenty of oranges, bananas and maize bread. They live in the hotter land and have plenty of food."

"Let us see how the journey progresses," I conceded. "If you permit me to go much more slowly than you, I can go on and on for as many days as my food supply lasts out."

"Good—very good." Jorge became wildly enthusiastic again. "Tomorrow I will show you the ruins of a very large fortress where the river Kechuamayo joins our river. It is called Takopampa—'the valley' in Quechua—and then we walk down the river Kechuamayo, and I will show you cities no one has ever seen before . . . No one except me and my brother."

On the face of it I should have been excited at the prospect of a really worthwhile expedition but, as usual, I was full of doubt. On the one hand, Jorge had never been guilty of total deception and deliberate lies, but quite clearly he was going all out to impress me, and he was so very enthusiastic himself. For the time being, I took all his claims with a large pinch of salt and prepared myself for 'large cities' to be tiny hamlets, and 'many Indians' to materialise as a small nomadic kinship group. But even without any remarkable discoveries, it was turning out to be a marvellously challenging expedition into remote and uncharted areas of spectacular beauty and idyllic climate.

CHAPTER EIGHT

Chuamayu

JORGE WAS RIGHT WHEN he talked about the particularly 'angry mosquitoes' on the river bank. I sprayed myself frequently with insect repellant, but still suffered a lot of bites, especially when I went to the lavatory!

After Tjara had prepared a camp-fire, we heated water to make soup and coffee which, with a packet of biscuits and cheese, made a reasonable supper. The word Tjara means 'worker' in the Quechua language, and our Indian companion was certainly that. Having made the fire, he leapt up to wash our tin plates and mugs, before helping me to pitch my tent higher up the river bank. Then, as darkness approached, and the wind began to whip up clouds of dust and sand, Tjara flitted in and out of the jungle at the edge of the river, carrying armfuls of vegetation. Soon he'd built himself a little platform of tree branches, presumably as a protection against snakes, and on this he carefully laid out a bed of foliage which he quickly and deftly twined together to make a solid and reasonably comfortable bed. Jorge had already told Tjara, with a gesture of superiority, that he was always allowed to share my tent, and I didn't feel inclined to slap him down in front of his worker.

We spent most of the next morning travelling no more than five kilometres down-river. We had to cross the river on three occasions in this short distance because of recent huge falls of rock that completely blocked the path along the river bank at three points. The river was not a torrent, and it was never more than four feet deep, but what made a crossing on foot such a hazardous undertaking was the very uneven and ever-changing surface of the river bed. One moment you might be walking knee-deep on a firm rocky surface and then, in one step, you'd plunge waist deep with your feet sticking in the sucking mud. And whenever you lost balance (which I managed to do twice on the first crossing), the turbulent current was strong enough to carry you away until you hit the next shallow patch.

After these minor misadventures, my two companions offered to select a reasonable path for the next crossings on a trial and error basis. Jorge stripped off with a show of bravado, and I think he secretly enjoyed an occasional buffeting when he was swept away and given the opportunity to show his strength and ability as a swimmer. Tjara proceeded much more carefully, and I noticed that he always chose to walk with the mule where the surface of the water was most turbulent and, therefore, shallowest. He never came to any harm, and I don't think the water ever reached above his thighs. It was just as well, I thought, because the mule was carrying all my filming and camping equipment.

For most of the journey the river sliced through the range of jungle-covered hills, which rose steeply on either side, as if someone had lowered the shaft of a red-hot poker into a block of butter. Occasionally, however, the massively overpowering wall, which squeezed the narrow river into a thin pencil of racing water, was broken by an individual hill, standing magnificently alone in a challenging position overlooking the river. Ahead of us, just such a hill rose out of the valley floor, like a witch's hat with the sharp point blunted and levelled out smoothly on the top.

"On that hill is a great city," Jorge claimed dramatically. "Chuamayu it was called."

The great hill was no more than one kilometre ahead of us, but I could see nothing but trees and scrub on the hillside, and the vague outline of what might be a few stone buildings on the naked peak. I must have expressed my doubts and disappointment rather harshly, because Jorge turned on me and, with a trace of bitterness, assured me that he was not going to drag me out on such a journey to see any ordinary ruins. If I were not going to trust him, there was no point in struggling ahead on the long journey into Paititi.

Since we were so near Chuamayu it was obviously too late to challenge Jorge's claims. I might just as well complete this part of the trip and see the ruins for myself, but I confess that I was quite prepared to be thoroughly disillusioned. Indeed, my first sight of what was supposed to be another lost city tended to confirm my worst fears. At the foot of the steep hill there was a narrow pathway leading to an area of level land about the size of a football pitch, covered by vegetation which looked to me but fifty years old.

"There are the ruins of many stone houses on this piece of level land," Jorge announced triumphantly. "You can see them when you walk through trees."

"How many is many?" I asked.

"At least fifteen," Jorge replied.

My heart sank. This was just what I had feared: a city of fifteen houses might seem important to an unsophisticated country boy like Jorge, but if this were Paititi . . .! My pent-up anger and suspicion finally burst, and I turned on Jorge.

"Fifteen houses, and you call this a city?" I stormed angrily.

"No, no—don't be doubting me again," Jorge protested. "The city is here, " he said, waving his arm over the hillside above. "This is just the fort to protect it. I will show you. Down here there are the houses of the soldiers, and on the far side is a magnificent fortress wall. Above us on the hillside are the ruins of fifty or sixty large houses, and a temple and another fortress wall with a garrison on the top. On the other side of the hill there are twice as many houses. There must be more than a hundred altogether. Isn't that a city?"

Ruefully I admitted that so many ruins would qualify Chuamayu as one of the largest ruined cities ever discovered in Bolivia, but I wanted to see it all for myself.

Tjara held the mule while it picked at the wild grasses, and Jorge led me through the trees and the undergrowth. He continually beat the ground with a heavy stick he had broken off one of the trees to disturb any snakes that might get in our way.

The plants were well separated at ground level, but as they grew upwards they threw out thin branches which intertwined, blocking with a thick green curtain the view even a few metres ahead. Brushing through the first leafy barrier, we suddenly came to a partly overgrown row of stone ruins, built alongside what must have been a meeting-place. The row of twelve houses had been built on a very large bank of stones that was about thirty-three metres long, five metres wide, and one metre high. As was the case at Iscanwaya, I had to stretch to reach the top of the wall and the patio of a house in one step, and I am over six feet tall. Both Jorge and Tjara had to lever themselves up on to the patio of the first house. Presumably the houses had been built on top of this thick stone wall for the same reasons as were those at Iscanwaya: as a protection against reptiles and the water which might cascade down the hillside in the wet season.

All the buildings were made of large pieces of stone, which had been squared off before being placed one on top of the other. Very much larger stones had then been placed in the wall at irregular intervals and, although most of the stones were about thirty to forty centimetres deep, the surface area varied considerably. Since the builders had not laid identical stones side by side, but had used different sizes with overlapping ends, it meant that they supported each other at the point of overlap, and this provided a very solid construction. The stones had not been shaped and fitted together with the superb skill of the Incas of Peru, and there was evidence that a small quantity of wet earth had been used occasionally to cement a few stones together. So, while it would be inaccurate to compare the standard of stonemasonry with that of the Incas, there was ample evidence to show that these houses had been built by relatively skilled workers, and the sheer size and scope of such a construction suggested that this had been a permanent and long-term settlement of indigenous people. The fact that the walls were still standing a little more than two metres high in most of the houses bore testimony to the strength of the construction. Much reminded me of Iscanwaya: the constructed stone bank, the provision of running water to all the houses by means of precisely constructed stone channels. The houses, too, were identical in size and layout.

"Come and see the *muralla,* the fortress wall," said Jorge enthusiastically. "It's the best in all Bolivia."

He led me along the stone path to a very solid-looking defensive wall, built of pieces of stone of all shapes and sizes. On the inside, the wall measured three and a third metres high and was almost two metres thick. On the top of this section was yet another narrow stone wall making the total height of this defensive position almost four metres. It was possible to walk along the top of the original first thicker wall, sheltered by the second narrower wall. As you walked along you could peer down through square peep holes at regular intervals. Through these holes, defenders could have hurled stones and bolas, or fired arrows, at would-be attackers beneath them.

So that defenders could have climbed with speed on to this ledge from the inside, large flat stones had been built into the wall with one end sticking out to form a step. Each flight of four stone steps had been placed at an angle of precisely forty-five degrees, and each was exactly sixty-six centimetres from the next; certainly this was no haphazard construction.

Below the fortress, which was a hundred and seventy-five metres long, the hillside dropped away down to the river Kechuamayo at the point where it rushed down a canyon to join the river Cotacajes. On the opposite bank, Jorge pointed out another fortress wall of about the same length. At the lower end of the stone wall I was standing on was a massive platform which matched another similar platform on the far bank. Jorge assured me that, according to local Indian lore, there had been a suspension bridge built across here in ancient times which had still been in use up to about sixty years ago, although there was no vestige of it left now.

A few metres inside the boundary wall I noticed the remains of a narrow stone channel, no larger than a drainpipe which, Jorge confirmed, ran two hundred metres back up the valley and would have once brought running water from a reservoir right to the houses we had been looking at.

I unpacked my camera, so that I could at least take some close-up shots, even if it were not possible to film panoramic views of the ruins; then, leaving Tjara with the mule on the level courtyard, Jorge and I took the very steep pathway of small stone steps up the hill. In ten minutes we broke through the curtain of bushes, and I was very excited to see that the towering slope ahead of us had been completely re-shaped in exactly the same way as the hills of Iscanwaya. Four enormous terraces had been laid out one above the other by building massive curved stone walls about two metres high on the face of the hill, and then, by filling the space behind them with earth and stones, four giant steps of flat level land had been created.

As we walked along the first of these terraces I counted the ruins of twelve stone houses, and I also noticed that a stone channel carried running water into a tank dug into the ground and lined with stones. There was also what looked like a huge communal stone oven, and a small courtyard of paved stones in front of the houses. The only difference between these houses and those of Iscanwaya was that the houses here in Chuamayu were not built on a separate stone bank over the level of the ground; so apparently the early Indians had not been threatened by rain water flooding down the hillside, or by reptiles and insects at this higher level on the hillside.

When I looked at the other two terraces, I saw that they all sloped away a foot or so from the centre, and this minute slope might have been enough to divert any surface water. The fact that each terrace had twelve to fifteen houses built on it would have given a total population of around two hundred in quite a restricted space, so that it would have been extremely unlikely that reptiles or wild animals would have ventured into the area occupied by such a busy and tightly-packed community.

Above these large terraces was another terrace, only half the size, on which were built two much larger houses. They were both of two storeys, and the walls on the ground floor were faced with what looked like a coat of cement. I found that I could not make any impression with my thumb nail on this coating, but when I chipped some away with a knife it had the appearance of very hard-baked earth which was almost as solid as pottery. The ground floor was divided into two rooms of four by four metres, and the ceiling, which was barely two metres above the level of the floor, was built of large stone slabs supported by the dividing wall and two stone pillars in each room. The whole ceiling was not built of stone, however. There were spaces of between seventy-five centimetres and one metre between the stone slabs, which suggested that timber joists had also been used. In spite of these gaps the ground floor was in a fair standard of preservation. The second floor, however, was only the shell of a tumbledown ruin. Clearly the walls and divisions of this upper storey had been built of stone and timbers laid precisely on top of the stone walls and supports of the ground floor, but very little was still standing. Three stone pillars, which were joined together by a stone lintel, showed the outline of a room; the stone walls of the perimeter had almost all fallen away to leave short sections no more than one metre high.

According to what local Indians had told Jorge, these large houses had been where the 'Ingà' and his ruling council lived so that they could look down on their subjects. This might have been true, or it might have been only hearsay and speculation, because there was no evidence whatsoever to support or disprove this theory.

As I walked around the house I noticed that only the outside of the stone walls had been coated with this plaster, or whatever it was, but at the back of the house there was a cylinder about the size of a fifty-gallon oil drum, made out of stone and covered with this hard mud plaster. I asked Jorge if this were some kind of food store or a device for cooking, but he stated categorically that it was 'the bath of the Inca', and that there were many of them in the area—at least one in almost every ruin. It just happened that we had not seen one of the others. "They used to fill the stone drum with warm water for the families of the elite to bath. They were also used for purification ceremonies," he added.

I searched the two houses, looking for ceramics, but found nothing, not even pieces of broken pottery. I expressed my surprise to Jorge, but he just pursed his lips in resignation. "I expect the Spaniards were here," he said, "and after them came the grave robbers."

"Did the Spaniards really come as far as this?" I asked incredulously.

Jorge nodded gloomily. "My father said they came this far, to the edge of Paititi, the legendary lost empire. In fact, the only part of Bolivia they did not reach was there in those hills, the centre of Paititi. Everywhere else they visited, even if only in small parties."

This was confirmed to me much later on by Dr. Carlos and the archaeologists in La Paz. On more than one occasion they told me that the Spanish *conquistadores* had looted almost every settlement in Bolivia, except in the Mosetene country north of Cochabamba.

On the very topmost terrace of the hill was a circular stone tower about three metres high, with a crude rampart built at the top, and with square holes like small window-frames let into the wall about two metres above ground level. This most certainly had been a look-out tower, to judge by its position on the highest point and by the manner of construction which was exactly the same as that of many known defensive positions built by the Incas in Peru.

Just below the look-out tower the penultimate terrace was almost filled by a substantial stone building in a good state of preservation, in spite of what looked like a liberal covering of lichen or moss. I told Jorge that I was anxious to examine this building in some detail.

"Yes, this is the most important part of the city: their temple," he claimed.

"How do you know it was a temple?" I challenged him.

"I know," he said. "The Indians have always said so. They used to come from very long distances. Apart from those that you have seen, I know of another fifty Indian villages from ancient times between here and Inquivisi, which is approximately fifty kilometres up the river, and there are many more down-river in Paititi."

It was unworthy, perhaps, but I took everything Jorge told me with a pinch of salt, in spite of the fact that all his claims so far had been fact, or at least founded on fact. Where he said there were ruins, we had found ruins, and this settlement was indeed turning out to be the significant city he said it would be. In my judgment, it had indeed been a city inhabited by a settled community. It was not a pure fortress or defensive position, as Creston appeared to be. Certainly there was the splendid look-out point on the top of the hill, and there was the magnificent fortress wall almost on the river bank, but such limited defensive positions might well have been necessary to protect only the city itself, and not an extensive surrounding area.

If I accepted Jorge's claim that this largest of all the buildings was indeed a temple, then it was additional evidence. The purely defensive fortresses never had a temple, only the cities with permanent residents. It is also probable that only genuine cities like Iscanwaya and Chuamayu would have had elaborate systems to supply running water to each house or group of houses.

I entered the temple through one of the three narrow doorways with trapezoidal arches, and looked around the almost-empty hallway. The ghostly silence was the first thing I noticed. Outside, there was always the steady roar of the river far below, as well as the rustling of the leaves and the almost imperceptible stirring of other flora and fauna. Here, inside the building, the thick stone walls seemed to shut out all noise and movement. There was the same air of peace and majesty that you might find in a modern church, in spite of the fact that the roof had long since rotted and fallen, leaving the great hall open to the skies. The floor was made of large stone slabs which had been cut and fitted together so precisely that nothing had been allowed to grow through.

The temple itself was certainly constructed on an east-west

axis, but I could not tell if this was a precise orientation or only an approximation, because, unlike Incallacta, there did not appear to be any other celestial orientation in the construction. There were only three doorways instead of the twelve at Incallacta, and, with a measurement of twenty metres by fourteen metres, it was only a fraction of Incallacta's size. The short wall at the eastern end had been lightly covered with hard mud plaster and perhaps painted with yellow ochre, because a faint sheen of yellow was still apparent. There were no alcoves in the walls on the inside such as we had seen at Incallacta, and the only object in the eerie empty hall was a type of stone altar in front of the painted wall. It stood one metre and thirty centimetres high, and its surface area was one metre by thirty centimetres. The fact that a groove had been carved out at each corner led me to believe that it may well have been the same kind of sacrificial altar as those found in Inca temples in Peru and Bolivia. According to the Spanish chronicles of Gamboa, who witnessed such a ceremony, the grooves or depressions were used to hold the victim's arms and legs during sacrifices.

Apart, however, from this sacrificial altar, there was no evidence to show that this was a true Inca temple. There can be little doubt that, by the very nature of its construction and location, it must have been an important meeting-place. The sacrificial stone tended to support the supposition that it might also have been a ceremonial centre, but the comparative simplicity of construction did not put it in the same category as other known temples of the Inca.

One thing puzzled me; so I asked Jorge. "Where did they grow the quantity of food needed to feed such a large community?"

"They had much food," was his answer. "On the small plateau of flat land all along the river bank they grew enough food for themselves, and some for the city. On my father's land they used to grow huge quantities of maize, beans and fruit. On the other side of this hill is a valley which is full of terraces for growing maize, coca, peppers—all the food the Indians of those days used to eat. Plenty of food," Jorge exclaimed emphatically.

I walked up to the watch-tower and looked over the other side of the hill. There, indeed, on a much more gentle slope were the ruins of two small groups of stone houses surrounded by hundreds of metres of neat stone terraces, like stone steps. Obviously the ground was very rocky, and there was little depth of soil, because there were hardly any trees to be seen; but the fact that the terracing stood out so clearly and there was so little scrub or jungle growing made me wonder whether these settlements had not been abandoned until comparatively recent times. All that Jorge could tell me was that a few Indians had still lived in the valleys when his father arrived thirty years ago, but they all disappeared about that time.

"But there are still Indians living in the hills of the Isiboro and Ichoa over there," Jorge voluteered excitedly as he pointed across the river to east. "Do you want to visit them?"

"Let us get our camp ready for tonight," I replied, looking at the sinking sun. "We will talk about it."

We camped that night in comparative comfort on the stone floor inside the ceremonial centre, and I spent most of the next day filming and photographing the city.

Although this area was not too overgrown, I was limited to filming almost all of it in a series of close-up shots, because there was no vantage point from which I could get a good panoramic view. Ideally, I would have taken film from the top of the opposite hills, but that would have meant a formidable climb up the steep wooded slopes and would have wasted at least two more days.

I was becoming more and more excited at the prospect of visiting some of the Indians deep in Paititi, and that afternoon and evening, round the campfire, I tried to nail Jorge on exactly how we would get there, how long it would take, and what we would see when we arrived.

"We follow the river round the next curve to the foot of that hill," he explained, indicating landmarks that I could see. "There is a good path that winds around and over the range of hills on the other side of the river. The hills are not so steep as they reach down to the lower land of Beni."

"Is it a easy footpath to walk along?" I asked. "Or is there much clearing to do? Could the mule carry our equipment?"

"We can walk quickly," Jorge assured me, "but the mule cannot come. Once we cross the next range of hills and the valley beyond, we come to the hill of the rivers Ichoa and Isiboro. This is where the Indians live. We can walk there, but not the mule, because there are two places where we have to jump down a rocky face. It is only two or three metres high, but the mule could not jump. Then we cross a boundary wall, and climb one short outcrop of rock. I will carry everything you need, and I will help you, but the mule cannot come, anyway. He has to return today."

This last sentence gave me the clue to the problem. Almost certainly Jorge did not want to admit that he'd only arranged to hire the mule for a few days. I discounted the story of having to jump down rock-faces, but obviously I was powerless to argue.

"How long will it take us to reach the Indians on foot" I asked.

"Not more than two days," Jorge replied eagerly.

I made a mental note that this would mean at least three days. Then, when I had considered the idea carefully, I put my last queries to Jorge.

"If we send Tjara back with the mule and my filming equipment, can you carry my haversack with the tent, the medicines and the food?" I asked.

"I can carry it easily," said Jorge with the sort of optimism and enthusiasm that characterised his determination to take me to the ruins at all costs. "And when we reach the Indians we shall get plenty of food," he added. "Take one of your shirts for the chief, and some of those cigarette lighters. Then they will give us food."

"If we go," I said at length, "can you arrange for Tjara to come back with a mule, and meet us along the river where the footpath starts? Then I can ride home if I am tired."

Jorge must have seen that he was winning, because this enthusiasm knew no bounds. "Yes, I will arrange it," he cried. "Tjara will come back with the mule in ten days. We have one mule with a saddle; so you can ride all the way back to Independencia. Give me a pen and paper, and I will write a note to my brother. I well tell him to have the mule on the river bank in ten days, and he must wait until we arrive."

What lingering doubts I had were gradually swept away by Jorg's immense enthusiasm and by the tremendous excitement I felt at the prospect of visiting the little-known Indians in the heart of the unknown area which might possibly be Paititi.

"All right, tomorrow we go," I said, and Jorge whooped with delight.

CHAPTER NINE

The Indians of Sacapampa

NEXT MORNING, AFTER A good breakfast of maize bread, cheese and coffee, I filled my metal can with water and added the purifying tablets so that I'd have a good supply of drinking-water for the journey. Then, after we'd all crossed the swirling river, Tjara and the mule set off up-river towards Munai Pata, Jorge's father's farm, while Jorge and I followed the river downstream for about two kilometres until we reached the footpath leading into the hills to the east. To start with, it was certainly very narrow, and we had to brush aside the branches of trees which were growing over the pathway. I scuffed away a layer of dry earth on the surface and found a bed of stone beneath; so I guessed that it had been a good, clear, stone track in years gone by, and had only deteriorated through lack of maintenance and regular use. At one point on the trail I noticed a pile of dung that must have been deposited by a mule or a llama, and I questioned Jorge about the present-day use of this trail.

He told me that, as far as he knew, it was not used very much, but certainly the Indians we were going to visit made occasional trips along it with their llama trains loaded with coca and peppers for the people of the High Plateau, the inhabitants of La Paz and Oruro and other towns on the top of the Andes.

"So they do have contact with civilisation?" I said, whistling in surprise.

"No, they don't," Jorge replied. "They know that there are towns in the Altiplano (High Plateau), of course, but they merely trade on the river bank with an Indian merchant from Independencia or Inquisivi. In ancient times they followed the stone road of the Incas all the way from the Yungas here up to Cuzco and all the other Inca cities."

I remembered Dr. Carlos telling me much the same story. He had pointed out that coca leaves (for strength and power) and chili peppers (for body heat and energy) were an essential part of the diet of the Indians living high in the Andes in Inca times, and that was why the Inca soldiers had gone to so much trouble to conquer the tribes of the Yungas in Bolivia, since this was one of the richest areas of production east of the Andes.

That was also the reason they had built roads, set up important communities in Bolivia, and protected them so capably against the Guaranees from the jungle, and later from the Spanish invaders. After some length of time in deep thought Dr. Carlos had added a rider. "Or possibly the tribes of the Yungas were first conquered by the Aymara long before the Incas," he surmised, "and the Aymara may have built the first roads which the Incas took over when they came to power."

This was certainly food for thought as Jorge and I trudged on up the fairly steep path which wound round the hill. Since Jorge was weighed down by my haversack and tent, I did not find it difficult to keep up with him, and indeed I stuck very close behind him for safety reasons. He was carrying the army pistol at the ready and, to judge by the way his eager eyes searched the jungle alongside the trail, he was longing to take a pot-shot at something.

As it happened we saw no sign of any animal or reptile during that morning's march, and soon after midday we emerged from the jungle into the wide open spaces of the higher slopes. Here it was much like the countryside around Independencia and Pocanche. The slopes were much more stony, with so little depth of soil that no trees grew. It was similar to a Yorkshire moor or heathland, and I could see a long way ahead.

"We cross the river," said Jorge, pointing to a valley only two or three kilometres ahead, "and then we cross the next range of hills to find the Indians in the next valley, where the river Isiboro rises. There is a small community of about four Indian families before we reach the next river. Perhaps it is just possible that we might be able to pay them for a mule for you to ride. Have you got something for them?" he asked.

"Cigarette lighters, sweets and my own clothes, " I told him.

When we reached the Indian families in their timber-built houses in the valley, my resourceful companion had everything organised in a very short time. Triumphantly he returned from his earnest discussion with two of the Indian men, to announce that, in exchange for one of my shirts and a cigarette lighter, they would let me have a mule for a few days to travel to the Paititi Indians over the hills. More good news was that, if I paid them some money as well, we could camp there for the night and they would feed us. I gave Jorge the lighter, a shirt and twenty pesos (one dollar), and when he had clinched the deal, we pitched our tent between the houses.

At once I questioned Jorge about this mysterious group of Indians, several of whom had come out of their houses to pay us close attention. Living out in these remote hills, it was most unlikely that they knew much about civilisation, and yet there were anomalies. Two of the men wore trousers under their traditional knee-length tunics. One wore a belt with a metal buckle, the kind you buy in a multiple store. A woman emerged from one of the houses, carrying a metal cooking-pot that must have been bought in a town and, of course, they had surprisingly asked for money.

Jorge explained. These families might have come from a small town like Independencia in the first place, and now they were the merchants or the middlemen who traded between the Indian tribes of Paititi in the interior and the travellers who came from Cochabamba to Independencia, or from La Paz to Inquisivi. Jorge thought that all the men of the group would travel regularly to the nearest small towns, and some of them might even have been as far as Cochabamba.

A strange little family group they turned out to be. There was not the slightest hint of hostility, but neither did they offer to take even the first tentative steps towards a friendly contact. They provided maize, yucca, beans and bananas when Jorge went to collect them, but none of the Indians approached us or spoke to us, not even the children.

Jorge advised me to stay in the tent that evening while he went to talk with some of the men. He returned after an hour to reveal that they were highly suspicious of me, and assumed that I was after gold. We both agreed that quite possibly they had already had some contact with white men looking for gold and, since those confrontations had probably been distasteful if not thoroughly unpleasant, this would explain their animosity.

Apparently Jorge had tried to convince them of our good

intentions, with some small success. He had been given an animal bone, which was about the size of a femur of a small llama and painted with an intricate pattern in black dye. This was supposed to be our 'passport', or card of introduction to the Indians of Paititi. It would tell them that we came as friends, and were not going to rob or harm them. Once again Jorge had turned up with a trump card, it seemed to me, and the fact that the Indians would accept currency made payment for the hire of the mule an easy negotiation without dipping into my limited supply of suitable gifts.

It may sound a little premature to talk of 'the Indians of Paititi' when neither the classification of the people nor the identification of the area has been verified to the satisfaction of serious scholars, but by now I was personally convinced that the Indians' own claim to be in Paititi was probably justified.

After an uneventful night we packed our camping gear, bought a large shawl from the Indians, loaded it with food, and tied it on to the mule, together with my haversack. The mule had no saddle or bridle, and riding it down the fairly steep path to the river Santa Elena would scarcely be very comfortable; so both Jorge and I decided to walk.

Crossing the swiftly-flowing shallow river was made easy, by walking over the level pathway regularly used by the Indians. The same could be said of the open trail, which wound round the hillside on the opposite side of the river. For two reasons it was much less arduous than the trek had been up to that point: as we marched eastwards towards the plains the hills were becoming much less steep, and the fact that the trail was the only means of communication between the tribes of the interior and the merchants meant that it was not over grown with scrub and jungle.

Since Jorge was anxious to reach the Indians of the river Isiboro before sundown, I rode the mule up the hills and walked down. In this way we made very good progress indeed across the magnificently empty countryside of Chapare. Lonely it may have been, but it was a reasonably hospitable wilderness.

We crossed two more shallow rivers tumbling down the hills and flowing eastwards towards the Amazon, and when we stopped for some refreshments I tried to trace our route on the army map. Jorge's criticism of the inaccuracies seemed to be entirely justified. The last two rivers we had crossed were not even shown on the map, and the comparatively large river east of the

Santa Elena was shown, but not named. On the map the distance between these two rivers appeared to be about fifteen kilometres. In fact they were separated by one range of hills, and were no more than four kilometres apart. I put the map away, and relied on Jorge's personal knowledge of the area.

He told me that, by late afternoon, we should reach the settlements of Sacapampa ('dry valley' in Quechua), and his forecast was absolutely right. About two hours before sunset we climbed to the top of the range of hills, looking down on a much lower hill that divided two fertile valleys just before they joined together in a v-shape to form one wider valley.

On all four slopes of the hills at this apex where the two rivers met were small groups of timber-built, thatched houses. This idyllic setting was made even more attractive by the little parcels of cultivated land surrounding the groups of dwellings. At first sight I judged that there would be about nine or ten houses in each of the four groups; so I might expect a community of something like one hundred and fifty Indians altogether.

I saw four or five Indians working in the plantations, and a few more walking around the houses. Another group of about a dozen men was walking down the open hillside across the river towards one of the settlements and, since Jorge and I were standing on the open heathland, the Indians must have seen us. Following the normal custom, Jorge yodelled loud and long as we made our way down the gentle slope. Apparently our presence did not alarm the Indians, because none of them scurried for cover, nor did they seem to be the slightest bit interested in our imminent arrival.

As we approached a bend in the trail about four hundred metres from the first settlement, however, four men emerged from the trees and stood blocking the trail fifty metres ahead of us.

"Stand here and wait, Mister Ross," Jorge commanded. "I will go and talk to them."

I faded into the shelter of the trees while Jorge, still leading the mule, walked confidently towards the reception committee, who looked very similar to the Mosetene Indians of Santa Ana, on the banks of the river Beni. They were dressed in knee-length cloaks that appeared to be made out of beaten bark or animal skin: I could not be sure from that distance. Just like that of the Mosetenes, their hair was tied back by a plain headband.

Their conference with Jorge seemed to be held in a perfectly calm and dignified atmosphere with very little gesticulation or animation, but it went on and on. After a quarter of an hour with no apparent progress I grew uneasy. Then, when Jorge unpacked my haversack and laid our most of the contents on the trail, I became decidedly apprehensive. I had almost decided to give up waiting and approach the group, when I realised that Jorge could be having some success. One of the Indians, who might have been the leader, because he was doing most of the talking, held up one of my shirts that Jorge had offered. The thought that this might be a payment of some sort was confirmed when Jorge re-packed my haversack, and led the mule back along the trail, while the Indians departed in the direction of their houses, taking my shirt with them.

"It was difficult," said Jorge, pursing his lips, "but it is all right. We can stay with these people."

"Well done, indeed," I said, patting Jorge on the back. "But what was so difficult?"

"They do not like other people very much," Jorge admitted, "not even me, and they know were I come from. You are a total stranger to them, and I think they are a little bit afraid that you may be a soldier. When I told them you have presents, and when I showed them the message from the merchants, it was all right," and he held up the painted bone that had proved to be a satisfactory card of introduction.

We just had time to follow the Indians as far as the first group of houses and to pitch our tent on an open space before darkness fell. We made no further contact with the Indians that night, but the next week in Sacapampa turned out to be one of my most memorable experiences in Bolivia. We spent the whole of our time with this one small community of between forty and fifty people, calmly integrating and trying to win their approval. The Indians neither avoided us nor did they approach us or try to communicate at first. It was as if we were not there: an eerie feeling.

Our only minor successes were due to the fact that Jorge could converse in fluent Quechua while I made a few crude attempts, from which I judged that some of what I said could be understood.

On the second evening, when a cluster of twelve men and women gathered round to watch us eating, I heard Jorge tell his audience that I was a stranger to this land, a visitor from the world where the sun rises. According to Jorge I was an important and influential person whom they could consult about any problems. I was a good person, who would help them.

I had already told Jorge to make it clear to any Indians we might meet that I only wanted to study their way of life and help them if possible. I told him to make it abundantly clear right from the outset that I offered no kind of threat. I did not want their land or their possessions, or intend to harm them in any way. It worked, inasmuch as the Indians responded at once to my offer of help. At first they only wanted another sweet or an item of clothing; so I gave them what little I could spare. Then one man, who was the only one with a very light growth of facial hair, and who seemed to command the respect of the others, turned to Jorge with a much more serious request. I did not understand exactly what he was saying until Jorge translated for me. Apparently this man was a *chunka camayoc,* the Inca term for a leader of ten families, and he would like to take us for a conference with *Sinchi Kooto*, who was, according to Jorge, the leader of all the four communities. What they wanted me to do was to get the builders from the big cities to reinstate the old road from Sacapampa to Cuzco.

"That's a tall order," I observed.

"Not such a big job," said Jorge reassuringly. "They mean, clean up the old Inca stone road and rebuild a few bridges over the rivers, that's all. And then they can take their coca and peppers and sell them direct in the towns."

Jorge broke off while the Indians' leader spoke again. "Then they want you to give them their herd of llamas which they used to have," Jorge added.

By now the Indian was getting quite worked up. According to Jorge, he was making the point that the people of the High Plateau, or top of the Andes, would perish without their regular supply of coca and peppers, which they have always needed since the time anyone could remember. But the merchants paid very little because goods were so difficult to transport, and the Indians of Sacapampa would not prosper until they could take their llama trains up into the Andes, as they used to do in days gone by.

It was a most interesting story, and provided further evidence to support the hypothesis that the Yungas of Bolivia might have been very important to the people of the Andes, even as far back as the time when the Aymara and then the Inca empires flourished.

It obviously meant a great deal to these isolated and relatively impoverished Indians of Sacapampa to have their road to the Andes once again, and I nodded my approval of their request. I told Jorge to explain that I would do all I could when I returned to La Paz, and I can only hope he did not paint too rosy a picture, because the Indians were absolutely delighted with his reply. Clearly I was very much a welcome guest from that moment on.

I was absolutely thrilled with the change in my relationship with the Indians, from the silence of their grudging acknowledgement of my presence to the chatter and cordial offer of friendship. Clearly they wanted to please me and impress me to a certain extent in return for my intervention with the authorities in the big city.

I had to admit that they might have overestimated my influence, but I had every intention of trying to help them on my return to La Paz, and from that point of view, as well as for the value of my own studies, it was essential that I should learn as much as possible about their way of life and that of other Indian tribes they might know in this remote and unexplored territory.

Jorge told the *chunka camayoc* what I wanted, and he said that, while they would show me everything in their small *ayllu* (kinship group), the other three *ayllus* had their own *chunka camayocs*, and I would have to talk to them if I wanted to visit the whole area of Sacampampa. When Jorge translated all this to me, I suggested that we might take full advantage of the friendship we were establishing in this *ayllu,* and think about travelling further afield later on if the opportunity presented itself. The obvious conclusion was that, if we won the friendship and trust of this small group, it would be so much easier to establish a rapport with the others.

That evening as we sat on a tree stump near the tent, the *chunka camayoc* and two other men, whom I took to be his assistants, came over to press their case for the rebuilding of the old road. They went on at some length about the vagabonds from civilisation who had destryed some bridges over the rivers and about the merchants who cheated them over the value of their crops and, in some cases, made off with a cargo and never returned with the money. They felt very bitter, and with some justification it seemed to me; so I listened carefully, and gave them a toffee each as a token of my sympathy for what 'my people' had done to them.

As soon as they saw the sweets being handed out, a group of about ten women and children, who had been watching from a respectful distance, came over to join in the conversation. I gave them each a toffee, to their obvious delight, and then, with Jorge's help, I started to question them about their past history as well as their present way of life. The hesitant way they talked of their past soon made it clear that they were speaking within the bounds of their own memories, or perhaps those of one generation past. For example, they said they had *always* lived in these valleys, not necessarily in these same houses, but in the surrounding valleys. They did not measure time accurately in years, so much as in periods of years such as 'until that baby reaches manhood', or 'between that woman's first and third child'; so the conclusions I reached are based at best on interpretation and a lot of guesswork.

On that basis I offer my opinion that these four *ayllus* in Sacampampa had formed themselves into a reasonably strong and united group of about two hundred people, living under the threat of attack by stronger groups of indigenous people from the interior who came to rob them of their crops and take their women and children as slaves, as well as being at the mercy of colonists and semi-civilised Indians with whom they had to trade in order to buy cooking- and eating-utensils, matches, machetes and similar items which had not been so very important years ago, but which were now regarded as necessities.

To judge from what they said, it seemed that they established a centre like Sacapampa every ten or fifteen years, and then moved on, either because they had extracted all the fertility from the land, or else because they were driven out by a more powerful group. Because they could never establish a permanent home, they no longer built their houses of stone as their ancestors did. The timber dwellings with thatched roofs could be constructed 'while the moon rose'—two weeks, perhaps.

I asked Jorge to get more information about the stone houses of their ancestors, and in a very short time he had persuaded the *chunka camayoc* to take us to see some of these buildings. With an Indian guide, Jorge and I walked for several kilometres on both sides of the steep hill that plunged down to the point where two rivers met. At one point we saw the remains of eighteen stone houses, most of them overgrown by trees and scrub, but quite recognisable once we had chopped away the undergrowth with machetes. It was also apparent that these stone houses had been built an artificial terraces, just like the Mollo city of Iscanwaya. The construction of what remained of the stone walls was also very similar. The stones had been squared off and carefully placed one on top of the other with some earth used as cement.

We also found what proved to be a remarkable and perhaps unique fortress wall protecting this group of houses and five other similar groups around the hillside and about three hundred metres above the level of the river. The fortress wall built in a series of v-shapes, all pointing down to the river and all bounded by one continuous wall. An enemy would have to struggle up the steep hill and then, from whichever direction he approached the fortress wall, he would be shot at from two sides. When the fortification was in use the wall was probably at least two metres high, with turrets built on the top, but after many years of tropical storms and decay not much now remains.

From a vantage point near the top of the hill we could see all four of the separate settlements that made up Sacapampa, and the whole scene bore an air of order and organisation. The houses were neat and in good repair, and the many small plots growing coca and peppers, maize and potatoes, looked tidy and productive.

Surprisingly, we did not see a solitary reptile or mammal of any sort during our journey on the hillside, and later I got Jorge to ask the Indians what food they ate, other than the crops from their fields. The answer was: fish from the rivers, because, according to the Indians, all the deer and wild pigs in the area had been either eaten or driven away by bad spirits.

During the week I spent with this Indian *ayllu* it seemed to me that they were obsessed by spirits and the need to communicate with them and placate them.

At the start of each day four or five men were detailed off to work in the fields, either cleaning out weeds and secondary growth or, at this particular time, harvesting and drying the coca leaves in the warm sunshine. Before they set off every morning, the men gathered in a bunch at the edge of the rows of houses, and performed a little ceremony, though perhaps ceremony may be too extravagant a term, for there did not appear to be any set ritual or group participation. They stood close the each other, certainly, but facing in any direction, with each man quietly mouthing his own personal incantation, while each of them tossed coca leaves into the wind, or placed coloured threads and small maize-flour biscuits on the ground beside him. This routine, I was told, was the day's offering to Patchamama, the Goddess of the Earth. According to the Indians she controls everything to do with Mother Earth, and only she can say whether anything will prosper, be it crops or a journey or a new house. She is said to be an irascible spirit always in need of coca to chew, biscuits to stave off hunger, and threads to make pretty clothes. Apart from the daily offerings at harvest time, the Indians held regular Patchamama ceremonies, when all the four communities sent their representatives to take part in a communal tribute and homage.

Continually during my brief visit I saw an almost non-stop demonstration of spirit worship in every aspect of the Indians' lives and, as I won their trust and confidence, they began to explain the meanings behind some of the ceremonies.

At the end of each day I noticed that a group of nine or ten Indians—both men and women and not always the same people—went down to the river, talked to themselves in another of these private rituals, and finished up by throwing a bundle of sticks in the river.

"They are throwing away all the bad things of today, so that we will start clean and strong in the morning," I was told.

Apparently one member of each family 'collects' the sins of the others, goes down to the river, recites a list of the family misdemeanors and ties them into a package of twigs and foliage and floats them away down the river.

I asked Jorge to find out what they regarded as sinful, and back came this interesting answer: *Ama Kelya* (do not be lazy): *Ama Suya* (do not steal) and *Ama Yuya* (do not lie). These three commandments were all part of the doctrine of life in the time of the Aymara and the Incas, and I have often thought what a different world it would be if all people observed these three commandments.

Spiritism in some form or other affected all the Indians regularly throughout their lives, much of it obviously focused on ancestor worship. I was able to trace much of this influence through personal observations, or by listening to their stories, or, very occasionally, by persuading them to enact a ceremony for my benefit.

No children were born while I was there, but they told me that the mother goes to stay in the houses of *Sinchi Kooto* (the Chief of all four communities), where there is a woman in charge of childbirth, and when the child is born *Sinchi Kooto* inspects it. If he considers that it will grow up to be a useful member of the community, he washes it (or dabs it?) with his own urine to ward off evil spirits, and the woman and child are sent home the same day. If however, the child is deformed or weakly (as many probably are, as a result of years of inbreeding) the Chief kills it, and the mother returns alone.

This ritual murder may sound a barbaric custom to people of civilised communties, but when life is such a constant battle for survival for the fit members of these small communites, and when they may, at any time, be forced to abandon the villages they have established to look for another valley, to start all over again, the burden of incapacitated members would be intolerable. Older women or widows were sent to the houses of *Sinchi Kooto,* who was paid 'tribute' by all the Indian families, so that he alone never had to work. He had to maintain his court, the midwife, the Shaman and all those in need of help in this mini-version of a welfare state.

A man could have as many wives as he could afford but, since every wife had to be fed and clothed by her husband, only the strongest and the youngest men had more than one. To obtain his first wife a young man had to pay a tribute to her family, generally an agreed period of free labour in their field. Wives could then be bought and sold second-hand; so it was quite usual for a middle-aged man to sell his wife and buy a younger and stronger girl to share the labour of looking after his children. His older wife would be purchased by a young man, who already had a wife of his own age. The older woman would be given the job of cooking and looking after the children, thus releasing the young wife to work full-time in the fields with her husband, who was then able to sow and reap a much bigger harvest.

I did not see this happening, but I was told that it was quite customary to swop labour with a friend during the busy times of sowing and harvesting. If a man worked for two days in his neighbour's field, he would expect two days' labour in return.

Each man needed good harvests because, apart from having to feed a family of five or six through the year, he had to give one third of his crop to *Sinchi Kooto* as a tribute or tax.

Certainly *Sinchi Kooto* was a person apart for during my stay I was never allowed to meet him, nor was I even shown where he lived. The Indians talked freely about almost any aspect of their community life, and I was guided all over their settlement, but *Sinchi Kooto* was kept a closely-guarded secret. No bribe or payment would persuade the Indians to lower the barriers.

In this *ayllu* there were no other secrets, and precious little personal privacy. The rough wooden door which covered the entrance to each of the one-roomed dwellings was always open, and I saw that it was quite acceptable for anyone to walk in and out of any house without formality. Most surprisingly in such a clean and well-kept hamlet, I noticed several instances of men urinating for a second against the doorpost of a house before entering. When I expressed my surprise, Jorge told me that urine keeps away evil spirits—a belief held by many Indians, both in the wilderness of the Yungas and in the towns.

There were only two babies in the *ayllu*; they were still in their comfortable cradles made of fibre ropes tied on a wooden frame, which was higher at one end so that the child always lay with its feet lower than its head. The two babies were still being suckled by mothers who knelt over their infants and dangled a breast for them to feed from. The babies were never cuddled because, according to the Indians, they could become fractious when they were put down.

Another of the customs which they told me about might well have explained why there were so few babies in what appeared to be a healthy community. Sex for any mother who is suckling her child was banned, because it was supposed to taint the milk, and, since one of the infants I saw must have been eighteen months to two years old, this served as a most effective method of birth control.

I wondered if, after such a long period of breast-feeding, the date of weaning was a ceremonial occasion. There certainly would be a ceremony, I was told, when the child, who up to that point had been known only by its mother's family name (generally a plant or a flower), would be given its own personal name by the father. A boy would have his hair cut for the first time, and a girl would have hers tied back with a length of cord.

The next ceremony in a child's life was at puberty, which I judged to be about fourteen years by the look of one boy who had recently been initiated into manhood. At this ceremony a young man is given his first breech clout to wear under his cloak; a girl has her hair plaited for the first time, and is given two gold spoons tied to a cord necklace. On ceremonial occasions these spoons were tied so that they pointed upwards for single women and downwards for those who were married.

I dare say there are other parts of the initiation ceremony in which a boy proves himself a man in some way, but the Indians did not volunteer this information and, not wishing to antagonise them, I did not press them. They did tell me, however, that the girls were sent to the *Sinchi Kooto* after the puberty ceremony. Here the Chief and his women taught the girls 'how to serve men: all they need to know'—whatever that may mean.

My relationship with the Indians was very delicately balanced, and while they were being so forthcoming (with Jorge's prompting), I did not want to jeopardise everything by overstepping the mark; so I resolved to be patient and not to turn a conversation into an inquisition.

I longed to know how the Indians preserved enough potatoes, yucca and maize for the whole family group for long periods. When I enquired, I was taken about a hundred metres from the village to a very short, steep bank into which four entrances had been cut, each large enough for a man to crawl through on his hands and knees. Inside was a large chamber about the size of one compartment of a modern train. On the floor was a layer of coca leaves still attached to their twigs; they looked as fresh and green as the day they were picked, and what was even more extraordinary was the the maize and potatoes hidden beneath this layer of foliage were fresh and cool to the touch.. I was assured that these vegetables were the left-overs from the previous harvest and that, buried in this chamber, they would remain fresh for 'two or more harvests'. "You must cover them with coca leaves, for they have magic properties." It all seemed so simple. It clearly worked.

The Shaman, who lived in the house of *Sinchi Kooto*, was a regal-looking figure who seemed a little older than most of the other members of the tribe. His cloak was much more ornate then any others, with elaborate decorations made of coloured thread. He wore a band of gold around his head and several gold pins in his cloak. Round his waist he wore a thick belt of animal hide, and this too was festooned with gold pins and ornaments.

I don't think a day passed when the Shaman did not make one

or two visits to our *ayllu* and, since he must also have been the medical practitioner for the other three *ayllus* as well, he would have been a busy man. To find out the exact nature of the medical problems of his patients without intruding was not easy, but in casual converstion and by sometimes looking in through the ever-open doorways, it seemed that the majority of the medication was needed for damaged limbs, especially for various joints that were giving trouble.

I saw the Shaman giving medicines by mouth and by spreading ointment or rubbing leaves on affected limbs. I suggest, therefore, that there was some herbal medicine practised, but there was also much black magic, with the Shaman chanting quietly, making offerings of small objects to an unseen spirit in the roof of the house, and almost always going through the ritual of tossing the coca leaves.

According to Jorge the Shaman was also summoned to dispense blessings and curses and sex potions, but the Indians themselves would not confirm this. They did support Jorge's interesting observation that, although the Shaman's services were very expensive, you only paid after a cure had been effected. It was a case of no cure, no fee. I asked Jorge what would happen if the Shaman failed completely, and his patient died.

"He will tell you that he expected the sick person to die," was the innocent reply. "He knew it was going to happen, and so no one can blame him."

The Shaman was also a key figure in the preparation and execution of the big Patchamama ceremony which, I was delighted to learn, was to take place very soon on the banks of the river Ayopaya where the Indians were to establish new areas of cultivation for the small town of Independencia. It was interesting to learn that the Indians who professed to live the civilised way of life in Independencia still believed in at least one of their traditional ceremonies.

When I was assured that I should be allowed to watch the ceremony, I asked Jorge to return the mule I had hired from the Indian traders and to fetch my camera and film on the mule Tjara had. This he did.

Before leaving to make the first-ever film of a Patchamama ceremony, I hoped to persuade the three other *chunka camayocs* to visit me. There was some doubt about this at first, but eventually a man was paid about fifty pence to search them out and ask them to come.

CHAPTER TEN

The Patchamama ceremony

THAT EVENING TWO REGAL figures strode into view. There was no doubt the they were the *chunka camayocs*: their dress was much more elaborate than that worn by the average Indian. The long, flowing cloaks were decorated with coloured threads of fibre or cotton, which were woven into intricate patterns. Their headwear, too, was much more ornate. The wide headbands were decorated with vividly-coloured birds' feathers and tiny figures made of gold. At a respectful distance came a party of five or six Indians carrying loaded string bags and large parcels wrapped in leather containers. It looked as if these young men were escorts for the two *chunkas*.

I jumped to my feet and hovered expectantly. The two leaders of communities on the other side of the river had been invited to meet me, and I expected them to make the first approach.Instead they walked straight past me as if I were not there, and they strode purposefully into the house of our own *chunka camayoc*. I sat down again and waited patiently for half an hour or more and, when they did not reappear, I asked Jorge to go and find out what was happening. For the first time he refused to carry out my request, merely blurting out an explanation with regret.

"You can't do that, Mister Ross. They are *chunka camayocs*, and they will come when they are ready."

"I thought there were three of them," I said.

"There are, but perhaps the other one cannot come," Jorge replied.

"Do you know what they are called? Do they have names?"

"They are simply called *chunka camayoc*," he assured me. "*Chunka* means ten, and *camayoc* means family. Each one is the chief of ten families, but they are very important. We cannot tell them what to do."

It must have been nearly noon the next day before anything happened. A woman emerged from the Chief's home, and sidled up to Jorge nervously. As she turned and scurried back to the house, Jorge smiled triumphantly.

"It is a message from the *chunkas*. They invite us to eat with them. At last we can talk."

As we walked over to the house, two young Indians came round the corner, sat at the entrance, and began to play their typically melancholy non-rhythmic music on a flute and drum. The musical instruments were just like those I had seen in other parts of Bolivia and, indeed, very similar to those used by the Indians of Venezuela and Colombia. The flute was a hollowed-out bamboo stalk with four finger-holes burnt into the stem, and on the end was a chamber made out of a mixture of wild bees' honey and wood ash, into which a bird's quill had been inserted as a mouthpiece. The drum was a small crudely-made instrument with a piece of animal leather tied across a short butt of wood that looked like a piece of hollowed-out tree trunk.

The door of the house was half open; so Jorge and I walked into the dingy light of the one room where the three Indian *chunka camayocs* were sitting. Two women and three children were busy preparing food at the other end of the uneven mud floor.

There were no introductions and no formalities; so Jorge and I just sat down alongside the *camayocs*. We rested against the wall made of saplings stuck into the ground and tied together with twine, with two heavier pieces of timber tied across to support the slender construction.

The Indians carried on talking as if oblivious of our presence until, after a few minutes, the women came over, carrying wooden platters with cooked maize in the form of corn on the cob, boiled and baked potatoes, and what looked like burnt yucca.

While we ate with our fingers the conversation ended, and the only diversion was when I saw a small black beetle crawling across the floor towards us.

"Is it dangerous?" I asked Jorge urgently, as I lifted my foot to squash it.

"No, don't touch it," Jorge hissed at me out of the side of his mouth. "All insects are spirits of their ancestors. Don't touch them."

Fortunately our *chunka camayoc* saw the creature and, when he leaned over and put a potato beside it, presumably as an offering, the beetle fled to the other end of the room at great speed.

As we came to the end of our simple meal, one of the women came over with a calabash of water, and we all washed our hands. I dried my fingers on my handkerchief, and reached into my pockets for the presents I had brought, since it seemed an appropriate time to break the ice. I laid out a selection of things I could spare from my dwindling stocks. I offered presents I thought the Indians would appreciate, like toffees, small disposable cigarette lighters, a pair of socks, a handkerchief and a penknife. I told Jorge to offer these gifts as well as twenty pesos (two dollars) each in exchange for information.

Jorge made the announcement, which drew a gruff response from the Indians, who were obviously keen to get their hands on my presents.

"They want to know what sort of information you require," said Jorge.

"About their way of life, their beliefs and their ceremonies—that sort of thing," I replied. "It is nothing sinister, so don't alarm them. What do they know of other Indian tribes and family groups in the hills of Paititi?"

Back came their detailed reply that there were many communities living in the valleys to the east. Some of them lived in large settlements where they had always lived, in permanent cities built of stone. Others moved from valley to valley trying to grow more and better food. The big communities were much more powerful, according to Jorge's translation, because they had a surplus of food. What was very interesting indeed was their account of the methods used by these powerful tribes for growing crops.

They built steps on the side of a hill (like the terraces of the Incas, I assumed) and, because they gave food to Patchamama (Mother Earth), she always grew good crops. They gave her food from the lake which they had constructed on the side of the hill; plants, fish and snails from this lake were very pleasing to Patchamama.

This sounded like the system of fertilisation used by the people of the Mound culture in Beni. Was this a link between that prehistoric culture and the people Paititi?

The *camayocs* went on to explain that, because these tribes always had plenty of food in a settled community, they had enough left over to maintain an army of soldiers who were only used to protect their cities and to fight battles. They never had to work in the production of food like all the Indians of Sacapampa.

I asked whether it might be possible to meet these Indians to the east, and take them presents. The answer was an emphatic no. Apparently they guarded their territory jealously, and killed other Indians if they went near. There was no chance of making friends with them, because they were feared by all other tribes.

I scribbled down these details at great speed, but when I tried to establish precise locations and numbers, I found it very difficult to differentiate between truth based on certain knowledge, and wild guesses just for the sake of answering my questions and earning their fees. I cannot possibly be dogmatic about the accuracy of these statements, and indeed I offer them only as interesting possibilities which, I consider, would be well worth a detailed investigation in years to come.

From what the Indians told me, together with my own travels and explorations plus the detail and, I am sure, the truthful descriptions by Jorge of his own journeys in much of the area, I draw the following conclusions.

There is ample evidence, most of which I have seen with my own eyes, that a line of substantial stone fortresses stretched from Lake Titicaca south eastwards to Inquisivi, Independencia and Cochabamba and eastwards to Comparapa, Samaipata and Santa Cruz, then northwards through the foothills of the Andes to Santa Ana and westwards to Iscanwaya and back to the lake. This line of defensive positions would enclose an area of almost unknown and unexplored jungle-covered hills and barren mountains about the size of Britain, and within this great wilderness there were smaller fortresses which enclosed sections about the size of an average English county. These smaller areas might have been the territories claimed and defended by indigenous cultures, some of which would have been conquered by the Incas, but not all.

It is a well-known fact, documented by Gamboa, the Spanish chronicler, that the Mostenes, for example, were never conquered by the Incas who, to save face, said they did not want the jungle territory, anyway. At the same time it is another fact well known to Bolivian anthropologists that the Incas of the highland areas were totally dependent on an ample supply of coca and peppers from the sub-tropical valleys of the lowlands to the east.

What has never been recorded, or established with any authority, is how many Indian tribes live in the area drained by the rivers Isiboro, Ichoa, Secure, Cotacajes and Chapare, as well as a dozen smaller, un-named rivers. No one knows how many Indians inhabit the vast area of fertile hills and valleys, nor to which culture they belong. Five years ago settlers in the village of Todos Santos were attacked by a tribe of savage Indians emerging from the surrounding jungle, and Todos Santos is only forty or fifty kilometres to the east of Sacapampa, on the other side of the range of hills which, the *camayocs* said, was the home of powerful and numerous tribes of Indians living in stone-built cities.

I tried to get some idea of numbers from the *camayocs,* but they only waved their arms and held them wide open to indicate a vast quantity. When I asked them to compare the jungle settlements of the Moxos, as they called the tribes to the east, our own *chunka camayoc* clenched and unclenched his fists over and over again, showing his ten fingers at least six times. Did this mean that there were sixty or so Indians in a tribe, or sixty times as many as at Sacapampa? I asked Jorge, and after a further converstion he ventured his opinion that there must be one thousand Indians in those hills: but, frankly I would be prepared to encounter almost any number, from a handful of primitive nomadic family groups to great cities inhabited by several hundred.

I longed to make the journey to find out, but, alas, no present and no sum of money would persuade the Indians of Sacapampa to take me. They insisted that the Moxos were a barbaric people and, as if to frighten me to death, they told me about the punishments handed out to those foolish enough to enter the Moxos' territory. Apparently they took savage delight in pummeling you to death with wooden clubs, and they did it slowly over one whole day. Or they might tie you to a *palo alto,* and let the ants eat you. Worst of all, they suspended people upside down from the branch of a tree and, over a period of one or two days, lowered them slowly, head first, into a pit of snakes. I hurriedly agreed that it would be foolhardy to try to make friendly contact.

Perhaps a much bigger, well-organised expedition might

make the trip in years to come, and find out if this is indeed one of the areas to which some of the Incas might have escaped after the conquest.

I am not suggesting that there are marked similarities in the way of life of these Indians to whom I was talking and the ancient Incas of Cuzco and Machu Picchu, but there is certainly a great deal of evidence to link them with some of the tribes which were conquered and absorbed into the Inca empire.

The pyramid structure of the social organisation of Sacapampa was based on the Incas' system. *Sinchi Kooto* was the head of this community and, like the Incas of old, he was allowed more than one wife as well as a court, which included a Shaman, a council and a religious leader. These *chunka camayocs* ruled over *ayllus* of ten families; Incas' tribal groupings were similar, and *Ama Kelya* (do not be lazy) *Ama Suya* (so not steal) and *Ama Yuya* (do not lie) were the three chief commandments of the Incas.

Other typical Inca customs practised by the Indians of Sacapampa included the puberty ceremony for a male, at the end of which he was given a breech clout, and a puberty ceremony for girls, when they were given gold spoons to be worn pointing upwards for single girls and downwards for married women. The method of storing food in underground chambers with a great deal of fresh foliage was also the method used by the Incas.

There were the stone road and the suspension bridges in need of repair; the ornaments of gold worn by the leader; the worship of Patchamama; tributes (or taxes) paid to the *Sinchi Kooto* and his court; the throwing away of sins at the end of the day; the exchange of labour called *ayne*. There were many similarities between the way of life of the Incas and that of the Indians of Sacapampa—surely too many to be rejected as 'independent invention'.

The terraces of levelled earth with irrigation and drainage on the steep hillside of the settlements on the bank of the river Cotacajes were exactly the same as those of Peru, but there are, of course, many other examples of cultivation on man-made terraces in many parts of the world. There are also plenty of examples of stone walls built as defensive barriers, and of cities built of stone like those deep in Paititi, which the Indians of Sacapampa described to me. I am certain that a detailed archaeological investigation would produce enough evidence to establish firm and indisputable links between the Incas and the present-day Indians of the vast unexplored area centred on the river Isiboro, but I reckoned that my own lack of academic training, as well as my shortage of time and money, would inhibit any more efforts to come up with immediate answers. I would have to be content merely to open the door for others to complete a scientific investigation.

What I could do, however, was to obtain a unique film record of the Patchamama ceremony, which perhaps few other Europeans had ever witnessed.

But no sooner had we packed my haversack than Jorge straightened up an let out an exclamation of surprise and disgust and he pointed to the far end of the village, where a small squad of six Indians was walking away up the hillside. They were departing without waiting for us.

Thinking we might have at least an hour's notice of departure, I had planned to take some film, fill a can with purified water, and barter for some food to take on the journey, but obviously we would have to depart at once if we were to be spectators at the Patchamama ceremony.

"Do you think it is still all right for us to go with them?" I asked Jorge. "They're not trying to avoid us, are they?"

"No, no," he replied in good humour. "If we want to go we have to be ready. We have to watch out for them. This is what they are like, and this is how they will behave all the time. They have given permission, and that is enough. They will not look after us like children, because we are not their children."

It did not sound very friendly but, on reflection, the logic was indisputable. So Jorge and I set out in pursuit, following the Indians along a well-defined trail across empty heathland, down into fertile valleys, across narrow, rocky river beds, then up again into the hills. The Indians stopped for neither food nor water but plodded on ahead, with us in hot pursuit.

Early in the afternoon we struggled up to the top of yet another range of hills and looked down at long last on the river Ayopaya at its junction with a smaller stream. We could see below us ten or twelve people grouped together on the only level piece of land by the river. This was to be the site of the Patchamama ceremony and so we slithered down the hillside as fast as we could. Grabbing camera and film-case, we hailed a canoe and were paddled over to the other side.

"Where are the Indians from Sacapampa?" I asked Jorge.

"They will come in a minute," he replied. "Get your camera ready, because the ceremony will start as soon as they arrive."

I loaded a reel of colour film and, while I was waiting, I decided to get out my small cassette tape recorder to tape the music of the flute being played by one of the men from Independencia. While I was doing this I missed the arrival of the Sacapampa Indians and, when Jorge called to me to join him, the six of them were already walking up the trail from the river bank. I was amazed at the change in their appearance. All were dressed in what I took to be their ceremonial costumes, which they must have been carrying when they left Sacapampa. Most striking of all was the vividly-coloured feathered headdress which each of them wore. The feathers were long, ornate and intricately mounted on a large headband, much more startlingly and colourful than the simple headdress of short, shabby feathers worn by the Mosetene Indians of the river Beni settlements. They also wore coloured cotton streamers tied to their plain smocks, and each one carried an enormous wooden sword in the shape of an outsize machete.

They walked slowly and with exaggerated dignity up the trail to the small clearing which had a tall, straight-limbed tree in the centre.

I filmed their arrival without meeting any protest but when I followed them into the clearing to take some close-up shots, the leader, whom I recognised as the Shaman, glared at me.

"*Yoxi* ('go away')" he spat at me ferociously.

I dropped the camera to my side and looked appealingly at our own *chunka camayoc,* who had agreed to my filming. He looked straight past me as if I were not there; so I turned to Jorge.

"Better not get too close to the ceremony," he suggested. "Why not film from over there just outside the clearing. I will make it O.K. with the Shaman."

This suited me perfectly well since, with my zoom lens, I could get some reasonably close-up shots without intruding at all.

The Shaman knelt down beside a tree at the edge of the clearing, and unpacked a number of small items which he had brought, wrapped up in a piece of cloth. As the pitifully sad dirge from the flute player whined on and on, I edged slowly towards the Shaman to see what he had laid out on the ground. First there was the inevitable heap of coca leaves, together with a bundle of brightly-coloured fibres that appeared to be lengths of dyed wool. There were pieces of maize bread and a dozen or more small biscuits, similar to the maize biscuits they always ate, but made in definite shapes. Some were circular discs that might have represented the sun or the moon, and others were in the shape of animals and trees.

Then two *mestizos* dressed in shirts and jeans came into the clearing, carrying between them the wizened, shrunken body of a baby llama. The fact that the two men were carrying the body must have had a ritual significance, because it was less than one metre long, and could not have weighed more than a kilo. When they had placed the body reverently on the ground in front of the Shaman, the two men returned behind the tree where I was standing. As I furtively raised my camera to focus on the clearing, I noticed that the whole group of six or seven men and women from Independencia were standing beside me, shielding me from the Shaman as I began to film the ceremony.

The flute-player came and stood just inside the clearing and continued to play his mournful music as the *chunka camayocs* and their three companions came dancing into the open spaces. The dance fitted the music well enough in the sense that it was slow, not very spectacular or energetic, and almost without rhythm. The Indians looked colourful enough in their bright costumes, but their movements were desultory and without animation or enthusiasm. They merely shuffled around the clearing in no particular order, taking half-hearted swipes at imaginary bushes with their wooden machetes.

Thinking that I must have missed some deep message hidden in this pale imitation of a ceremonial dance, I sidled over to Jorge to ask him to explain.

"They are clearing the land", he whispered, "so that Patchamama can enter without hindrance. Now they will call her," he added excitedly as the dancers shuffled over to sit in a tight circle about the Shaman. The music stopped, and the onlookers, who had been moving around to get a good view, stood motionless and silent.

I focused my camera on the Patchamama offerings which were spread out in front of the Shaman. The almost imperceptible whirring of the camera made quite a loud noise in the oppressive silence, and the Shaman turned round and glared. Jorge tugged my sleeve, and indicated that I should stop.

This was not a bitter blow, as it turned out, because the rest of the ceremony was almost statuesque in its lack of movement or excitement or clamour. For three or four minutes the Shaman sat motionless and silent, as though he were in a trance. Then he slowly picked a handful of coca leaves from the heap, and one by one, with great deliberation, he tossed them into the air. When the *chunka camayocs* joined in and started to throw an occasional coca leaf, the Shaman seemed to stiffen his body as he closed his eyes and dropped his head on to his chest. He remained absolutely motionless for ten minutes as if he were in a hypnotic trance. Then he slowly raised his head and, with his eyes still shut, he chanted to the skies.

One of the *camayocs* handed him a few biscuits, and the Shaman replaced them on the ground beside him while he chanted to Patchamama that here was food for her journey. When he was given the coloured ribbons. he tossed them high into the air, telling Patchamama that they would make fine clothes to keep her warm. The biscuits in the shape of trees were thrown into the air with a message I did not fully understand, but afterwards Jorge told me that they were offered as shelter and protection against the storms she might encounter.

By now the Shaman was becoming much more voluble and excited, and when he lifted the shrunken body of the llama about his head his incantations were delivered with emotion bordering on hysteria.

The others in the ceremonial group remained silent and apparently unmoved. It was left to the Shaman to shriek his incantations to Patchamama. He thanked her for coming to them, praised her for her goodness, and acknowledged that she and she alone could bring prosperity to the new 'camp of cultivation'.

I did not dare approach the Shaman, since it had been made quite clear that I would be interfering with the ceremony. Not even the 'civilised Indians' of Independencia went near, but I was just able to record the much quieter incantations that followed. I got Jorge to place my cassette recorder on the ground quite near to the Shaman, before we both retired some distance away.

The Shaman subsided on to his haunches. He sat absolutely motionless, speaking softly, as if he were engaged in an earnest conversation with some unseen spirit.

"Patchamama has come," whispered Jorge urgently, and he held his finger to his lips. No one moved or spoke, and for fully five minutes the only sounds were the distant roar of the river and the occasional cries of the birds. Later, when we replayed the tape, we found that the Shaman had again offered Patachamama comforts for her journeys, so that she might often return to bring prosperity to their cultivations. At the end of his quiet incantation he closed his eyes, and let his head sink on to his chest while the group of Indians from Independencia took up the theme, and they also spoke to Patchamama. Quietly they reinforced the Shaman's plea that she might accept their offerings and bring good fortune to their cultivation.

Five minutes later the Shaman rose to his feet slowly and melodramatically. He threw his arms upwards, looked to the sky, and shrieked out one long, desolate cry such as you might expect from a man falling from a high building. Then he dropped his arms, turned and strode briskly away from the ceremonial site back down to the river, followed by the dancers still dressed in their feathered headdresses.

The villagers from Independencia gathered round the spot where the Shaman had been sitting. They quickly collected all the offerings to Patchamama, heaped them together and set fire to the threads of fibre and cotton.

Now that the Shaman had left, it seemed safe to get out my camera once again. No one objected, and so I was lucky enough to get a filmed record of the offerings before they burned slowly into a pile of cinders.

At once the local people started clearing the area, and two of them began to dig small channels with a special spade, which was like an enormous metal arrowhead tied to a wooden shaft. There was a thick stump of wood tied across the shaft just above the metal tip, so that the digger could use one foot to thrust the sharp point downwards into the earth and pick out a narrow channel, which would obviously be the seed bed. They were wasting no time in preparing for the sowing of a new crop.

Jorge and I loaded all our equipment on the canoe, paddled back across the river to collect the mule, and set off on the long uphill walk to Independencia. Surprisingly we found the army jeep and driver still waiting for us. We drove back to Cochabamba and then took the regular flight to La Paz.

I spent the entire evening with Dr. Carlos Ponce Sangines. I suggested that there seemed to be many important and unknown ruins down the river Cotacajes, and that a large-scale expedition by professionals would be well worthwhile. I also told him that there was still gold to be found in the ruins of the interior. Even though I would keep my promise, and not reveal the exact location of any significant caches of gold ornaments, the publication of my own personal adventure story might draw attention to the area, and make it another target for the *huaceros*.

Dr. Carlos may well have made a mental note of this information but, to my great disappointment, he received it all with an air of resignation rather than the unbounded enthusiasm I had hoped for.

I drew the circle of forts from Cochabamba eastwards to Santa Cruz, northwards to Santa Ana and Aucapata and southwards through the Yungas to the river Cotacajes, Independencia and back to Cochabamba. This comprehensive system of defensive barriers seems to be guarding the hills and fertile valleys around the area of Isiboro and Chapare, I suggested.

"The Indians on the perimeter tell me there are many large settlements of indigenous people in this unknown and unexplored area," I added. "Could these possibly be the Incas who escaped from the *conquistadores*?"

Dr. Carlos looked dubious.

"They might be people who have always lived there," he replied. "They may have been conquered by the Incas, and they may have been absorbed into the empire, but we do not know. We shall never know until the anthropologists study their way of life, and until we archaeologists can study their buildings and their ceramics."

"What about the immense circle of forts?" I demanded. "Surely they were built to guard an area of great importance?"

"That does seem to be the most logical explanation," Dr. Carlos agreed, "but there might have been other reasons. Perhaps each fort was built to guard one comparatively small area where one tribe lived, although I admit that this is a less likely explanation. We know about the line of forts between Cochabamba and Santa Cruz," he went on, "and we have always supposed that they were built to protect the valuable and fertile valley of Cochabamba ('the rich valley', in Quechua) from the nomadic Guaranee Indians of the Matto Grosso and the jungles on the borders of Bolivia and Brazil."

"What about the large settlements and cities I heard about in Chapare and along the river Isiboro?" I insisted.

"As you say, you have only heard about them," Dr. Carlos replied dubiously. "We would have to carry out a long and detailed study before we could say anything."

The Director's next remark explained most, if not all his discouraging and disappointing reaction.

"There are no more than three qualified archaeologists in the National Institute, and we have much work to do in Bolivia," he said rather sadly. "An expedition to Chapare would take most of our resources, our staff and our money. Furthermore, we are already engaged in three important projects: the excavations in Iscanwaya, the study of the Mound culture in Beni, and new investigations around Lake Titicaca."

He must have sensed my frustration and disappointment, because he underlined the problem. "I would like to carry out a preliminary investigation, and we certainly will do so one day, but I cannot say when. Our present projects have been approved by the Minister, and they must be completed first. Perhaps in two or three years' time we can organise a study, and you could give us tremendous assistance."

I had one last card up my sleeve.

"Supposing I can go back to England and tell about my discoveries so far," I suggested. "Possibly I could get academic and financial support. Could we mount an expedition from England?"

Dr. Carlos looked thoughtful as he considered the proposition.

"If you tell only a few of the scientists we know and approve of, it is a possibility. If they contact me, and agree to work under the jurisdiction of the National Institute, it is just possible that I may get permission," he concluded. "But don't build up too many hopes."

His message was quite clear. He was not wildly enthusiastic about my hypothesis, but it might be something to attract the National Institute in the years to come. He was not closing the door, but neither was he giving the idea any priority. If, however, I could come up with the finance, and the whole-hearted enthusiasm of some of Britain's top scientists, there seemed to be the distinct possibility of a much earlier start.

My precarious financial situation made it imperative to return home to work, but I did so with a fair degree of hope and expectation, which lasted only a very short time. None of the qualified experts I consulted when I returned to Britain in October 1976 would even consider the possibility of the existence of Paititi or of unknown Indian tribes who might have been descended from the Incas who escaped at the time of the Spanish conquest. A few of the scientists were interested in some of the news I brought back from Bolivia, but they all derided the hypothesis that any Inca descendants could be living in Bolivia today. In nearly all the conversations I had with the academics I was left in no doubt that a poorly-presented hypothesis by a person without qualifications was not really a subject for serious consideration.

I wrote at once to Dr. Carlos to tell him of my abysmal lack of success; that there was no support for the argument that there had ever been a significant occupation of Bolivia by the Incas or that there were pure-bred Inca survivors anywhere in South America. That was the end of my search, or so it seemed.

To my immense joy and satisfaction, Dr. Carlos, the most conservative of all scientists, leapt to my defence. He telephoned from La Paz to pour scorn on the doubters. With nationalistic pride he claimed that Bolivia held the key to the history of South America. There was no doubt in his mind that his country had much to tell the world about the Inca culture and, most important of all, there were communities of the descendants of the Incas still living in Bolivia, which the scientists of La Paz knew all about. I might be guessing about the unknown Indians of Paititi, but if I would return he would take me to known descendants of the Incas in northern Bolivia in a mountain range called the Nudo de Apolobamba.

"It is said that they know an old Inca road which leads to the Lost City of the Incas—as you people always call it. This is the city supposedly discovered by your Colonel Fawcett," he said.

Why he had never told me this exciting news before I shall never know, but I have my suspicions. I believe that he was dead set against anyone who might be merely hunting for gold, and it had taken me a long time to demonstrate beyond all doubt that this was not my motive. He was also angered by the way his country had been written off by some English scientists; he certainly seemed very anxious that I should return and film more evidence of Inca occupation. He also dangled another carrot. "We have also made new discoveries near Lake Titicaca," he told me, "and you can film there, as well, if you return."

Before I put the telephone down my mind was made up. I

knew I had to return. The big question to resolve was the financing of one last expedition. I had two mortgages on my house and an overdraft at the bank beyond which I could not go. There was only one piece of property I now possessed which would raise enough money if I sold it, and that was my car, and as I was a freelance reporter for the B.B.C., covering the south west of England, the car was an essential tool of my trade. Unless I returned with instant success, and with the material to sell in order to replace the car at once, I knew I should be on a downward spiral.

For weeks I thought about all the ramifications, and in the end I decided that a brave death would be better than an empty existence in the doldrums of frustration. I sold my car, and prepared for the final journey.

When I told Dr. Carlos, he outlined his plans to have me escorted to Lake Titicaca to film the new discoveries in that area. Then I would be taken to the Callawaya Indians in Northern Bolivia, who might take me to see their camps of cultivation in the lowlands, where I might also see the Lost City, or at least *another* lost city. This would be a long and arduous journey, Dr. Carlos warned me.

With this warning I made my preparations. Clark's, the local shoe factory close to my home in Plymouth, spent two weeks making me a special pair of extra-strong hiking boots. Made of very fine soft leather, they laced up well above my ankle to afford some protection from reptiles and insects, and they were extremely comfortable.

I visited the Survival School at nearby R.A.F. Mountbatten, and they were also most helpful. I showed them some of the methods the Indians had used to trap animals, and how to cook eggs and heat water in orange peel, cook fish wrapped in brown paper, and roast bodies in clay. They showed me some of their methods for survival training, and, most useful of all, they gave me a complete survival kit including medicines, small knives and tools, and a supply of dehydrated food and chocolate. It was a special chocolate with a very sweet and deliciously strong taste. I could not resist it and, I'm ashamed to admit, I ate the whole half-pound block before I even set out.

My daughter was married at the end of May 1977, and two days later I was on the aircraft, once again bound for La Paz.

CHAPTER ELEVEN

The Callawayas

I ARRIVED IN LA PAZ on 3rd June, knowing that I had three to four months of dry weather during which I could travel anywhere in Bolivia in order to obtain enough material to demonstrate that it would be well worth while for large and well-organised, professional expeditions to enter this little-known world. Lack of finance would certainly prevent me doing any more than that.

Time was short but, to my delight, Dr. Carlos had everything organised. He introduced Oswaldo Rivera, one of the bright young university graduates attached to the National Institute of Archaeology. As I understood it, he was working on a Ph.D. thesis, but would like to take some time off to conduct me on a tour of Tiwanaku, Lake Titicaca and Copacabana.

This area, said by some Bolivian archaeologists and anthropologists to be the cradle of civilisation in South America, would form an essential chapter to any story about the Incas, but I had reservations. With so little time left, I felt bound to point out to Dr. Carlos that both Tiwanaku and Lake Titicaca were very well known. They were even on the package-tour itinerary of some tour operators, and they had certainly been written about by many professional archaeologists in the last twenty years. Dr. Carlos himself was recognised all over the world as the main authority on the subject of Tiwanaku. Surely I could extract all the relevant information from his many books on the subject? Then I could spend my limited time on obtaining the essential evidence of the little-known descendants of the Incas who, according to his letters, still live in Bolivia.

"You can film both," Dr. Carlos said firmly. "We are making important new discoveries in Tiwanaku, as well as much deeper studies of known sites on the shores of Lake Titicaca. Oswaldo will show you all these things, and will then arrange for someone to guide you to the communities of the Callawayas in the mountains to the north near the Peruvian border. I think you will find this visit very interesting, because the Callawayas are direct descendants of the tribe who were the medicine men of the Inca culture. They still practise their cures with herbal medicines all over South America even today."

"What will this cost me?" I asked anxiously.

"The journey to Lake Titicaca will cost you nothing except for your own food and lodging. You will go in our own jeep as our guest and, if you sleep in your tent most of the time, it will cost very little."

"And the journey to see the Callawayas?"

Dr. Carlos was thoughtful. "You will have to pay a guide," he answered, "and you will have to hire a jeep. Perhaps Oswaldo could arrange to organise both the vehicle and the guide for something like one hundred dollars per week, plus the cost of petrol and food for the guide."

I made a quick calculation, and it seemed that I might be able to spend about six weeks in the mountains, if I lived frugally, eating the native food, and sleeping in my tent. I had barely two thousand dollars left, and that would have to be my total budget. I could see no way in which I should ever be able to borrow any more money—ever. This would have to be the 'make or break' trip.

During the two days of earnest discussions with Dr. Carlos, I wrote a detailed summary of the facts and the theories we had established so far.

In theory the Mound culture of the Plains of Beni was the first organised nation of indigenous people in South America. The nation may have been founded about twenty thousand years ago and, to judge by the thousands of earth mounds they built, and the thousands of miles of man-made canals and irrigation channels they constructed, there must have been several millions of them. Their territory stretched from the coast of Brazil, and encompassed all the lowland area as far north as the Caribbean coast.

All the available evidence shows that this enormous nation flourished until the epoch of excessive rainfall, about ten thousand years ago. As most of their crops failed year after year, they were forced to migrate into the Andes, taking with them a political and religious organisation and a knowledge of agriculture.

Exactly what happened over the next six or seven thousand years nobody knows, but the excavations carried out by the National Institute of Archaeology show the emergence of settled communities in the Altiplano between three and four thousand years ago. During the epoch of wet weather, the climate would have been much warmer than it is today in the high Andes. Agriculture could have thrived and, with an endless supply of stone available, it is reasonable to suppose that permanent cities of stone houses were built.

Next, following his excavations and carbon dating of ceramics, Dr. Carlos has established the fact that a culture called the Wankerani settled in the area north of lake Poopo in the southwest of Bolivia about the year 1200 B.C. Twenty-one settlements have been uncovered, seventeen of them on the high plateau, and four in the nearby lower valleys. By counting the numbers of dwellings, it is possible to estimate the total population at about ten thousand, or twenty per square mile. They appear to have lived a completely communal life, and never progressed beyond village status, surviving until the first century A.D.

Near the shores of Lake Titicaca (which would have covered a much larger area then it does today) the Bolivian archaeologists have unearthed the remains of two more early cultures. On the western shores, the Chiripa culture was formed around 1200 B.C. and, like the Wankerani, survived until the first century A.D. when, again like the Wankerani, it was taen over by the Tiwanaku. All the evidence shows that the Chiripas also reached village status with some higher skills, like stone sculpture, smelting of gold and copper, and the manufacture of well-made pottery.

The most important of all these early cultures in Bolivia was the Tiwanaku. It was founded on the southern and eastern shores of Lake Titicaca around 1500 B.C., and developed beyond village life in the first century A.D., when the Tiwanakotas reached urban status.

The Bolivians are satisfied that they have the evidence to prove that the Tiwanaku culture flourished in various cities from thefirst to the fifth century A.D., during which time it developed further and expanded to form an empire. The people obtained gold from the rivers to make sumptuous jewellery; sea shells from the Pacific coast; and copper from the mines of Corocoro and Quimsachata.

By the time the empire reached its maximum power in A.D., 900, it covered the whole of the Andean mountain range and the temperate valleys of the country of Bolivia, together with a wide coastal strip covering about one third of what is now Peru. So far, one hundred and twenty five settlements have been identified as belonging to this empire which covered an area of 230,000 square miles. Dr. Carlos estimates the total population, all of whom spoke Aymara—the language of the Tiwanaku culture—to have been three and a half million people, giving a density of population of about six per square mile, much greater than that of today.

But why did this brilliantly successful empire disintegrate during the thirteenth century A.D.leaving absolutely no evidence of a cataclysm or of conquest by a more powerful race of people? Scientists are baffled, but I think a likely explanation is another complete change of climate. I refer to the two notable volumes by Professor H. H. Lamb, Director of Climatic Research at the Universiry of East Anglia. He shows that an epoch of colder, drier weather developed around A.D.1000. It was nothing like an Ice Age, but it was cold anough to transform the high Andes into the bleak, barren wilderness it is today.

Without a surplus of food supplies, the Aymaras would have been forced to migrate to the lower, warmer slopes and valleys of the Andes in search of a better environment in which to grow food.

I suggest that it is not unreasonable to suppose that some groups of intelligent, well-organised Aymaras kept together and formed smaller cultures, like the Mollo, in the temperate valleys, and when the climate improved, some of the later generations of the Mollos might have returned to the higher slopes around Titicaca. Although it is very much an unsubstantiated theory, I believe it is possible that, at Lake Titicaca, the Mollos may have met and joined an advanced culture from Central America, or perhaps even some Europeans shipwrecked on the Caribbean shores, and so founded the Inca culture, some time during the thirteenth or fourteenth century.

It seems that the Incas were more intelligent than other Indians in South America, and extemely skilful in engineering, building, and, above all, organisation. As Dr. Carlos writes in one of his books, "The Inca Empire was a flaming streak. It brought cohesion into all the Andean region as it united the hundreds of tribes and small cultures scattered through the western half of South America after the disintegration of the great Aymara nation."

The Incas introduced the Quechua language and the pyramid system of government to all the tribes they conquered or assimilated into their empire. It seems possible that the small percentage of Aymara Indians who remained on the high plateau may have submitted to Inca control without completely giving up their own culture. There is still a significant number of indigenous people living in and around La Paz who proudly claim Aymara ancestry, and who still speak the Aymara language.

The Inca control of the Andean peoples lasted for only eighty-three years, from 1440–1523, so it is difficlt to see how they could have built all the magnificent stone cities and paved highways with which they are credited.

Dr. Carlos agrees with me that it is more likely that these were built by Aymara and the Mollos, the small culture which developed after the disintegration of the Aymara empire. Bolivian scientists are increasingly favouring the theory that the Incas were the organisers and administrators of one of the great empires of the New World, but not the builders of it.

I put my theory about the dissolution of the Aymara empire to Dr. Carlos, and he agreed at once that an epoch of cold, dry weather could have brought about the fall of the empire. He agreed that it was a possible explanation, and offered some further support for the suggestion. He pointed out that, if the crops failed year after year, the farmers would blame the leaders and their gods, who would then lose credibility and authority. A breakdown in government would hasten the breakup of the empire, as disillusioned masses migrated in search of both food and leadership.

Two days after my arrival in La Paz, Oswaldo and I set out in the archaeologist's jeep to visit Tiwanaku and Lake Titicaca. For a fortnight I visited the impressive ruins at Tiwanaku, and more than five magnificent sites on Lake Titicaca and Copacabana. All were interesting, but none held out for me the harm and excitement of finding a site in the jungle. I wanted to know what happened to the Incas after the Spanish conquest, rather than what they were doing at the height of their powers. I longed to be off into the interior.

I saw exactly what everyone meant, however, about the skill and precision of the stone-masons. Flanges, niches and curves had been cut and matched to perfection. One extensive ruin near some hot springs held a great stone bath two metres high and a metre in diameter. It had four stone steps on the outside and another four inside. A Spanish chronicler said that on the first day of every new moon the Inca would be carried on his litter down to this bath, which was almost filled with warm thermal water. He stood in the bath with the water up to his shoulder and then, with due pageantry and ceremony, he was bathed by his concubines in what must have been an idyllic setting, looking across the sparkling waters of the lake.

Finally I managed to convey to Oswaldo my impatience to be off and he then produced my guide, Geraldo de Plata. Aged about twenty-five, Geraldo said that he was descended from the original people of Titicaca before the Incas came. However, I soon realised that I was talking to an educated and knowledgeable man, and was not at all surprised to learn that Geraldo's sophisticated manner was the result of having studied in the University of Lima in Peru. Later I asked how an Indian family could have afforded to send their son far away for a university education, but he could only hazard a guess. "I know his father is very wealthy," he said. "Perhaps he found gold on his land. I think you will find Geraldo very useful, because he has so much local knowledge. He can speak Quechua; he has his own jeep; he knows the people; he is ver interested in helping you to make your film."

Two days later we set out towards the mountains which form the border between Bolivia and Peru. For most of that first day the jeep crashed and shuddered along the stony track which had been bulldozed out of the vast, empty hillsides. None of the hamlets we passed through enjoyed the luxury of running water, lavatories, electric light or asphalt road, but they all had at least one shop and a café, where weary travellers could stop for a can of beer or a cup of coffee. To judge by their appearance, the inhabitants were nearly pure Indian, but the fact that they wore western clothing, listened to the blaring transistor radio in the café, and obviously had a regular trade with the larger centres of populaton, all created a air of decadent civilisation, a dull acceptance of their way of life. There was no animation, no pride or pleasure in their lives and, to judge by the way they paid scant attention to our arrival, they must have seen many travellers passing through. Indeed, in Puerto Acosta on the north-eastern tip of Lake Titicaca we found a mud hut loaded with fifty-gallon drums of petrol for sale, and Geraldo topped up our tanks so that we could keep our five gallon containers strapped on the back of the jeep as a reserve.

When we reached Apolo, Geraldo explained our plan of campaign.

"I will leave the jeep at the army post here, and hire two mules to take us on the two-day journey to the Callawayas. I know the army officers, and I know a farmer who will hire us mules, if you will give me five hundred pesos to pay for them. While I am gone, you had better buy food for us to last a week at least."

"I've got packets of dehydrated food, as well as presents for the Indians," I told Geraldo, but he looked at me derisively.

"These are not people you can buy with trinkets," he said scornfully. "They want money, just as we do. And we want some proper food. It is cold up there, and I am not going to live on powder and water. We must have meat and eggs and tins of food."

"Well, you'd better get another mule to carry all this food and our equipment," I suggested.

"I'll try," Geraldo said, as he marched off down the village street.

I went into the two village stores and bought a sackful of meat, cheese, coffee, powdered milk, biscuits and raisins. An hour later Geraldo returned witn two Indians, leading three mules between them.

"I shall now take the jeep to the army camp," Geraldo announced. "My two *amigos* will load up the mule, and we can set out on our journey. This giant of a mule is for you. He is strong and, as you see, he even has a saddle. You are very lucky. I have to ride bareback. If you give all the cases to these two men we shall be ready by the time I return."

Geraldo's confident and authoritative manner was most heartening. He was in command of the situation, and knew his way around.

An hour later, when we set off on our two-day mule-ride to the headwaters of the river Tuiche, I asked him why he knew the area so well.

"I have been here on three visits in recent years," he told me. "I wrote a thesis on the Callawayas when I was at the University. That is why they asked me to guide you."

My heart leapt at this exciting piece of news. It sounded like an ideal introduction to the Callawayas in their remote and isolated villages. To visit them in the company of a sniversity graduate who had already made friends with them and studied their way of life—nothing could be better.

As we plodded slowly up the gently-winding pathway leading towards the snowcaps, I decided to take Geraldo into my confidence. I told him the whole story about my search for the last descendants of the Incas over the twenty-five years. I explained that I needed some tangible evidence, and that was why I was making a film record of my expedition.

Geraldo thought for some minutes about this before he came out with a firm proposal.

"I need the money for guiding you on this particular journey," he said firmly, "but I am prepared to help you much more, if you will do one thing for me."

My attention was riveted.

"I can show you Callaway ceremonies thet no white man has ever seen. I can arrange for you to walk the Inca road, and visit places that no one knows about. I can take you to prehistoric cities that are not known about—even in La Paz. I can do these extra things if you will teach me how to use that camera of yours."

"Of course I will," I replied excitedly. "If you make my journey worthwhile I will certainly share m camera with you, and show you all you need to know."

"Good," said Geraldo, smiling for the first time since we'd met.

Having broken the ice so successfully, I took the opportunity of discussing my theories with him. I told him about the primitive tribes I'd met in Colombia, and of their oft-repeated legend that Ijka, the Injka (or the Incas) were still hiding in the jungle-covered hills. Finally I put it to him that, according to official figures, more than one million Incas seemed to have vanished without trace, and it was quite conceivable that many, if not all, of their descendants could be living still in unknown and unexplored hills north and south of the headwaters of the Amazon.

"Is that what you say in your country?" Geraldo said scornfully.

"No," I admitted. "This is only my opinion. All they said in my country is that there is a lost city of the Incas in the Amazon jungle, which was discovered by an Englishman called Colonel Fawcett when he took an expedition to draw up the borders of Bolivia with Peru and Brazil."

Geraldo suddenly became excited. "You mean Fowsey of Peru," he asked, his eyes lighting up. "I heard of the Englishman Fowsey in Lima. He found a city of gold, it is said, but he never came back with the gold."

"That's the man," I agreed. "He was an officer and a man trusted by the governments of Peru, Bolivia and Brazil, and that is why they asked him to decide on the exact boundaries between these countries. He must have been a man of honour to be trusted; so we should believe him."

Geraldo did not soften his attitude of scorn and derision.

"All through the years people have talked about the fabulous lost city of the Incas made of pure gold," he said, "But it does not exist. It is a joke which the Indians played on white men to make them look fools."

Geraldo must have seen the doubt and disbelief on my face, because he pressed home his argument forcibly.

"The Indians of ancient times were clever people," he announced gleefully. "When they saw that what you people wanted was gold, they invented rivers of gold, cities filled with gold, and hoards of precious metals. They were all a long way to the east, in the Amazon jungle. Why did you think they were there? Now all stupid, greedy white men go searching the jungle and leave the Indians in peace." Geraldo doubled up with laughter. "There *are* lost cities," he concluded in a more serious vein. "I will show you some. There is also gold, especially along some of the rivers, but there is no fortune in gold lying around waiting to be collected, nor is there any city of gold. That is all a complete myth."

I was not particularly dismayed to hear Geraldo's version of the lost city, and was pleased to discover that he was not going to be a yes-man. He had made a thorough study of the history of his own people: I could take careful note of what he had to say.

I sounded him out on the subject of the Inca empire, and the possibility that many Incas might have escaped annihilation or slavery at the hands of the *conquistadores.* I asked him if he and his fellow students believed in the legend of Paititi, and specifically if he agreed that it could be in the hills, enclosed by the line of forts I had filmed north of Cochabamba.

Geraldo pursed his lips dubiously.

"I do not think it is possible, but I know some who would agree with you," he aditted cheerfully. "There are those who say there is much yet to be discovered in the eastern foothills of the Andes, and no one can deny your claims, because the area is unexplored." He warmed to his subject. "You Europeans keep on about the Incas all the time," he said n an accusing tone of voice. "Who are the Incas? Am I an Inca? I don't know. Nobody knows. Englishmen were a mixture of various tribes when the Romans came and conquered and made England part of the Roman empire, but are you a Romn? Do you consider yourself a descendant of the Romans?"

"That was a long, long time ago," I observed.

"So was the Inca empire," Geraldo protested. "Five hundred years ago, they cnquered nearly all the indigenous races in this part of South America, and made them all one people, one empire with one rule, and one language and way of life. To achieve this conquest the first Incas uprooted many of the tribes and races of people, and made them build new cities and new homes in different parts of the continent. They were so busy building and adapting themselves to a new way of life in strange surroundings that they did not have the time or the strength or the means to revolt. This enforced migration made them easier to control.

"When the Spaniards killed the Inca leaders, the whole empire collapsed, because it was like a huge body without eyes to see or brains to think. Many of the conquered tribes ran away when their rulers were gone. Maybe hundreds of thousands escaped back to the lower hills where they had lived before their conquest by the Incas. One of these areas could be the foothills north of Cochabamba. Another area could be on the other side of the hills we are crossing now, and in the fertile valleys beween here and the river Beni.

"We do not know for sure, but it is just possible that there are large communities of Indians hidden away in these forest-covered hills, but are they truly Incas? No sir, I don't think they are genuine Incas, and so I cannot agree that there is any lost empire of the Incas," Gerald concluded dogmatically.

"Not even living the Inca way of life?" I queried.

"Ah yes, that could be," Geraldo had to admit. "They could retain some aspects of the life-style taught them by the Incas. In fact, the Callawayas say that they control some tribes living down in the foothills. Perhaps we will try to visit them."

That evening, as we pitched my tent on a rocky plateau, Geraldo prepared to roast some pieces of meat on spits over the open fire, and I gave him his first lesson in filming. It was very difficult to keep his over-confidence in check, but he was exceedingly intelligent and certainly made rapid progress. Most important of all, he was obviously very pleased to have the opportunity I offered him, and I guessed that his genuine gratitude would pay handsome dividends when we reached the Callawayas.

Next day we continued our mule-ride higher and higher into the mountains and, as we nearly reached the snow line, the old problem of altitude sickness returned. I found myself in an almost permanent state of breathlessness, and my head ached until I took a dose of pain killers.

After crossing one snow-covered peak I was relieved to see that the path fell quickly towards a spectacular plateau enclosed by snowy peaks. As we descended towards the little village of stone-built houses nestling at the edge of the plateau, the surrounding hills offered some protection against the biting cold wind that had been cutting right through my protective clothing.

"This is where the Callawayas live," said Geraldo, indicating the village ahead of us. "There are more villages in the mountains all around, but this is one of their chief communities, and it is the one I know."

A cursory glance revealed about thirty dwellings plus one larger building in the centre of what looked like a traditional village square or meeting-place. Indeed, all the Indians that were to be seen—approximately twenty of them—were assembled in this central square. One man, dressed in a black cloak and black knee-breeches, was blowing a few mournful and tuneless notes on a horn that, from a distance, looked just like an old-fashioned hunting horn made of animal bone. To brighten his sombre black dress he carried two bright red woollen bags, one on each shoulder, and he wore a strange white hat that looked rather like an upturned pudding basin with a narrow rim.

"That is Humumari ('the bear', in Quechua) the son of the chief," Geraldo announced proudly. "He welcomes us; so they must remember me. The others are all women who have been sent to greet us."

The women also wore sombre black woollen shapeless dresses, but they all had bright-red, patterned cloaks around their shoulders, and the same white pudding-basin hats with coloured bands round the rims. As we approached, the whole reception party stood motionless and silent with their heads slightly bowed and their eyes looking down towards the ground. I noticed the the women wore two huge soup-spoons dangling from cords around their shoulders and resting across their breasts. Some of them wore the spoons hanging downwards and some wore theirs pointing up. I quickly asked Geraldo if this were significant.

"The spoons downwards means that they are married. Upwards means they are free, and can be bought as a wife. You want one" he asked, chuckling.

I was too preoccupied with the magnificence of this unforgettable scene to rise to the bait. In front of us was the colourfully-dressed reception committee and, beyond them, the lonely village surrounded by the pale-green, rocky slopes of the steep hills with the spectacular snow-covered peaks towering over all.

I may be wrong, but I doubt if many other white men have ever seen this particular setting because, if they had, they would surely have written graphic prose or poetry, and composed music to describe the magnificent and unforgettable grandeur of this unique scene.

We stopped, dismounted, and handed over the mules to the little group of five women who came trotting up to us with their eyes averted. My first impression was that their slightly blotchy, olive-coloured skins were not so pure and smooth as one might have expected in the crystal-clear atmosphere of this glorious environment.

Geraldo approached the horn-player, who stood meekly with head bowed, and spoke to him in Quechua. The horn-player did not answer Geraldo's question, but he led us across the parade ground, past the row of small, neat houses, whose doorways were full of curious onlookers.

Just beyond these houses built around the open parade ground was the one much larger building which, I assumed, was their meeting-place or community centre. Attached to the side wall of this building was a lean-to shelter, also built of stone with a thatched roof, just like all the other houses.

The wooden door was thrown open, and we were ushered into the one small bare room with no furniture or fittings of any kind.

CHAPTER TWELVE

Calling the condor

THE NEXT DAY WE were ushered into the presence of the *amautas,* the three wise men who ruled this community of Callawayas. Solemn and impassive, they sat on a stone bench at the side of the meeting-hall, showing no sign of recognition or greeting. There was not the slightest sign of hostility either, however; so I was not too disheartened at such an apparently chilly reception. The indigenous people of Bolivia seldom smile, for they do not have a light-hearted attitude to life. Their sense of humour seems non-existent; jokes and friendly japes are foreign to their nature, but this does no necessarily mean that they are bitter or antagonistic.

Geraldo held a long conference with the *amautas*, during which he negotiated in Quechua the terms of our stay with them. To house and feed us both would cost me a total of twenty pesos (one dollar) a day, which seemed ridiculously cheap and, at my request, Geraldo warned the *amautas* that we'd like to stay with them for several weeks.

"Tell them I want to study their customs, habits and way of life," I told Geraldo. "Tell them I will give them some money in exchange for this information, but don't tell them anything about filming yet. These primitive people are alway scared to start with: they think I am stealing their souls."

Geraldo, who had been squatting down to speak with the *amautas,* slowly drew himself upright, and his blood-flecked eyes gave me a withering glance.

"These are not primitive people," he snarled, "and they will understand what you are saying. Many of them have travelled all over South America. They are exceptionally gifted medical experts, who cure people that your own doctors have given up as hopeless cases. They are as civilised as you and me," he hissed angrily. "They know exactly what films and photographs are; so do not say these stupid things and offend them, not if you want me to help you make a good film."

"I'm sorry . . . I . . . had no idea," I stammered apologetically. "I'll leave it all to you," and I walked away very shamefaced, to drink in the gloriously spectacular scenery, and let Geraldo's bitter remonstrations sink in.

Half an hour later he rejoined me to say that he had arranged for us to stay.

"I am not sure that you will want to stay a long time, however, because they will not give you much information," Geraldo admitted dubiously. "To start with, they will tell nobody—not even their own womenfolk—the secrets of their medical cures. Secondly, they will not talk about their past life, because they think you may be some kind of government agent who wants to take their land away from them."

"What's that got to do with past history?" I asked.

"It has happened before," Geraldo replied. "If settlers want to move into Indian territory they can do so, unless the Indians have lived there for many years, when they can claim ownership. So agents have investigated the past history of some tribes, hoping to prove that they have not occupied their land long enough to claim ownership. Then they can throw the Indians out, and settlers move in."

"Can't you tell them that I'm not even a Bolivian, that I come from the other side of the world?" I pleaded.

"I'll try," Geraldo said. "They may not know England, but they know Europe. I'll try to persuade them that you do not want to harm them, but it will take time. We Indians are suspicious of you Whites, and you can't blame us."

In spite of his university education and his civilised upbringing, Geraldo still had enough pride left to make his claim to be an Indian. His previous bitter outburst also made it clear to me that I should show the respect he thought the Indians deserved, and never act in any superior fashion. Eventually Geraldo himself volunteered to tell me all he knew about these people—if I paid him an extra two hundred pesos.

According to him, this settlement which they call Urina (the centre of communication) was one of the three principal villages of the Callawaya culture in the hills of the Nudo de Apolobamba. He had visited all three and, following his years of study, he had found out much about these Indians, who were acknowledged to have been the medicine men of the Inca culture.

The present-day Callawayas do not, however, refer to or acknowledge the existence of the Incas. They merely told Geraldo that their ancestors were the doctors who cured the illnesses of people 'all over the world'. It is likely that their 'world' did not extend beyond central South America in those days, but that is still a large area.

"Today their world really is the world," Geraldo continued. "The older men train every Callawaya youth, and tell him all the secrets of their medicine. The trainee undergoes examinations all the time and, when he is qualified, he takes on one of their practices. There is a Callaway *brujo* (witch-doctor) in every South American city," Geraldo told me. "There are several in the United States, and they once claimed that there are two or three in Europe, but I think they may have been boasting."

"Can you be sure they are all over South America?" I asked dubiously.

"Oh yes, that is certain," Geraldo affirmed positively. "Every body knows that and, when you have lived in Bolivia for some time, you will know that also."

"Do they just treat the Indians in the towns?" I asked.

"*Caramba*, no," Geraldo replied, as if he could scarcely believe I could be so stupid. "They treat every body from professors to presidents. Many high officials and white men go to the Callawaya doctors for a cure when their own doctors can do nothing for them. In every, town and city the Callawayas have practices, and they earn a great deal of money, which they bring back to their *ayllu*, and they all live off the money until the next one comes home, and his place is taken by one of the younger trainees. Last time I was here there were a few more than one hundred women and only about thirty men in the *ayllu*. A word of warning. Don't talk to a woman with two spoons hanging downwards from her neck. That means she is married, and almost certainly her husband is away. You see, they make every young man marry and have one child before he is allowed to go away to earn money. Then they can be sure he will return, but his wife must be absolutely faithful while he is away."

"There must be a lot of temptations, if the women outnumber

the men by about three to one," I observed.

"Yes indeed," Geraldo agreed, "and to make matters worse there is a constant stream of Indians from all over South America who come here for a miracle cure from the medicine men who have returned from their travels. That's why their rules governing their womenfolk are so strict."

I was fascinated by this wealth of first-hand information which Geraldo was giving me with such authority and knowledge. I continued questioning him with the same respect that any student might have for his tutor.

"If they have so much experience of living in towns and cities, why do they live such a primitive and traditional way of life here? Why don't they introduce some of the comforts and luxuries of civilisation?" I asked.

"They do," Geraldo replied vehemently. "They buy tins of food, pots and pans for cooking, pressure cookers, hair shampoos, knives, scissors and matches."

"But their village looks just as it must have done hundreds of years ago," I insisted, "and their clothing and appearance are absolutedly traditional."

"Certainly they weave their own woollen cloaks and underclothes," Geraldo admitted. "They are beautiful garments for this cold climate up here in the mountains. There is nothing they can buy in the shops that is half so good." He was thoughtful. "There is one item of clothing each witch-doctor brings back with him," he mused. "They love our trilby hats. You will see some of the older men who always wear a trilby hat wherever they go. It is a sort of badge of office. It announces that the wearer is one of the senior witch-doctors, who has been away to serve his time in civilisation and has returned. Otherwise they bring back only the food and the other items which the whole community can share. And, of course, they bring back money to buy everything the community needs."

It sounded very much like a primitive communist way of life and, indeed, over the next two weeks of living with the Callawayas this impression was confirmed. They appeared to live a tranquil life without any pressures, even if it was a rather low-key existence. Everything was provided by the members of the community, and shared out equally. Apart from the necessities of life purchased with the money brought back by the travelling witch-doctors, some potatoes and quinoa and yucca were grown on terraces on the slopes below the village. The women spent much of their time weaving colourful cloth by hand as they knelt at the looms outside their houses. Bread was baked in one enormous stone oven near the parade ground, and that too was shared out among the households. There appeared to be a perfect balance between supply and demand. Nobody went hungry, and there were no apparent surpluses. There were no luxuries and no personal possessions. Everything belonged to the community.

I do believe that, over a period of twenty-five years, I have evolved the most satisfactory way of making friends with Indian tribes, whether semi-civilised or not. I have found that obvious and sustained generosity plus a total lack of superiority and pride in my attitude is the best method. I give constantly—anything from a sweet to a smile to physical assistance in carrying out a job of work. By taking a genuine interest in their day-to-day life, and never being too proud to assist with the most menial tasks, I can eventually get them to accept me as a friendly person who poses no threat whatsoever. That is why I took my time in asking anything from them, so that they would not think that I was there to take advantage of them or to take anything that was rightfully theirs. The days I spent allaying their suspicions were all well rewarded.

The oldest of the three *amautas* (wise men), who appeared to be the leader, spoke reasonably good Spanish, and I was lucky enough to hold long conversations with him. In spite of Geraldo's warnings that these Callawayas could not be 'bought in exchange for trinkets', he was quite happy to accept my offer of a packet of cigarettes, a lighter, and a regular supply of toffees.

Mamani (the hawk), as he was called, was quite prepared to make a straightforward business deal with me. He would tell me some details about their way of life for a fee of twenty pesos (one dollar) per hour, but he warned me at once that there were many secrets which money would not buy.

Obviously I did not try to plunge in at the deep end, into those areas about which he was sensitive. I talked about their present way of life, and Mamani confirmed what Geraldo had told me, that everybody worked for the benefit of the community. There were no individual possessions. Each man was allowed one wife, and she was selected for him by the *amautas,* according to each man's value to the community. The *allakuna* (selected virgins) were handed over to prospective husbands at the Feast of Intip

Raymi, the June solstice. The young men who had made the largest contribution to the welfare of the community were offered the strongest and most desirable virgins.

There was no ceremony. The couple merely took over an empty room in the house of the girl's parents, and lived together on trial for up to one year. During the trial period the young man could reject his new wife as being unsuitable, and he could ask for a new virgin at the next Feast of Intip Raymi. The girl was then allocated as a wife to an older man who was a widower, or she could be sent to join the 'pool of unwanted women', where she would work as a servant of the community. As Mamani pointed out, this sort of arrangement encouraged the young girls to be such good wives that they would not be rejected. Clearly the women of this Callawaya community were inferior citizens as far as the men were concerned.

I asked Mamani about their gods, but he did not seem to understand what I was talking about, and I had to call Geraldo over to explain. Back came the answer that they treated Patchamama (Mother Earth) as their Supreme Being. Just like the Indians I had visited north of Cochabamba, the Callawayas offered food and drink to Patchamama at every meal, and asked her blessing whenever they built a new house or road, or made a long journey.

Encouraged by Mamani's willingness to answer questions, I decided to take a bolder step, and ask about ceremonies, particularly at birth and death. It seemed that there was no ceremony associated with the new-born child who, as I saw for myself during the following weeks, was treated with almost cruel indifference. Immediately after birth the child was put into a wooden cradle packed with cloth so that its head was always well above the level of its feet. Just like the children of the Indian families north of Cochabamba, the Callawaya baby was never picked up and nursed or suckled. Indeed the Callawayas seemed to be obsessed with the idea of acquiescent behaviour, and they even carried out the Inca method of stopping tantrums and outbursts of temper by tying wide bands of cloth tightly round the baby's head, if it was obstreperous. I also saw one baby lying on its back, held in position by a small flat piece of wood tied across its forehead. Both the wooden clamp and the bandages had the effect of changing the shape of the child's head into what the Indians called 'the beehive'.

As the Callawaya child grew up it was never shown love or affection. As soon as it could walk, the youngster was put into a small cylindrical hole the the ground outside the house, where it spent most of the day. The child was effectively buried up to its armpits and wrapped up in lengths of woollen garments so that it was safe, warm, comfortable . . . and ignored. This was its life until, at the age of six or seven, it was taken to the terraces to help with the cultivations and harvests, or, in the case of a girl, was taught to weave and to cook.

I asked if there were a ceremony at death, and was told that there was no large-scale ceremony, merely a small private mourning within the family. The bodies of dead women were taken down to the river in the valley nearly three hundred metres below the village and buried in a large communal grave for women, but when a man died—especially the head of a family—there were strict rules to be observed, as I was to see for myself when the father of one of the three *amautas* died after I had been there for a fortnight. His body was wrapped up in a huge bundle of twigs, leaves and long grass which were brought up from the river bank. The tightly-packed bundle was hung from the wooden rafters inside his own house, while the women of his family chanted a mournful song which said '*Sasay T'ikaway Mansaway*', which, according to Geraldo means 'A creature that no one can control'. I supposed that this was a tribute to someone they considered invincible, and Geraldo agreed.

When I talked to Mamani about the significance of this ritual, he told me that the body would remain in the house until the spirit had flown away. Everybody is reborn as a winged creature, according to Callawaya lore. The insignificant ones among us are reborn as flies or moths, while the head of a family might come back as a bird. The great leaders of the whole nation are reborn as condors, the most majestic and awe-inspiring creature of the South American skies.

Another ritual during the period of mourning for the dead Callawaya man was to prepare food for his long journey. Because there are so few birds up in the mountains, eggs are considered quite a delicacy; so the four eggs that the women began to cook for the dead man represented a very special dish. They lit a small fire of twigs and placed a large stone on either side of the fire to support what looked like a thin sliver of slate, which rested above the flames and heated up slowly. The four eggs were placed on this piece of stone and were cooked in their shells. This is not an uncommon way for primitive people to cook eggs, and in the past I have seen them remove the eggs from the red-hot stone immediately the shell started to crack. On this occasion, however, the fire was built up to a furnace, and the eggs, instead of cooking slowly, suddenly began to explode. This must have been the intention, because, when the first egg exploded, the yoke flew into the air where, presumably, the dead man's spirit was flying around. The explosion brought forth howls of delight from the assembled family who were grouped around Mamani, as he muttered some incantations. I watched every detail of this ritual, so that later, when I had won their confidence, I could ask them to re-enact the scene for my film camera. All these thoughts were blown away when the second egg exploded, and the yoke shot out like a squeezed orange pip and hit me on the shoulder. I brushed off most of the mess instinctively before I suddenly realised that the ritual had stopped, and that I was the centre of attention. The other two eggs exploded, but no one took any notice, as Mamani walked slowly up to me and examined my shoulder carefully.

Geraldo was just inside the dead man's house at this moment and, although I was not frightened, I was apprehensive enough to call him over. He and Mamani walked over to the fire talking earnestly, and I must say I wondered what the outcome would be. After five minutes Geraldo came back, beaming with pleasure.

"That was very fortunate, Mister. As far as these Callawayas are concerned it was an extremely significant accident. Patchamama approves of you, so you are now a very welcome guest. They are your friends, and they will do much more to help you."

"What an extraordinary accident," I said in amazement.

"The same thing happened to Oswaldo near Lake Titicaca some years ago, and the people of that village have been his friends ever since. Let us talk to Mamani at once, and ask about your filming. Now might be a good time. You wait in the house, and I will talk to the leaders."

It must have been almost an hour before Geraldo returned, but his triumphant smile of success heralded good news. I was to attend a special meeting of the three *amautas* evening. Beside Mamani there would be Hukumar (the bear) and Chipana (number nine). They would consider all my requests and, according to Geraldo, I was in great favour because of the egg incident; so it was most likely that all would be well. The fact that I was teaching Geraldo the rudiments of filming had obviously earned his gratitude, and he gave me the impression that he was making considerable efforts to help in my project.

I felt rather like a job applicant at a selection board, as I faced the three solemn and serious Indians sitting in line abreast on their stone bench. With Geraldo's help I explained that I wanted to tell the people of my country about the interesting life of the Callawayas, and about their skills as doctors. Geraldo, as a passing thought, added that the people of England did not know anything about the Callawayas' ability to cure illnesses and diseases, and this casual remark was a turning-point in the whole negotiation.

"They do not know what we can do?" Hukumar asked incredulously. "Tell them that we can cure people who are beyond the help of your own doctors."

"We have always been known as doctors," added Chipana. "They must know. Our ancestors could work miracles. They could even transplant hearts and livers and brains, but we have forgotten how to do these things."

I must have looked rather dubious about these unbelievable claims, because Mamani chipped in.

"You are thinking that these transplanted organs will be rejected," he said knowingly. "What our ancestors did was to transfuse blood from a pregnant woman into the person's body before he had a transplant, and that stops rejection. Your doctors do not know this."

Later I read an article in *The Times* of 29th September 1977 under the headline 'Why a foetus is not rejected', which said that Dr. Oldstone of Scrips Clinic in California had "measured the production of anti-bodies by a mother's cells and found it could be suppressed by selected cells from the cord blood". The report went on to say, "The existence of such cells may prove to have important implications for control of the immune response in transplant rejection and in allergies and auto-immune diseases that result from over-activity of the immune system."

Mamani then collected three engravings on stone from his house, and tried to explain more of the advanced medical practices of his ancestors, which they—the present-day Callawayas—have 'forgotten how to do'.

With the help of Geraldo's translation and explanation of some difficult words, and with the illustrations of the rock engravings to work on, I came to the conclusion that Mamani seemed to be claiming that his ancestors practised acupuncture, skin grafting, brain surgery and Caesarian operations. I cannot be dogmatic about this, because the language barriers meant that there were areas of doubt, but I think these were the claims he made.

He went on to tell me, and Geraldo confirmed all this, that today their doctors are called upon to cure 'fevers, paralysis, imbecility, growths in the body and all the illnesses of the mind'. I told Geraldo to explain to the *amautas* that I would like to film some of these medical cures taking place, so that I could show my people the miracles performed by the Callawayas. The three wise men pondered over this request in silence for a moment, and then broke into an animated conversation between themselves.

"What are they saying? I asked furtively.

"I don't know," Geraldo admitted with a baffled expression. "They are speaking their own secret language. Nobody else can understand."

I was about to question him on this so-called secret language when the *amautas* stopped talking together, and Mamani turned towards me. Speaking in Spanish, he said, "We will never show you the secrets of our medical cures but, if you want to take back a picture of another secret, we will call the condor for you."

I looked at Geraldo, because I did not really understand what Mamani meant, but Geraldo shrugged his shoulders in ignorance.

"But we will do this only if you promise to tell your people about our miracle cures," Mamani continued.

"Yes, I will tell them," I answered enthusiastically. "They will see the film you allow me to take."

"Then we will call the condor for you," Mamani said proudly. "The condor is the spirit of Huayna Capac, the great leader of our ancestors. He will come down from the skies to talk to us, and we are the only people who can do this, because he is our ancestor."

"He will come here to the village and talk to you?" I asked incredulously.

Mamani nodded.

"That would certainly be a miracle," I said to Geraldo. "I have seen a few condors in South America, but always floating hundreds of metres up in the sky. It is one of the most shy and elusive of God's creatures."

Geraldo seemed uncertain what to do next.

"You go back to our room,' he said finally, "and I will discuss this and find out exactly what they mean."

Nearly half an hour later he returned, smiling broadly.

"We are in luck," he said. "Because you are in great favour after the egg incident, and because they think you will bring more business to them, they are going to re-enact the ancient ceremony of the calling of the condor, and we may film it."

I liked the way Geraldo referred to us as a partnership in filming, because his whole-hearted co-operation would be invaluable; so I encouraged him.

"It is an ancient ceremony which they used to perform during the autumn and the spring equinoxes," he explained. "They used to sacrifice a virgin to the condor, who is supposed to be the spirit of Huayna Capac, their first great ancestor and the founder of the Callawayas. They don't make human sacrifices any more, because they are civilised now, but they still hold the ceremony."

But Huayna Capac was one of the Inca chiefs," I observed. "In fact, I believe he was the Inca who conquered Bolivia and established Collasuya, the south-eastern quarter of the Inca empire. This seems significant, since they never acknowledge any Inca ancestry."

"They are direct descendants of the Inca," Geraldo affirmed, "but four hundred years is a long time, and they have forgotten much of their history, no doubt. Perhaps only their ceremonies and legends remain as conclusive evidence."

"So when will the ceremony take place?" I asked.

"They have to toss the coca leaves in another ceremony," Geraldo told me. "The leaves will tell them when the condor will be prepared to come."

"Coca leaves?" I queried. "They only grow in the hot valleys; so how do they get them? Now I come to think of it, where do they get the maize, fruit and peppers I've seen them eating?"

"Yes, that's a good question," Geraldo observed. "They have a little contact with civilisation and, of course, their doctors bring back supplies when they return from the towns, but this does not explain the regular supply of coca and fresh fruit and vegetables they are receiving. I will try to find out were they come from."

"Meantime, while we await the condor ceremony, I will teach you more about filming," I said, to Geraldo's obvious pleasure.

During the next two days I took pictures of Urina, of the terraces of cultivation down towards the river bank, and of women weaving their brightly-coloured woollen garments. Geraldo demonstrated his intelligence by the speed with which he mastered the basics of filming, to become a most useful assistant to me.

The supply of food kept arriving twice a day from the communal kitchen, but individual Callawayas did not offer any personal hospitality and, in general, they suffered our presence without hostility of any kind, but without friendship either.

By day Geraldo and I wandered round the village and the surrounding area, taking film and making notes. In the evenings we discussed the way of life of the Callawayas at great length.

First of all I asked Geraldo about what he had described as a 'secret language' spoken by the *amautas* at our last conference, and I must have put my question in such a way that my disbelief was blatantly obvious.

"Any student of the history of South American Indians knows that they have a secret language," he replied haughtily. "The language of the Tiwanaku culture was Aymara, and that is spoken by seventy per cent of the indigenous population of Bolivia today. The Incas introduced the Quechua language, which many Aymara-speaking people can understand after some practice, but there is also a third language. It may have been introduced at the time of the Spanish conquest, or it may have been in existence already; we shall never know. The Spaniards certainly knew about it, and wrote about it in their reports."

"Do you mean that the idea was for the Indians to speak to each other without the Spaniards understanding?" I asked.

"I don't know, Mister. I have never been told," Geraldo admitted. "But this secret language still exists today, and some Indian tribes speak it when they don't want others to understand."

I still found this difficult to believe, and I said as much. Geraldo almost lost his temper.

"Why do you ask me these questions if you do not believe me?" he exploded. "So many people know about the secret language that it is not even a secret any more. There have been books written about it. You could learn to speak it if you like, but not many non-Indians bother to learn it."

"What books?" I asked. "I might try to learn it one day."

"I know one such book," Geraldo replied. "We studied it at the university. It is called *El Idiona Secreto de los Incas*, and it is written by Enrique Oblitas Poblete. It contains a grammar and a dictionary and thousands of words."

I only wish I had known about this book before my journey to meet the Callawayas because, when I bought a copy on my return to La Paz, I found it a fascinating and scholarly work by a man who had spent years with the Callawayas. The book contained references to several authors who also acknowledged the existence of a secret language. Sir Clements Markham in his book *The Incas of Peru*; H. A. Wedell in his report *Journeys to the North of Bolivia* and Jose Dominco Cortes in *The Republic of Bolivia* all refer to the belief that the secret language is still spoken by the Callawayas who, they say, are known throughout the Americas as medical geniuses. In his book Enrique Poblete says that there are no more than two thousand Callawayas left today, and they live in what he calls an oasis in the middle of the Quechua-speaking communities in the provinces of Saavedra Munecas and Caupolican in Northern Bolivia.

Not having seen this interesting book at the time of my visit, I had to satisfy myself with questions to Geraldo. I asked him how many Callawaya communities there might be in the mountains. He told me that he had visited two more villages about the same size as Urina, and he believed there might be four or five smaller settlements as well.

I then questioned him about the extraordinary claims made by the *amautas* that they could cure conditions which baffled our own medical experts, and especially about their wildly improbable claims that their ancestors had been able to transplant hearts and brains. I expressed my opinion that many relatively primitive Indians spoke in hyperboles in order to impress people from civilisation, like us, and that these gross exaggerations were not to be believed.

Geraldo bridled. "You are talking about these people again as if they were jungle savages," he said accusingly. "They are very skilful medical men. If thousands of people all over the world believe in them, why should you condemn them?"

"I don't mean the ordinary day-to-day cures of illnesses," I said reassuringly, "but transplanting hearts and brains is something else altogether."

"Well, I believe them," Geraldo insisted in his militant manner. "Why don't you get your doctors to come and talk to them and examine their engravings?" He paused as he warmed to his subject. "We who are decendants of the first Americans think we have uncovered enough evidence to show that, thousands of years ago, America was inhabited by very advanced cultures, who were much more intelligent and more knowledgeable than anyone in the world today." He turned away. "But you won't believe that. You people from Europe think you are the most advanced civilisation that there has ever been, but you cannot travel in time and space, or make dead people live again."

Next morning Geraldo found me sitting on a stone bench writing up my notes.

"Come, Mister Ross, we must film the ceremony. It has started," he shouted, his voice ringing with excitement.

I collected my camera case and tripod from our room, and gave them to Geraldo to carry so that I could follow him as speedily as possible in that rarefied atmosphere. He led me to the parade ground area at the edge of the village, where the three *amautas* were standing in front of a large stone table. A small fire of tiny twigs burned in the middle of the table, and surrounding it were heaps of coca leaves, pieces of maize bread, meat, fruit and short lengths of coloured wool, not unlike the collection for a Patchamama ceremony.

Mamani put a handful of coca leaves on the fire, and a thin wisp of smoke rose up towards the cloudless blue sky.

"Start filming this," Geraldo urged me. "The *amautas* say you can."

"What is happening?" I asked, as I set up the camera with his help.

"I don't know exactly," he admitted. "I have never seen this ceremony before, but I have been told that this morning they will select the virgin for sacrifice, and they will ask the condor if he will come."

For half an hour I filmed the three *amautas* as they burned their offerings on the fire, blew the ashes into the air, muttered their own individual incantations, or else remained silent for minutes on end as if they were in a trance. Perhaps in my own mind I was being unjustly derisory, but it reminded me of a simple black-magic ceremony which a troop of boy scouts might invent for a district pageant.

Occasionally an Indian passed by, stopped for a moment to watch, and continued on his way. As the fire died away into a pile of ashes, the ceremony seemed to be coming to an end. Suddenly Mamani threw back his head and screamed one word: 'Wakchu'.

"She must be the girl they have selected," whispered Geraldo, and sure enough, within moments, a girl came trotting into the parade ground carrying a woollen cloak, which she spread on the bench for the *amautas* to sit on. They spoke to her quietly in their secret language for several minutes and she walked away, looking thoroughly alarmed.

The *amautas* did not move, and so Geraldo approached them to ask for an explanation of what was happening. They confirmed that they had selected the fortunate woman to be the sacrifice to the condor. There were no suitable virgins, and so they had selected the youngest mother in the village, because tomorrow the condor would come, according to the coca leaves.

"What happens to the girl?" I asked.

"She will be prepared," Mamani told me. "The musicians will play their flutes and will sing songs of celebration."

That evening and right through the night the flutes kept playing one mournful dirge after another, with the monotonous whining noise echoing around the hills. There was also an endless high-pitched chanting coming from all parts of the village, and the cacophony of singing, together with the droning of the flutes, made sure that no one got any sleep that night. I recorded some of this incredible noise on my cassette tape recorder.

As dawn broke, the dreadful monotonous cacophony of music finally ceased and, when I looked out of the door, the village was bustling with life. No one seemed to be cooking or eating or carrying out the normal day-to-day tasks; so it was no surprise when our breakfast stew failed to appear.

Geraldo and I shared some of my biscuits and raisins, and, since we were keen not to miss anything, we hurried out to the parade ground to set up the camera. On the way we passed the three *amautas* at their stone table, performing much the same ceremony as on the previous day, tossing coca leaves and maize bread to the heavens, and mouthing whispered incantations.

"They are beginning to call the condor; we'd better hurry," Geraldo said eagerly.

"Hurry where?" I asked.

Geraldo stopped in his tracks. "I suppose on the parade ground, but I'd better find out," he said, as he trotted over to a group of waiting Indians.

"They are coming now," Geraldo called, "We film them over here." He waved towards a large rocky plateau, about half the size of a cricket field, on the outskirts of the village.

No sooner had I joined him than two of the *amautas* Hukumar and Chipana—appeared from behind the houses, leading Wakchu between them. They walked straight up to a solitary wooden stake, about two metres high, which had been driven into the rock-strewn surface at the centre of this desolate area. When they reached the stake, Wakchu was unceremoniously stripped of all but her loin cloth, and in spite of the shivering breeze blowing down from the surrounding snow-capped mountains, she was tied to the stake. While this was taking place, the villagers came bustling on to the scene, apparently well aware of what was going to happen.

The women formed up rather like a choir and started a high-pitched chant, while the men created a discordant cacophony of sound on flutes, drums and tin whistles. There seemed to be no rhythm or metre or tune in the shrill whining noise that reverberated around the mountain top and must have been heard in the far, far distance

After about half an hour of the seemingly endless, dreary chanting, absolutely nothing happened. A child began to cry with frustration. The women chanted less as the tension mounted. Indeed, I saw the *amautas* hold an urgent conference, during which their hurried glances in my direction told me that I was the subject of conversation. Perhaps they were merely regretting having allowed me to see this sacred ceremony, or it could have been something much more sinister. Perhaps they were blaming my presence for the apparent lack of success.

At this crucial moment there came a triumphant cry from the *amautas*. Attention was suddenly riveted on the distant snow-capped mountain tops. There, silhouetted against the white curtain, were the unmistakeable dark shapes of a flight of three incredibly graceful condors. And they were heading directly for our mountain plateau. With their immense wings stretched a full twelve feet, they dived towards us like fighter planes with their engines cut. The smaller black females fell behind as the male leader, his white collar glistening in the frosty sunlight made two bold passes only thirty or forty feet above us.

The *amautas* were gloriously happy that the spirit of their renowned leader had arrived, and they renewed their chant. I was thrilled beyond words to see a magnigicent condor so close. Wakchu was uneasy. She struggled against the embracing rope, whose coils held her captive. She dropped her head and averted her eyes so that she could pretend to herself that the condors were not really there.

The chanting stopped, and the flutes were silent as the male condor landed, to a frenzied beating of the drums. He surveyed the scene. Not one of the silent crowd moved an inch. Nor did I. I felt spellbound to be almost within touching-distance of this magnificent creature.

There must have been fifty or sixty Callawayas sitting motionless at the edge of the plateau, and none of them moved as I darted to and fro, taking shot after shot of that was, to me, an incredible spectacle.

The great condor strutted around the centre of the arena like a gladiator and, at one breathtaking moment, he ran towards the helpless Wakchu with his wings outstretched and his wicked-looking beak pointing at her throat, She screamed, and struggled against the ropes that were binding her. Geraldo averted what might have been a nasty moment by running towards the condor and hurling a stone at it. The great bird took fright, sprinted down the slope until it gathered enough speed to take off and disappear in majestic flight away across the mountain tops with its two females in attendance.

At the time I was too busy trying to film the scene to think about possible explanations but, in retrospect, I believe there must have been a reason for the arrival of the condors. Assuming that the Callawayas do not possess any magical powers to persuade a wild condor to land at their feet, one must look for the reason.

Was it a tame condor, which had been reared by hand in the village? Did the Callawayas entice this particular condor into the village at regular intervals by feeding it some sort of meat? This was more likely because, to judge by the manner in which the condor strutted around the rocky plateau, it might well have been searching for the tasty morsels it expected to find.

Whatever the reason, the dramatic arrival of the condor almost within touching distance was a memorable and unique experience, and so incredible that I doubt if I would have had the courage to tell the story if my film and photographs had for some reason failed to materialise. Happily, all the film and the photographs survived their subsequent travels and in fact turned out to be of good quality, so that I have ample film evidence to corroborate every word I have written.

CHAPTER THIRTEEN

The Moxos

THE *AMAUTAS* WERE OBVIOUSLY pleased that all their claims had been justified so completely, and Mamani was both surprised and gratified when I gave him an extra one hundred pesos to express my own satisfaction.

I think that, by now, the three *amautas* were convinced that there was no ulterior motive for my visit, and the way they kept reminding me to tell my people about their skills made it obvious that they were expecting to cash in on their success. I suppose that, in a way, I was deceiving them, because I don't expect any Englishman will make the long journey to their mountain home seeking a miracle cure, but it always was my intention to write about the Callawayas, and to show the film they allowed me to take.

Geraldo and I had three more long conferences with the *amautas* and found them more and more forthcoming. We were allowed in to some of the neatly-built stone houses. Each of them consisted of one small room which was home for a family of two adults and one, two or three children. There were no large families, and this was probably due to the custom of forbidding sex while a mother suckled her child for the first eighteen months or two years of its life. Another contributory factor was well documented by the Spanish chroniclers. In that rarefied atmosphere at more than four thousand metres above sea level, sexual intercourse represents a daunting physical effort, and, as the Spaniards noted, the appetite for it almost disappeared.

The houses were extremely simple. There were no furnishings whatsoever beyond a crude table made out of one plank of wood propped up between two small pillars of stone. It seemed that the family must have slept on the piles of animal skins and woollen cloaks that were heaped in the corners.

From what I had seen of their life-style it was obvious that the men were the only members of the group to be educated. They were the thinkers, the scientists and the organisers of life, while the women were the work-horses, whose sheer physical efforts kept each family unit intact. They had no power or authority in their own family or in the community. They were possessions.

We talked to the *amautas* about the way they governed, and the rules that their subjects were expected to obey. As in all Inca tribes the three major sins were *Amasuya, Amayuya* and *Amakelya*—stealing, lying, laziness. These sins were very rarely committed, probably because the punishments were drastic. For a first offence the punishment was *hiwaya,* which consisted of tying up the offender and dropping heavy stones on to his back. He was not expected to work for several days after this injury, I was told, and, since he was contributing nothing to the communal coffers he drew nothing out: no food, no clothing. If one Callawaya steals from another he is tied up and hung by his ankles from a tree. Any member of the family from whom he has stolen is allowed to beat him with a wooden club for one whole day, but they are only permitted to break one bone for each article that has been stolen. A persistent offender is exiled, I was told. Generally he or she is banished to the lowland valleys, where he works for many years, growing food for the community and collecting the necessary materials for the preparation of secret medicines.

As soon as I heard this I turned to Geraldo and whispered, "Let us go to see these plantations." He nodded agreement, but the *amautas* took no notice. They were obsessed with the idea of impressing me with their skills.

"We not only cure all illnesses; we can also curse people or make potions for you to overpower women," Mamani claimed dramatically.

"All right. Let me film some of these ceremonies," I said.

"There are no ceremonies and, as I have already told you, we do not allow you to take pictures of our secrets, but I will tell you how some of them are carried out."

"What happens when you curse somebody?" I asked.

"Terrible things will happen to them, and the person will probably die," Mamani replied in a matter-of-fact tone.

He looked at the other two *amautas* and, when they offered no objection, Mamani said he would explain how it is done.

"You just have to tell me the name of your enemy, and whether it is a man or a woman. I make you an earthenware doll to represent your enemy, and I give you a special splinter of wood which possesses magic properties. All you have to do is to cover the doll with a mixture of some hair and some excrement from your enemy, and then stick the magic splinter in a place where it will hurt. If you do this many times great harm will befall your enemy."

I wrote down everything Mamani told me, but inwardly I was very cynical, of course. It was becoming increasingly difficult to reconcile such primitive beliefs with the claims of the Callawayas to be regarded as medical experts all over South America. It became even more difficult when Mamani elaborated on his belief that all diseases and disabilities are caused by spirits, and so only the spirits can cure them. The Callawayas, he told me, are in contact with the other world, and it is only by learning how to communicate with your ancestors that you can be told how to cure people in this world

Geraldo's loyalty to what he called 'his people' was stretched to the limit, and he grudgingly admitted that modern doctors could do more than the Callawayas to cure many modern diseases—(and he accentuated the word 'modern') but, primitive or not, the Callawayas had proved to many sceptical westerners that they had 'a power of the mind' that we have completely lost with the advance of civilisation.

Geraldo warmed to his favourite subject. "You people think that you have advanced compared to these retarded Indians who still live in the Stone Age, but have you ever thought that you may be progressing backwards? Have you ever thought that these people may not want your kind of development in their way of life? If they had invented the car, where would they drive? They do not want fine clothes when they have no need of them. For the same reason they do not want electricity or the telephone. Just because they do not have these things, it does not mean that the Indians are backward. They are absolutely content with their own way of life, and how many of you westerners can say that?"

I did not really want to get involved in an argument, but Geraldo had me by the coat tails and was not prepared to let go. "Until you brought your evil way of life to South America, things must have been so different, so much happier. Gold was a useful metal with which to make things the people needed. It was better than mud for making pots and pans. You people turned it into bullets which kill. Before the Spaniards came our currency was coca leaves, the same as it was with the Mayas and the Aztecs. You brought your religions, which may have been right for your way of life, but not for ours. We were content and happy until the Europeans came here, Mister Ross, and now look at us. We are all suffering like you and your people now—all except the lucky few like the Callawayas. Don't call them primitive or backward. In their own environment they are much more advanced than people from civilisation, because they have everything they want from life."

"What I would really like to do now," I told Geraldo, "is to see the Callawayas' camps of cultivation, where they grow their fruit, vegetables and plants from which they make their medicines."

"That is quite a long journey down towards the jungle," Geraldo replied. "It will take us several days even if you ride your mule, Mister. Do you have the money to pay for a guide?"

"You see what you can arrange with Mamani, and tell him that, if he wants me to spread the word about their medical powers, he must help us to make the journey," I said, and Geraldo understood exactly what I meant.

That evening he spent an hour with the *amautas*, and came back with the news that we had permission to visit their camps of cultivation, but the Indians living there—the Moxos—were giving trouble, and the Callawayas had sent a group of soldiers to keep them under control. According to Mamani, the Moxos were unfriendly even towards the Callawayas at this time, and so there could be trouble for a total stranger.

"I am no hero," I admitted at once. "I don't want to go if there is any real danger, but Mamani told us that he banishes members of his own tribe to the valleys as a punishment for crimes; so there must be Callawayas living there as well."

"Exactly. I understand that it is these exiled Callawayas who are leading the revolt," Geraldo replied.

"Well, what do you think?" I asked him. "Are you willing to give it a try?"

"We can always go part of the way," Geraldo offered grudgingly. "If we find that there is serious trouble we can turn back.

At least we will be able to film some of these lost cities of the Incas that you keep talking about."

I tried not to sound too excited as I asked Geraldo to tell me more about these cities.

"There are a number of ancient stone cities in the hills leading down towards the Amazon," he insisted. "The Callawayas know about them, because two are alongside the road to their plantations, and some archaeologists know of their existence, but very few people have ever visited the ruins. No one has ever taken film of them."

"Can you be sure they are Inca cities?" I asked incredulously.

"No, I cannot be certain, because I am not an archaeologist and I paid only a brief visit to one of them," Geraldo admitted, "but the Englishman Fowsey said they were Inca cities."

"Do you mean Colonel Fawcett?" I asked.

"Write down the name," Geraldo demanded, and I wrote FAWCETT on the back of my cigarette packet. "That's right," Geraldo enthused. "We pronounce that 'Fowsey. At the university we read the official accounts of his journeys through these mountains when he was given the job of deciding the exact border between Peru and Bolivia. He was in this area, that is quite certain; and he wrote about his journeys from the mountain tops down to the river Beni, and about the ruins of ancient cities he found."

"But how do you know it was right here in the Nudo de Apolobamba?" I queried.

"Because he said so in his reports," Geraldo affirmed. "He even mentioned the river Tuiche, which runs very near the road we have to take from Urina down to the plantations."

"Are they big cities which we can film?" I asked with bated breath.

"They were large cities in ancient times," Geraldo admitted, "But there is not much left today: just the fortress walls, and the ruins of many houses. There is also a ceremonial site on the peak of one of the hills that is almost untouched. In fact, the buildings on hilltops are in a reasonable state of preservation, because there is very little soil and hardly anything grows; but down in the valleys it is overgrown with jungle."

"Well, if you can help me to film one of these cities I will give you another hundred pesos, and I will let you take some of the film," I told him. "I wouldn't mind if it is not then possible to film the Moxos Indians at the plantations."

Geraldo became more enthusiastic about the adventure ahead, and we talked of little else as we waited for word from Mamani about our departure.

Before we left, two days later, I was fortunate enough to see just one miracle cure performed by one of the Callawaya witch-doctors called K'Aturikasti, which, according to Mamani, means 'puma' in their language.

An Indian boy from the town of La Paz had been half-carried by his parents up to the Callawaya village because he had a mysterious swelling around his knee, which had crippled him for almost a year. The doctors had not been able to cure the condition and, in desperation, the whole family had come to the Callawayas.

The teenage boy walked with a pronounced limp, and always used a walking-stick as he hobbled along. Both he and his parents were wearing western clothes, spoke fluent Spanish, and considered themselves perfectly civilised.

Geraldo got to hear about the imminent ceremony at which the boy would be cured, and he obtained permission for us to watch, although S'Aturikasti and Mamani were both adamant that I would not be allowed to film or take photographs.

The ceremony took place on the rocky slope at the side of K'Aturikasti's house. The witch-doctor was obviously a serious and experienced practitioner, because he wore a trilby hat and, according to Mamani, had worked in Lima and Guayaquil.

A little group of ten or twelve Callawayas gathered for the ceremony, including one teenage boy, who was apparently being taught medicine, since he was at the witch-doctor's side throughout. As K'Aturikasti prepared his potions on a stone table, he whispered instructions to the boy the whole time. They toasted coca leaves and boiled up a mixture of fruits and vegetables to which they added what looked like a few dead insects and a live frog.

K'Aturikasti stood back from the pot as it simmered over the fire, and carried out a ritual very similar to the one used in the ceremony to call the condor. He whispered incantations, tossed the coca leaves, blew the smoke from the fire, and gradually relapsed into a trance. As far as I was concerned, it was all very predictable and a pure caricature of a black-magic ceremony. While he feigned being in a state of trance, K'Aturikasti laid the crippled boy out on the ground, and silently waved his hands over the swollen knee. Suddenly, and with a dramatic cry, the witch-doctor fell on the boy and sucked vigorously at his knee. After a few moments he leapt to his feet, and, with his arms waving, he gyrated like a spinning top befor spitting a small grey object on to the ground. As he did so, he appeared to wake up from his trance in a state of collapse, and he called some of the Indians to his side to support him while he walked back to the crippled boy.

None of the assembled crowd took any notice of the small object that K'Aturikasti had apparently sucked out of the boy's knee, but I saw where it landed, and I never took my eye off it for a second.

I only saw the rest of the ceremony out of the corner of one eye, therefore, but it looked as if the witch-doctor and his young assistant were bathing the knee with the warm mixture which had been simmering over the twig fire, and then they tied several coca leaves to the affected part. Ten minutes later the crippled boy was helped to his feet, and he walked away with only a slight limp. The crowd dispersed, and I moved over to pick up the mysterious object which the 'doctor' had sucked out of the boy's knee. It was a small pebble, of which there were hundreds on the hillsides all around.

Later, Geraldo explained to me that this was a typical cure by the Callawayas. The boy's condition had been caused by a spirit, and that is why the doctors from La Paz had been powerless to help. As we had seen, the Callawaya doctor had been able to suck out the spirit, and soon the boy would be completely cured. Indeed, before we set out on our own journey next day, Geraldo and I saw the formerly crippled boy walking around a little unsteadily, but without assistance, and the swelling was almost gone.

I have thought about this so-called miracle cure a great deal since that day. I did not tell Geraldo or anyone else at the time that the evil spirit which had been sucked out of the boy's leg was nothing more than a pebble, or that, in my opinion, all the evidence indicated that it was pure suggestion or hypnosis, to put it mildly. Deceit might be a more accurate description, and yet the boy was cured. That was the mystery.

I suppose the only logical explanation is that the whole thing was a gigantic confidence trick staged for my benefit. The whole episode might have been a total charade, with the crippled boy acting out his part. That is possible, of course, but if it was staged deliberately, it was superbly acted out, and it succeeded in deceiving me, because I cannot see any rational explanation; as far as I am concerned it was a classic case of 'mind over matter'.

Geraldo and I spent a busy evening gathering our kit together and packing everything ready for an early start next morning.

At daybreak a Callawaya youth, who was intoduced as Siku, 'the little one', appeared at our door to tell us that he was going to guide us to the plantations in the valleys. Siku looked a suitable young man for the job. He seemed fit and strong, and the fact that he was not particularly forthcoming or friendly was probably due to his shyness. Since he did not speak a word of Spanish, I knew that I would be able to talk uninhibitedly to Geraldo on the journey.

I rode one mule, and the other mule carried our equipment, while the two young men walked, but it still took all the first day to cross the snow-capped mountains to the east. I would never have attempted such an arduous journey on foot at that altitude—about fourteen thousand feet. In fact, both the mule and Geraldo were affected by the rarefied atmosphere on the mountain tops, as they both puffed slowly along. I puffed too when Geraldo asked me to dismount and climb on foot to the top of a hill which rose steeply to the left of the Inca road.

"It is well worth the effort," he pleaded. "From that high point you can see for miles ahead down in the valleys where there are several unknown Inca cities."

That tortuous journey on foot up the snow-covered slopes was a gruelling experience I shall never forget. After two hours of slipping, sliding and gasping for breath, we finally reached the top, and I only regret that I was in such a state of collapse that I could not really appreciate what must surely be one of the most spectacular and beautiful views in the whole world.

The snow-covered mountain tops cut sharp white lines against the pale blue sky and sliced down steeply to rolling green hills as far as the eye could see. It was glorious virgin country, unknown, untouched by modern man, and majestic in its lonely splendour. If only the altitude had not imposed such cruel restrictions on my enjoyment of an unforgettable panorama!

The return journey down the hill was almost as exacting, but I was so relieved to get back that the rest of the journey, re-mounted on my mule, seemed easy by comparison.

Where the clearly-defined track passed across the tops of the mountains there was a thin covering of snow, and when we descended towards the lower land below the snow-line, some mud and dust partly obscured the superbly-made stone highway. Where the rain-water rushed down the hillside and gently spread across the road, it exposed the foundations, the square granite blocks placed neatly together and forming a smooth surface that must still be as good today as it was hundreds of years ago when it was constructed with such care, skill and superhuman effort.

We camped that first night on the open heathland at the side of the trail and, although there were no trees to provide wood for a fire, we ate some of my iron rations, and the mules grazed the coarse grass.

Next morning the sun rose above a horizon which was far, far below us, and gradually it lit up the most awe-inspiring views I have ever seen. In front of us stretched hundreds of miles of empty valleys and hills. The undulating carpet of green vegetation was the epitome of lonely grandeur, and the fact that the soft surface was broken by occasional sharp craggy outcrops of pure, naked rock only emphasised what was for me the majestic splendour of these lonely empty hills.

Once we left the snow-caps behind us and continued our steady descent, it became pleasantly warm and the air was much much easier to breathe. Soon we reached a crossroads where our narrow track crossed a much wider stone road at right angles. Here, in a small basin of rocks at the intersection of the two roads, Geraldo asked me to wait. He walked around, scuffling the ground with his foot like someone looking for a lost treasure. Presently he swooped to pick up what looked like a perfectly ordinary small stone but, judging by the way he turned it over in his hands and inspected it closely, Geraldo apparently saw something special in it. Nursing it tenderly in his outstretched hand, he walked over to a huge pile of stones nearly two metres high, and placed his stone carefully on the heap. He returned looking a little embarrassed. "It was always an Inca custom," he said. "They used to place a stone there every time they made a long journey. It was to placate the gods." Then, not wanting to appear unsophisticated, he added the rider, "I just did it so that you could see the custom."

With that he turned abruptly on his heel, and marched across the main highway, following our smaller trail eastwards down into the valleys. I was about to follow him on my mule when I saw a small party approaching along the main track. Three young men dressed in shirts and trousers were leading two heavily-laden mules up the hill. I asked Geraldo who they might be, and where they'd come from.

"They are civilised Indians," he replied. "We call them 'merchants', and they have been to the plantations belonging to an Indian village down in the valley to buy coca and peppers. They are taking it to sell in the towns in the mountains, even as far as Peru—this road leads right to Peru. I know it is a very long journey," he admitted, "but they get a good price for coca and peppers in the towns. They've carried out this same trade since the time of the Incas. That is why this road was built, to get supplies from the Yungas to the people in the high Andes who cannot live without coca leaves, which they chew to give them strength at high altitudes, and peppers to give them warmth in the cold climate up in the snow."

"But they had no mules in the days before the Spaniards," I pointed out.

"But they had llamas," Geraldo said. "Coca was considered absolutely essential to life in the time of the Inca; it was also their currency, as it was that of the Mayas and the Aztecs. Gold was just a useful metal until you Europeans came here. Before that coca was much more valuable."

"Do the merchants buy coca from the Moxos, where we are going?" I asked.

"No, the Moxos do not trade with civilisation," came the answer. "They belong to the Callawayas, and grow only for them. The coca plantations at the end of the main highway are much larger, and the people there have a regular trade with the towns. Nobody except the Callawayas travels down this track to the Moxos, because they are not friendly. They defend their valleys in case any colonists come to settle there."

For two days we walked the narrow Inca road across miles of barren hills. From a distance the hillside had looked green and relatively fertile but, as we walked the ribbon of road that snaked across the open countryside, I could see that there was so little depth of soil that only coarse grass and dwarf bushes covered the harsh, stony surface. It must have been an inhospitable area in prehistoric times, for we saw no sign of any ruins or of any previous settlements. The road must have been built through this windswept wilderness simply to reach the fertile, green valleys down towards the Amazon.

Eventually we reached the first line of trees. To start with, they were widely scattered, and seldom more than three metres high, but gradually the sparse woodland gave way to a much thicker forest of substantial old trees, whose foliage often covered the blue sky above the road. Here there was a depth of soil. There was leaf-mould underfoot, and on either side of the road small streams of clear water cascaded down to join the river Tuichi in the deep valley away to our left.

It was only mid-afternoon when Siku, the Callawaya youth, stopped and pointed to a treeless platform of flat land just below the level of the road and on the banks of the tumbling stream. He spoke quietly to Geraldo, who turned to me to say that this was where we would camp for the night.

"Siku says there are many ruins all around us," Geraldo confided; "so if we stay here tonight we could spend all day tomorrow filming them."

"Better check that we are not wasting our time," I said, as I scanned the hillside, vainly looking for signs of 'many ruins'. "I cannot see any ruins at all."

Geraldo questioned the Callawaya youth, who beckoned to me to follow him through a gap in the trees at the side of the trail. I dismounted, and followed him through an avenue of trees for about one hundred metres. Suddenly we emerged into a large clearing and there, on top of a large mound of earth and rocks, was a magnificent ruin.

Built on a square platform of stones were eight stone pillars supporting an impressive carved lintel and a massive stone roof. On top of the flat roof was another two-storeyed building consisting of sixteen single rooms, each about the size of a prison cell. The whole building was very much larger than anything I had seen so far. It had the appearance of a temple or meeting-hall with living-quarters above, and the immense size of some of the stones used, plus the ornate carvings on the pillars, and the fact that this huge edifice was three storeys high, showed a degree of skill in the workmanship that was unequalled in any of the other ruins I had visited.

Next day, with the two young Indians carrying my heavy

filming equipment, we walked about half a kilometre down the stone pathway. Siku explained that, in the jungle-covered hills that towered above us on the right, were more large 'temples, palaces and ceremonial centres' which were hidden away like the building he had already shown me. On the left of the trail, where the vegetation was much less thick, there were terraces of cultivation on the more level stretch of land, drained by the mountain stream that passed our camp-site.

We turned off the trail to the left to look at this area which, as I soon realised, must have been the focus of life for the ancient community. Dozens of terraces of cultivation stretched down the gently-sloping hillside, covering a area of about forty hectares (one hundred acres) before reaching a sheer drop of two hundred metres (six hundred feet) into the canyon through which a much larger river flowed. Looking at my map, I believe that this was the river Tuichi but, since the maps one buys in the shops are notoriously incomplete, and since I had no way of taking accurate measurements during my journey, I cannot be certain.

On a promontory of rock overlooking the terraces were the ruins of what appeared to be a large communal building alongside eight one-roomed houses. By the side of these ruins was an area of levelled land about half the size of a football pitch. This may have been the site for dozens of adobe houses long since eroded and washed away by the tropical rainstorms. In the centre of this rocky plateau was a large stone oven, and what looked like a stone water-tank. This leads me to believe that this may well have been a centre of population inhabited by the workers or the less important members of the tribe. On the top of the canyon wall, just before the sheer drop down to the river bed below, there was a line of superbly constructed stone fortifications. The large oblong windows in the stone walls looked straight down on to the river. It was easy to see that any would-be invader approaching from the direction of the river would have to scale the sheer rock-face with the skill of a mountaineer, and then face a barrage of stones and arrows from the fortifications directly above him. In other words, it would have been quite impossible for a large, well-armed force of jungle Indians to have invaded this ancient Inca settlement from the south or the east, since the fortifications appeared to be impregnable.

My opinion that this was indeed an Inca site was reinforced by my inspection of some of the palaces and temples, and the ceremonial site the next day. I visited three more large buildings, which were all constructed of stone, and the quality of masonry, as well as the engineering and construction skills, was of a very high standard; no cement had been used: the stones fitted exactly; it showed greater knowledge and ability than any of the buildings of Iscanwaya, Incallacta or Sacapampa.

We slowly climbed to the top of the steepest hill of the group to see what Siku described as the ceremonial site of 'the people of yet before'. This again was magnificently impressive, and how the huge stones were brought to the very peak of the hill and laid out there is quite beyond my understanding.

The centre-piece of the ceremonial site was a huge oblong-shaped stone, five metres long, two metres wide, and one metre deep. It must have weighed more than one hundred tons, and it rested on a bed of large stones in such a way that it must have been placed there by hand. No earthquake or cataclysm could have placed it so precisely on the narrow pinacle of the hill. Carved into the surface of this gigantic rock was the figure of a matchstick man: a body with two arms and two legs, where the sacrificial victim must have been laid out before having his throat cut. There was a channel carved out from the top of the figure (where the head would have been) leading to a bowl-shaped indentation which could have collected the blood. At one corner of the platform (or altar) was a thin, very straight stone pillar just over two metres high. The base of the pillar had been squared off and smoothed over, but it amazed me to find that it was just standing there perfectly upright, with no support whatsoever, and without even a basin cut into the great rock into which its base might have nestled. When I pushed against the pillar, it did not move an inch. According to Geraldo it had been precisely placed so that, when its shadow reached a certain point, this would have been the signal for the sacrifice to begin. He was probably guessing, but this does seem to be a logical explanation.

From the four corners of the altar great slabs of stone had been placed so that they sloped down to ground level, forming causeways on which people could walk up on to the altar stone. From one of these causeways a stone road snaked round the hillside, following the line of the river until it came to what looked like another very substantial ruin on the bare slopes below us. We set off to inspect it. After half an hour's walk we came to what turned out to be the most remarkable ruin of them all.

The lower level of this three-storeyed mansion consisted of a line of fortifications, behind which were four sentry-boxes alongside a flight of stone steps leading to twelve single rooms and one much larger room. A flight of steps led up to the next level, which also had a stone wall to protect the one very large building, which appeared to have been a communal dwelling, like a barrack room. Yet more steps led up through another stone wall to the top level of this pyramid-shaped construction. Here were two more small stone watch-towers guarding the narrow entrance of a platform on which was built a substantial single-roomed dwelling of superb masonry, significantly higher than any of the buildings. Some of the stone joists and rafters were still in position; only the roof had gone. The flagstones of which the floor was constructed had been fitted together with care and precision to form a perfectly smooth surface. At the back of the large room was an archway leading into an annexe room that must have been carved out of the hillside. Unfortunately, I had not brought my torch; so the Indians collected some brushwood which we placed inside the archway entrance and set on fire.

The flames lit up a small, dank room with stone walls; at the far end there was a gap in the wall flanking what looked like another flight of stone steps leading even further up into the hillside. We could not see exactly, because a quantity of earth had cascaded down the tunnel and made a large heap at the foot of the stone staircase.

Geraldo became quite excited and, after borrowing my box of matches, he climbed over the pile of rubble and disappeared up the stone staircase.

A few minutes later he returned, triumphant.

"It is just as I thought," he clamoured excitedly. "This was the palace of the Inca. Look, Mister Ross. The lower level is the fortress where the soldiers lived who protected him. The next level is where all his courtiers and concubines and their children lived, and here on the top is where the Inca lived. If an army tried to attack the palace, they could not have reached the Inca without killing every single soldier, and even then the Inca could have escaped up that stone staircase. It leads out on to the hillside, which cannot be seen from below, and he could have walked past the ceremonial site and gone to the big city for protection."

I knew that this was all pure guesswork on Geraldo's part but, since we shall never know the truth, I accepted it as a perfectly reasonable hypothesis, and thanked him for all his efforts.

"Come up the staircase, Mister, and you can see down into the valley were the Moxos live," Geraldo urged me.

I explained that I was not so young and nimble any more, and did not care to take risks so far from help. So we re-traced our steps down through the ruins and up the hillside, after I had taken some film of this spectacular setting.

I have given my word to the Bolivian authorities; so I'll only mention in passing that there were gold figures scattered around in the shape of animals, human heads, human figures and skeletons. Some of them were quite easy to identify, but some were grotesque and completely out of proportion with, perhaps, huge hands or feet. There were also many axes, knives, pins and drinking-vessels that appeared to be gold, or else gold alloy. They were certainly very heavy.

It is easy to get excited about lost cities of the Incas, fortunes in gold and so on but, having talked to the Bolivian scientists, I refuse to make any such claim. All I am prepared to say is that this is possibly another lost city of the Incas, one of many which have not yet been discovered and excavated by modern scientists. The fact that there was some gold in the ruins leads me to believe that this may have been one of the ruins not discovered by the Spaniards. On the other had the *conquistadores* may well have ransacked the place and, since there is gold in all the rivers of the Andes, the few trinkets I found may have been manufactured by the Indians who survived the massacres of the sixteenth and seventeenth centuries. This to my mind is a far more exciting possibility: that some Incas escaped to areas like this and lived long after the conquest.

When we reached the pinnacle of the hill-top above the ruins we had a magnificent view down the valleys and the canyons that cut spectacular slices in the hills.

"There are the Moxos," Geraldo cried, pointing to the far bank of the river about two to three hundred metres below us. "From here right down the river they live, as far as the eye can see."

At first sight this settlement of the Moxos was not unlike those on the banks of the river Cotacajes. On the one piece of level land on the river bank, the Indians had constructed a small hamlet of about twenty timber houses with thatched roofs. All the surrounding land—about twenty hectares or fifty acres of it—was neatly divided into small plots, growing what looked like maize, beans and potatoes, and peppers. Obviously there was coca as well, since that is what the Callawayas purchased or exchanged.

A stream of water cascaded down the steep hillside in clouds of spray until it reached the plateau on the river bank, where it turned into a wider stretch of water that flowed more gently into the river. With this constant water supply, and warm temperatures right through the year, the Indians probably grew an ample food supply with two, or in some cases three, harvests a year. I could see a few men and women working on the cultivations, and others walking around their group of houses where a huge log fire was blazing.

"We will tell them we are here and then send Siku down," said Geraldo, and he yodelled loud and long. Most of the Indians below stopped what they were doing, looked up the hill towards us, and then carried on with their jobs, as though they were completely unconcerned.

On the face of it we were looking down on a very primitive community. They appeared to be dressed in plain cloaks made of animal skin or beaten bark. There was no sign of mules to help with the cultivation, nor sheep or chickens. Nor could I see any sign of even the most simple machinery or implements, not even the first necessities of life that semi-civilised Indians acquire when they first come into contact with civilisation. The Moxos tribe appeared to be untouched by civilisation. For a moment I wondered whether such a group might protest at the disturbance we represented, and I said as much to Geraldo.

He rejected the suggestion at once, pointing out that, since they traded regularly with the Callawayas, they probably knew of civilisation, and probably sent expeditions into the villages around Titicaca to do their shopping, with money they might receive from selling coca and peppers. But they probably preferred their own way of life.

Soon after down the next day, Geraldo and I were cooking some maize for breakfast when Siku returned, leading a party of eight Moxos men. We smiled our greetings as the solemn-faced men walked boldly into our clearing. They were dressed in the same grey, shapeless cloaks as the Mosetenes I had met near the river Beni. Their long hair was tied back with braid made out of lengths of fibre, and they walked barefoot. Each of them carried a wooden club about the size of a baseball bat, and some of them also carried a flat piece of wood shaped rather like a sword or a machete.

In spite of their sullen expressions, their weapons, and their refusal to acknowledge our greetings, I did not sense any particular threat, as they just stood there surveying our camp site.

One of the Moxos, who was apparently the leader, walked over to Siku and spoke quietly to him. I did not hear what was said, but the leader turned back to his companions and gave the word to proceed. They walked quite slowly and deliberately over to my tent, and slashed it to pieces with their clubs and wooden swords. They then pulled away its tatters to reveal my kitbag and filming equipment. The cases containing my camera and my tripod and tape recorder were all smashed by ferocious blows from the clubs. My kitbag was torn open and my clothing was shared out among the Indians.

Hardly a word was spoken. The Indians seemed to know exactly what they wanted to do and, of course, Geraldo, Siku and I were powerless to stop them as they destroyed everything I possessed.

It was heartbreaking to see the savage destuction, and yet, strangely enough, I had no fear whatsoever for my own personal safety. The Indians were not showing any sign of anger or animosity, and I noticed that Geraldo, although he must have been horrified, was taking it quite calmly. Somehow the stony-faced Indians made it quite clear that they intended to destroy all our possessions with cold-blooded thoroughness, and then leave. That is exactly what they did do, without a word to us, and without any kind of threatening gesture towards us during the whole strange drama.

After they'd left we were silent for several minutes. I turned over the wreckage just to confirm that indeed everything was smashed to smithereens.

"Well, that's the end of our trip," I said quietly.

"We'd better go at once," Geraldo replied. "They could come back soon, and then it could well be us they'll be after. They must resent us very much. I don't know why. Who knows what Siku told them?" he added meaningly.

"At least I've got my film," I said turning to more cheerful subjects. "I put all the film I'd taken in the stream to keep it cool."

I retrieved my tape recordings from the broken cassette, and lifted the bag of film out of the river. Geraldo and Siku collected the packets of food we had stored in a cave, fetched the mules, and we all set out on the long journey home in a state of bewilderment and, for my part, considerable sadness as well.

I had completed my last expedition. I was already heavily in debt, and now, with one thousand five hundred pounds' worth of filming equipment smashed and abandoned, it seemed to have been a costly caprice.

Looking on the bright side, it had been the experience of a lifetime: there might even be a story to tell in the end, whilst still honouring my promises to the Bolivian authorities. I told Geraldo that I would not yet reveal the exact location of this lost city, because the quantity of gold there would only attract thieves, who might tear these historic ruins to pieces and certainly disturb the tribe of Moxos living nearby.

For the time being it is enough to say that, somewhere in the hills of northern Bolivia, there are more lost cities of the Incas, and that I have seen and filmed one of them. They are a long, long way from civilisation, it is true, but only a few days' journey from the Callawaya communities. Why didn't they collect some of the gold treasure and sell it in the modern towns up in the Andes? I asked Geraldo this question, pointing out that the Callawayas must know that gold could buy them the food and household articles they need.

Geraldo's answer was revealing.

"They do," he said. "They take a little at a time, but they dare not take very much, because these ruins belong to very important people in the white man's cities. The men who own each ruin bring their own soldiers once a year, and take a small amount of gold on each trip. They dare not take huge quantities at one time, because that would draw attention to their treasure-trove, and they would be found out. By taking a little at a time they are slowly building up a fortune. There are many people in high places who are very rich because they 'own' an Inca ruin. Reputable scientists like Dr. Carlos must deplore this stealing of irreplaceable gold artefacts, but it is so well organised by groups of influential people that they are seldom caught. The money they get by melting down a small quantity of gold will give the organisers a comfortable income, and will buy the silence of those who help them. The Moxos we met are probably bribed to keep others away. They have forced you to retreat very quickly, and they know that you haven't taken any gold, don't they? I did not take any, and you can be sure that, if you and I returned to any of these ruins to loot the gold, we should soon disappear mysteriously."

What I learned on this and all my other expeditions persuades me that there are still a lot of gold artefacts in many little-known ruins in Bolivia, especially those hidden ruins on the banks of the rivers that rise in the Andes and flow eastwards through Paititi towards the Amazon. According to the analysis of some of the pieces I brought back with me, a small percentage of them are made from high-quality gold, but much more than half the items are gold alloy of much less intrinsic value.

Fortunately the National Institute of Archaeology in Bolivia is slowly winning control over the professional *huaceros* and the casual robbers who plunder any newly-discovered ruins. The same tight control may not be so easy to establish where ruins are 'owned' by influential people in high places, but the steady flow of priceless antiquities into the melting-pot is now carried out on a much smaller scale. Many beautiful gold artefacts of the Inca and the pre-Inca period are now being saved, and future studies of these treasures may help to build the picture of a pre-conquest South America inhabited, I believe, by intelligent people of the greatest and most advanced culture of the Middle Ages.

My lifetime's search for El Dorado, Paititi, the lost empire of the Incas—call it what you will—may lack position and comprehensive proof to satisfy the academics, but I hope I may have opened the door. I sincerely believe that some of my discoveries and, more important, some of my research and filming for the Bolivian archaeologists, has uncovered fresh evidence which may be worthy of much more detailed study and assessment by professional historians and South American experts.

I shall particularly look forward to hearing the results of the four-year project by the Smithsonian Institute in the plains of Beni and the lowlands of the eastern half of South America. Was this, as I suggest, the home of the first settled community of man, the first nation in South America? Will the investigators prove that these lowland Indians migrated into the Andes at the time of a great flood, and founded the enormously powerful Aymara culture? Did an epoch of cold, dry weather lead to the collapse of the Aymara, and was the legendary Inca nation founded on the scattered remains of some of the surviving Aymara rulers who joined the first explorers from Europe? Was the Inca empire even larger and more advanced than we believe at present? Did it have a sophisticated language, or medical skills even more advanced than those of today?

These questions may not be answered for many years, but the most important question of all, from my point of view. could be answered in the next decade. Did more than one million Inca subjects escape the Spanish *conquistadores?* Did they re-group in the hills and fertile valleys north of Cochabamba on the banks of the rivers Chapare, Isiboro, Cotacajes and Ichoa? Do a few of their descendants still live there today? Is this vast, unknown and unexplored area the Paititi of Inca legend?

In this account of my travels and explorations over the last twenty-six years, I have sometimes refrained from giving the exact locations of some sites so as to thwart irresponsible vandals and adventurers who could destroy Bolivia's heritage, but I have more detailed maps and precise locations in safe custody, and I will gladly pass on all this information to any reputable scientific body, if it obtains the agreement of the National Institute of Archaeology in Bolivia. If my personal story pays this dividend, I shall consider my twenty-six years well spent.

Index

Index

adobe huts, 28, 90, 111, 113, 237
agriculture
  crops, 78–9, 178
  cultivation, 89, 109, 151–2, 162, 174, 182, 229, 241
  irrigation, 79–80, 118, 151–2
  on man-made terraces, 118, 185
Alaska, 15
allakuna, 212
Amaru, Tupac, 127
amautas, of Callawayas, 208, 212, 214, 226, 229
  at meetings, 215, 217
  condor ceremony, and, 221–4
  government, and, 227
  medicine, and, 216–7, 220, 227–8
  secret language, and, 217, 219
Amazon, river, 73, 75
  basin, 100
  headwaters, 202
  jungle, lost city in, 203
  lowlands, 125
  rivers flowing to, 168
Americas, first migrants, 15
Andes, 20, 75, 105
  copper, silver and tin mines, 110
  entrance to, 33
  foothills, 89, 106, 114
    and line of fortresses, 183
  Inca cities in, 87
  pass, 23
  Upper, 114
  volcanic eruption, 120
Apolo, 201
Arellano, Jorge, 115–16, 118–19, 120, 121, 122–3, 124–5
Aucapata, 118, 124, 126, 132
  garrison of *conquistadores*, 127
  Iscanwaya, and, 115–16
  Karrie, and, 128–30
  line of fortresses, and, 191
  Mollos and Inca settlements at, 125
  Quechua, and, 130
  rebuilt by Spaniards, 127
  tourism, and, 143
ayllu, in Sacapampa, 172, 173, 174, 210
  chunka camayocs, and, 185
  day-to-day life in, 177
  Shaman, and, 179
Aymara Indians, 166, 198
  culture, 74, 117, 199, 244
  doctrine of life, 175
  downfall, 125, 244
  empire, 117, 171
  Iscanwaya, and, 124
  language, 37, 58, 130, 198
  roads, 166
  writing (Kelkanya), 137
ayne, 185
Ayopaya, river, 179, 186
Aztecs
  currency, 229, 235
  pyramid cities, 138

Baranquilla, 14

B.B.C., 19
  identity card, 146
  reporter for, 69, 194
Beni
  plains of, 75, 85, 87, 88, 163
    prehistoric ruins in, 74
    project in, 244
  province of, 74, 81, 89, 102, 115, 116
  Paititi Indians in, 82, 84
  Spaniards arrived, 78
  river, 85, 86, 107, 114, 205, 230
    Mosetene Indian settlements on, 101, 169, 187, 241
Bering Straits, 15
Billings, Noel, 136–7
Bogota, 14
Bolivia Magica, 126
Bolivian National Institute of Archaeology, 69, 115, 118, 143, 145, 195, 224, 245
  excavations, 197
  Lost City of Incas, and, 74
  projects, 192
  Rosinda culture, and, 81
  Sangines, Dr. Carlos Ponce, and, 70, 71
breastplate, discovery of at Pukarilla, 135
  hieroglypics on, 135–7
Bustos, Dr. Victor, 74, 76–8, 79–84
Butanan Institute of Brazil, 145
Byrne de Caballero, Mrs. Geraldine, O.B.E., 21, 44

Cajmara, Juan, 34–5
calendar, agricultural, 38–9
Callawaya Indians, 194, 201, 205–33, 241
  allakuna, 212
  amautas, 208, 212, 214, 215, 217, 219, 220, 221–4, 226, 227–8, 229
  brujo, 210
  ceremonies, 202, 218, 221–4
  children, 213–14
  clothing, 206, 221
  communities of, 196, 243
  condors, and, 214, 217–8, 221–4
  cultivation, camps of, 229
  death, 214–15
  government, 227
  houses, 226–7
  Incas, and, 218
  Intip Raymi, Feast of, 212–13
  medicine, and, 196, 209, 210, 216, 217, 220, 227–8, 231–3
  Moxos, and, 229
  Patchamama, and, 213
  secret language, and, 217, 219–20
  way of life, 211–12
Capac, Huayna, 36, 37–8
Capachachal, 63–6, 68
Caracaras, tribe, 37
Caracas, 14
Carib Indians, 16
Caripo, river, 89
Carlos, 21–2, 25, 27–8, 30–3, 36, 40, 41–2, 43–4
Carratera Marginal de la Selva, 90
Carya, 85, 86, 87, 88, 90, 91–2, 93, 94, 97, 100, 101, 102–3, 104–15
Caupolican, 220
Chapare, 71, 72, 107, 192
  countryside of, 168
  line of fortresses, 191
  hills of, 153
  river, 184, 245
Charcas, tribe, 37, 38
Charparini, river, 89
chicha, 94–5
Chichas, tribe, 37
chili peppers, 131, 165, 166, 171, 184, 235, 241
Chipana, 215, 216, 223
Chiripa culture, 197
Chuamayu, 155–64
  agriculture, 162–3
  houses, 156–7, 159–60
  look-out tower, 160
  muralla, 157–8
  temple, 161–2
    altar stone, 162
  terraces, 158–9, 160
Chuncho tribes, 125
chunka camayocs, 171–3, 179, 180–4
  at Patchamama ceremony, 187, 188
  clothing, 180
  government, 185

Clark's, 194
clothing, Indian, 167
  at Tablas Mayu, 47
  of Callawaya Indians, 206
  of Sacapampa Indians, 169, 178, 180
    at Patchamama ceremony, 187
coca, 114, 131, 152, 165, 171, 184, 235, 241
  as currency, 37, 47, 229, 235
  leaves, 47, 166, 175, 178
    in ceremonies, 218
    in medicine, 179, 231–2
    at Patchamama ceremony, 187, 189
Cochabamba, 42, 66, 72, 146, 167, 190, 204
  line of fortresses, and, 43, 106, 183, 191
  road from, 43, 47
  ruins discovered near, 145
  shops, 47
  Spanish frontier post at, 36
  State of, 42, 71, 107
  University of, 21, 30, 36
  valley, 37
    cultivation in, 131
    Incas in, 38, 127, 245
Collasuya, 218
Colombia, 14, 48, 60, 140
  Incas of, 32
  Indians, 62
  jungle, 54, 57., 112, 141
  musical instruments, Indian, 181
Comparapa, 74
  line of fortresses, and, 183
condor, 32
  ceremony of, 217–18, 221–4
  death, and, 214
conquistadores, Spanish, 21, 70, 130, 135, 160, 240
  Capachachal, and, 68
  garrison at Aucapata, 127
  Incas, and, 191, 204, 245
  written material of, 14, 15, 29, 36, 73, 106
Copacabana, 195, 199
copper, 198
  mines, 110
Corani, 44
Cordillera de los Mosetenes, 44
Corocoro, 198
Cortes, Jose Dominico, 220
Cotacajes, river, 146, 150, 153, 158, 184, 245
  gold, and, 151
  line of fortresses, and, 191
  ruins on, 145, 190
  settlements on, 185, 240
Cotapachi, 37
Creston, the, 152–3, 161
Cuzco, 20, 165
  Inca roads from, 37, 171
  Incas of, and Sacapampa Indians, 185
  walls of, 110

Darillo, 85, 86, 87, 88–115
Davies, Dr. David, 20–7, 30, 33–6, 41–6, 48–50, 54–69, 145
de Plata, Geraldo, 200–24, 226–44
Dobokubi, tribe, 14, 19
  legends of, 32
Dolmatoff, Professor, 14
Dorset, 95

East Anglia, University of, 198
Edinburgh, University of, 43
Ecquador, 69
El Dorado, 73, 82, 244
El Idiona Scecreto de los Incas, 220

Far East, 15
Fawcett, Colonel, 73, 74, 193, 230
  Lost City of the Incas, and, 203
fortress walls, 24, 157, 161, 174, 185
forts, 106–7, 108, 113
  Creston, the, 152–3, 161
  Incallacta, 24, 32
  in valley of river Llika, 125
  line of, 43, 106, 183, 191
Fowsey of Peru, 203, 230

Gamboa, Spanish chronicles of, 162, 183
Ger, Jorge, 146–90
Gillingham, Professor John, 43
Giza pyramid, 137

gold, 15, 70, 73, 167, 193, 229, 235, 243
as currency, 47
city of, 73, 203
mines, 125, 127, 130
objects, 24, 42, 66, 68–9, 71, 74, 130, 135, 191, 240, 244
rivers, in, 48, 73, 110, 130, 151, 198
Gomez, Professor, 84, 85–8
Great River, 73
Greek empire, 117
gringos, 30
Guaranee Indians, 38, 43, 166, 191
Guayaquil, 231

High Plateau of the Andes (Altiplano), 84, 85, 165
people of, 171, 197
houses
adobe, 28, 90, 111, 113, 237
Callawaya Indians, 226–7
Chuamaya, 156–7, 159–60
Incallacta, 28
Iscanwaya, 120–1
Pukarilla, 134
Sacapampa, 169, 173–4
Tablas, Mayu, 47
huaceros, 70, 71, 130, 191, 244
Huaqui, 50–68
Huayna Capac, 217, 218
Hukamar, 215, 216, 223
Humumari, 206

Ichoa
hills, 163
river, 163, 184, 245
Ilyapa, 49, 50, 55
Incallacta, 21, 22, 23–36, 38–41, 59, 71, 74, 109, 111
agricultural calendar, 38–9
altar stone, 134
breastplate, 135
houses, 28, 98, 129, 238
Huayna Capac, and, 36, 37–8
Inca holy waterfall, 25, 28, 39
site of, 23–4
temple, 30, 38, 65, 162
Temple of the Moon, 32, 40, 41
Temple of the Sun, 32
view of, 31
walls of, 60, 132
Inca Museum, University of Cochabamba, 34
Incaracay, 42
Incas, 20–1, 32–8, 73, 184
ancestors, 75, 244
army, 29–30
brain surgery, 34–5
building, 30, 65–6, 99, 157, 160, 200, 237–8
Callawaya Indians and, 218
cities, 24, 28, 87, 166, 230, 233, 237
culture, 74, 117, 118, 193
currency, 229, 235
customs, 29, 30, 34, 185, 234
descendants, 193, 195, 202, 245
distinctions from Mollo culture, 124
doctrine of life, 175, 185
empire, 30, 127, 171, 193, 204–5
government, 36–7
language, 118, 124, 199, 219
Mosetenes, and, 101, 183
rise to power, 118
roads, 31, 151, 165, 166, 193, 233, 235
from Cuzco to Tiwanaku, 37
from Incallacta, 26, 33, 41–2
from Sacapampa to Cuzco, 171
from Cochabamba to Santa Cruz, 43, 44, 59
skulls, 34–5
soldiers, 166
style of cities, 123, 138
surgeon's knife, 42–3, 66, 96, 135
temples, 29, 162
theory that descended from Mollo tribe, 125, 198
tribal groupings, 185
waterfall, holy, at Incallacta, 25, 28
for purification, 123
at Karrie, 129
written language, and, 135–7
Incas of Peru, The, 220
Independencia, 146, 151, 164, 165, 167, 179
countryside around, 166
Indians from, at Patchamama

ceremony, 188, 189, 190
line of fortresses, and, 183, 191
Indians *see* under individual names
'Inga', 159
Injka, 17, 18, 19, 32, 202
Inquivisi, 161, 165, 167
line of fortresses, and, 183
International Archaeological Conference, Equador, 69
Inti, the Sun God, 29, 40, 62
Intip Raymi, Feast of, 212–3
Intisuyu Indians, 54, 56
cities, 53
Iscanwaya, 115, 116, 119–24, 125, 132, 238
Aymara Indians, and, 124
breastplate, and, 135
Chuamayu, and, 157, 158
crops, 123
day-to-day life, 121–2
excavation of, 192
footpath from Carrie, 131
garrison, 122–3
hills of, 158
houses, 120–1, 174
importance, 143
line of fortresses, and, 183
Mollo culture, and, 117, 118
palace of the Inca, 122
Pucanwaya, and, 133
road from Lake Titicaca, 143
tombs, 121
Isiboro
hills of, 163
Indians of, 168, 186
line of fortresses, 191
river, 163, 166, 184, 245

jaguar, 26, 32, 57, 113
Jiminez, 16–17
Jones, Professor Hugh, 20
Journeys to the North of Bolivia, 220

Kapachachal, 54
Karrie, 125, 128–30
footpath to Iscanwaya, 131
K'Aturikasti, 231–2
Kechuamayo, river, 153, 158
Kelkanya, 137
Kunaguasaya, 14, 19, 29

La Guara, 14
Lamb, Professor H. H., 198
La Paz, 21, 37, 115, 126, 131, 146, 160, 165, 167, 172, 190, 195
province of, 89
Lee Kenneth, 75
leucotomy, pre-frontal, 34
Lima, 47, 231
University of, 200
Liverpool School of Tropical Medicine, 142
llama, 33, 325
at Patchamama ceremony, 188, 189
path, 131
shape, in Inca cities, 32
trains, 165, 171
Llika, river, 115, 118, 119
Mollo ruins on banks of, 124, 130
ruins in valley of, 125
Loma Mendoza, 76
Loma Ortiz, 76, 77, 78
Lost City of the Incas, 21, 65, 71, 74, 203, 240, 243
Callawaya Indians, and, 194
Capachachal, and, 68, 72
Inca road to, 193
myth of, 73, 117
Lost Empire of the Incas, 66–7, 71, 117, 143, 145, 205, 244
gateway to, 116
location of, 114

Macchu Picchu, 115, 143
Incas of and Sacapampa Indians, 185
Magdalena valley, 14, 17
Mamokoro, 133, 138–40
Mamani, 212–5, 216, 217, 221, 226, 227–8, 229, 231
Mamore, river, 75, 79, 89
Maniqui, river, 85, 89, 103
Maracaibo, oilfields, 13
Markham, Sir Clements, 220
Matamonte, river, 56, 60
Matto Grosso
Guaranee Indians, 191
Maukallacta, 125

breastplate, and, 135
Mayas
currency, 229, 235
pyramid cities, 138
Mayka, river, 52
Medellin, 14
mestizos, 14, 114, 146, 188, 203
Mexico, ancient, 138
missionaries, 15, 48, 72
mitimae, 37
Molino, Antonio, 126–8
Mollo tribe, 117
culture, 74, 117, 118, 198
distinctions from Inca culture, 124
fortifications, 126
Iscanwaya, and, 123
pre-Inca culture, 123
Pukarilla, and, 138
Quechua, and, 124
ruins on Llika river, 124
settlements, 118, 199
theory that founded Inca culture, 125, 198
Titicaca, Lake, 125, 198
Mongolia, 15
Morales, Don Alfonso de, 36
Mosetene Indians, 63, 101, 105, 107, 109, 160
clothing, 187, 241
Incas, and, 183
Indians of Sacapampa, and, 169
village, 107, 108, 114
Motilon Indians, 16
mounds, 30,75–84, 88
in Beni, 84
in Bolivia and Ecquador, 76
in Colombia, Venezuela and Brazil, 76
Mound culture, 79, 80–82, 89, 182, 192, 196–7
Moxos tribe, 82, 87, 105, 242
Callawayas, and, 229, 230, 235
clothing, 241
jungle settlements of, 184, 240, 243
Munai Pata, 165
Munecas, hills, of, 126, 127, 130, 131, 138
cities of, 139
muralla, 157
musical instruments, 181

Nudo de Apolobamba, 193, 210, 230

Oldstone, Dr., 216
Orinoco, plains, 13
Ortiz, 89
Oruro, 165

Paititi, 73, 82, 86, 87, 143, 145, 150, 153, 182, 193, 204, 244, 245
cultivation, 182
empire, 82, 160
gold, and, 244
Indians, 84, 85, 87, 100, 101, 105, 163, 167, 193
card of introduction to, 168, 170
temples, 161
Pakari, river, 53
Pamparacay, 42
Patchamama, Goddess of the Earth, 175, 182, 185
Callawaya Indians, and, 213, 215
ceremony, 179, 186–90
clothing at, 187
Payapaya, 133
Peru, 20, 127
Plymouth, 194
Poblete, Enrique Oblitas, 220
Pocanche, 146, 147
countryside around, 166
Poopo, lake, 197
Potosi, 38
silver mines, 21
Pucanwaya, 132–3
Puca Puca, 42
Puerto Acosta, 201
Pukarilla, 133–6
breastplate, discovery of, 137–8
buildings, 137–8
pumas, 26–7, 32, 57, 113

Quechua, 53, 58, 91, 92, 94
Aucapata, in, 130
Incas, and, 118, 124, 199, 219
Mollo tribe, and, 118, 124
Sacapampa Indians, and 170
Yuko Indians, and, 17
Quimsachata, 198

Rafael, 44–6, 47–8, 54–5
R.A.F. Mountbatten, Survival School, 194
Ramon, 21–2, 25, 27, 30, 33, 36, 38–43
Reid, Dr. Alistair, 142
Republic of Bolivia, The, 220
Rio de Oro, 63
Rivera, Oswaldo, 195, 196, 199
Rockies, 26
Rojo, Hugo Boero, 126, 127, 128
Roman empire, 117
Rosinda culture, 81
ruins, city, 109–12, 115, 145, 236–40

Saavedra Munecas, 220
Sacapampa, Indians of, 169–90
  agriculture, 174, 178
  ayllus in, 172, 173, 174, 177, 179, 185, 210
  childbirth, and, 176
  child rearing, 177
  clothing, 178, 187
  diet, 174
  fortress wall, 174
  houses, 169, 173–4, 238
  Inca customs, and, 185
  Incas of Cuzco and Macchu Picchu, 185
  marriage, and, 176
  medicine, 179
  music, 181
  Patchamama ceremony, and, 179, 186–90
  puberty ceremony, 177–8
  road to Cuzco, 171
  Shaman, 176, 178, 179, 185, 187–90
  Sinchi, Kooto, 171, 176, 177, 178, 185
  social organisation, 185
  spirits, and, 174–5
Salisbury Plain, 95
Samaipata, 74
  line of fortresses, and, 183
Sangines, Dr. Carlos Ponce, 70–4, 83, 110, 116, 117–8, 123, 124–5, 146, 153, 160, 166, 190–2, 193–9, 243
San Ignacio, 107
San Ignazio de Moxos, 85
Santa Ana, 114
  line of fortresses, and, 183, 191
  Mosetene Indians of, 169
Santa Cruz, 76
  Inca road to Cochabamba, 43, 44
  line of fortresses, and, 106, 183, 191
Santa Elena, river, 168, 169
Scrips Clinic, 216
secret language, 217, 219–20
Secure, river, 184
Shaman, 176, 178, 179, 185
  at Patchamama ceremony, 187–90
Sierra de Perije, 14, 16, 19
  Indians of, 15
Sierra Indians, 100
Siku, 233, 236, 238, 241, 242
silver, 15, 110
Sinchi Kooto, 54, 171, 176, 177, 178, 185
Smithsonian Institute, Washington, 83, 244
snakes, 96–7
  bites, 140–3
Sorota, General, 127
Spanish explorers, 15, 160, 166, 193
  army, 127
  mission, 82
steles, 136, 137
Stonehenge, 95
Suarez, 89
Sucre, 83

Tablas Mayu, 44, 45–7, 50, 62, 99
Takopampa, 153
temples, Inca, 29
  Capachachal, 65
  Chuamayu, 161–2
  Incallacta, 30, 38
    of the Moon, 32, 40, 41
    of the Sun, 32
  Karrie, 129
Temple of the Moon, 32, 40, 41
Temple of the Sun, 32
Thapka, hills of, 53
Time magazine, 48
Times, The, 216
tin, 110
Titicaca, Lake, 20, 86, 115, 125, 195
  Chiripa, and, 197

cultivation, 131
discoveries near, 192, 193, 194
line of fortresses, 106, 183
Mollo culture, and, 118, 198
Paititi, and, 84
road to Iscanwaya, 143
sites on shores of, 196, 199
Tiwanaku, and, 117
Wankerani, and, 197
Tiwanakota tribe, 130, 197
Aymara language, and, 130
Tiwanaku, 117, 124, 130, 195, 199
culture, 37, 197–8
Aymara language, and, 219
Chiripa, and, 197
Wankerani, and, 197
Tjara, 150, 153–8, 164, 165, 179
Todos Santos, 184
Trinidad, 76, 77, 84, 88, 89
Tuiche, river, 201, 230, 236, 237
Tupaco, 95, 96, 97–8

Urina, 209, 219, 220
road from, 230

Venezuela, 13, 14, 148
jungle, 54, 112, 141
musical instruments, Indian, 181

Wakchu, 222, 223, 224
Wanaku, 127–35, 138–42
Wankerani culture, 197
Wedell, H. A., 220
Wiltshire, 95

Yanakaka, 53
Yuko Indians, 14, 17, 19, 29
Yungas, 84, 85, 87, 101
Bolivia, of, 171
de Corani, 43, 44, 60
de la Victoria, 44,
Inca road from, 165
line of fortresses, and, 191
tribes of, 166
Yupanki, Topa Inca, 37